Pathways in Theodicy

Pathways in Theodicy

An Introduction to the Problem of Evil

Mark S. M. Scott

Fortress Press
Minneapolis

PATHWAYS IN THEODICY
An Introduction to the Problem of Evil

Cover image: Aslan is Coming by Dawn Waters Baker; 2014 (www.dawnwatersbaker.com)
Cover design: Alisha Lofgren

Library of Congress Cataloging-in-Publication Data
Print ISBN: 978-1-4514-6470-2
eBook ISBN: 978-1-4514-6980-6

The paper used in this publication meets the minimum requirements of American National Standard for Information Sciences — Permanence of Paper for Printed Library Materials, ANSI Z329.48-1984.

Manufactured in the U.S.A.

This book was produced using PressBooks.com, and PDF rendering was done by PrinceXML.

Dedicated to the memory of my dear nephew
Justin David Scott (1994–2014)

Contents

Acknowledgments

I wish to thank my students at Harvard University, Concordia University (Montréal, Canada), the University of Missouri-Columbia, and Villanova University who explored the problem of evil with me in various contexts over the years, and who have sharpened my thinking on theodicy. Their enthusiasm, diligence, and insight made courses on evil ironically good, instructive, and memorable. I am confident the subject will continue to elicit engaging discussion and illuminating analysis in future courses on the problem of evil.

Thanks also to Villanova University for awarding me the Veritas Faculty Research Grant for the present study, and for providing a collegial environment to complete the project, truly embodying the Augustinian spirit of *veritas*, *unitas*, and *caritas*.

Finally, let me express my deepest thanks to my wife Esther, the joy of my heart, and to our four children, James, Hannah, David, and Rebekah, who make our joy complete.

Preface

In Christian theology, the problem of evil refers to the logical tension between belief in divine goodness and omnipotence on the one hand and the ubiquitous reality of suffering on the other, especially unjust or innocent suffering. In its basic form, it asks: "Why does God allow evil?" Theologians from the first century until today have debated the many permutations of this quandary. Alvin Plantinga catalogues the constellation of questions that comprise the problem of evil: "Why does God permit evil, or why does he permit so much of it, or why does he permit those horrifying varieties of it?"[1] This multifaceted problem has both theoretical and existential dimensions. Theoretically, it explores the complex interrelationship between God and evil within Christian theology, broadly conceived. Existentially, it expresses the feeling of divine abandonment and absence that overtakes us when we descend into our own valley of the shadow of death, or when we internalize the agony of the world around us, which elicits the cry of Godforsakenness: "My God, my God, why have you forsaken me?" (Mark 15:34).[2]

Karl Rahner delineates the existential scope of the problem of evil in his essay "Why Does God Allow Us to Suffer?" He calls it

1. Alvin Plantinga, "Supralapsarianism, or 'O Felix Culpa,'" in *Christian Faith and the Problem of Evil*, ed. Peter van Inwagen (Grand Rapids, MI: Eerdmans, 2004), 2.
2. Throughout I will employ the NRSV unless stated otherwise.

"one of the most fundamental questions of human existence . . . which is universal, universally oppressive, and touches our existence at its very roots."[3] We cannot dismiss it as irrelevant, since suffering impacts all humanity, eventually. While some theological questions are experientially and existentially remote, the question of God's permission of evil remains perennially proximate and urgent. It appears in ancient and contemporary Christian texts with devastating theological force, and it appears in the news with equal force, raising the question anew with every natural disaster or heinous crime. It does not discriminate based on temporal, spatial, or social location. It is not reserved for specialists writing from the safety and comfort of the ivory tower. It is a basic question of human life. We suffer. We cry out. We wonder. We hope.

Jürgen Moltmann also notes the force of the problem and posits the provisionality of theodicy, that is, the attempt to vindicate divine justice or, more simply, to explain suffering. Despite its ubiquity and urgency, we search in vain for definitive, final answers to the problem of evil. Moltmann argues that "the problem of theodicy" cannot be answered *or* ignored. Theodicy does not promise conclusive answers, but it does give us resources to engage the problem of evil: "No one can answer the theodicy question in this world, and no one can get rid of it. Life in this world means living with this open question. . . . It is the *open wound of life* in this world."[4] Living with the open question of theodicy, for Moltmann, requires the willingness to suspend final judgments until the eschaton while we work toward the realization of God's new creation.

3. Karl Rahner, "Why Does God Allow Us to Suffer?" in *Theological Investigations* XIX, *Faith and Ministry*, trans. Edward Quinn (New York: Crossway, 1983 [1961]), 194.
4. Jürgen Moltmann, *The Trinity and the Kingdom: The Doctrine of God*, trans. Margaret Kohl (Minneapolis: Fortress Press, 1993), 49.

My study strives to promote dialogue on the problem of evil through an analysis and assessment of the major models and motifs in Christian theodicy, and to recommend some ways forward. I do not purport to offer any definitive solutions. When you turn over the final page of the book, you will not have discovered *the* answer to the problem of evil. In fact, you will probably have more questions than you had when you opened the first page. Theodicy, in the end, does not provide solutions as much as it provides perspectives that help us come to terms with suffering. My study seeks to equip readers with tools to contribute to a dynamic, nuanced, and open-ended conversation with diverse interlocutors. It identifies several pathways in theodicy, not just one. It is the beginning of a conversation, not an end to it.

Do not tread lightly on the paths of theodicy. The journey taxes the heart, mind, and soul. To encounter even a slight fraction of the breadth and depth of evil in the world outstrips our intellectual, emotional, and spiritual capacities, and leaves us winded and wounded. Theodicy traverses the shadowlands of suffering, where dangers await at every step and darkness shrouds the long, tortuous road ahead. It is an arduous, perilous, but, finally, wondrous journey into the sacredness of a broken world awaiting redemption, tilting between despair and hope, moving toward the Light. The bush burns but is not consumed, and God speaks from within the flames.

We are standing on holy ground.

Introduction

Does God exist? When Thomas Aquinas (c. 1225–1274) addresses the foundational question of theology in his *Summa Theologiae*, he first entertains the strongest possible objection to God's existence. On the surface, he says, the reality of evil undermines the concept of God:

> It seems that there is no God. For if one of two contraries were infinite, the other would be completely destroyed. But by the word "God" we understand a certain infinite good. So, if God existed, nobody would ever encounter evil. But we do encounter evil in the world. So, God does not exist.[1]

With peerless precision, Aquinas expresses the lethal theological force of the problem of evil. God and evil cannot coexist, he says, at least not without further theological explanation. As ontological antitheses, the reality of one should cancel out or preclude the reality of the other. Put simply, we presuppose that God, as the infinite good, would prevent evil. And yet, experience clearly reveals that he does not, which begs the crucial question: Does God exist at all?

1. Thomas Aquinas, *Summa Theologiae* Ia, q.2, a.3, *ob* 1 in *Thomas Aquinas: Summa Theologiae* Questions on God, eds. Brian Davies and Brian Leftow (Cambridge: Cambridge University Press, 2006), 24.

Where Is God?

If God exists, where is he? Why does he not intervene to stop at least the worst of evils? When we observe the plethora of evils in the world around us and in the pages of history, God seems like an absentee landlord. Divine absence in the face of evil suggests divine nonexistence, does it not? The slow decay of time has not abated the force or blunted the edge of this abiding question. It remains the gravest threat to the Christian doctrine of God. It is aptly called the formidable "rock of atheism," that is, the intellectual stronghold of atheism.[2] Despite its intractability, however, not all Christian theologians have declared it insuperable. Aquinas, for instance, refutes the atheological argument from evil by appealing to a general "greater goods" theory of evil.

> As Augustine says, "Since God is supremely good, he would not permit any evil at all in his works, unless he were sufficiently powerful and good to bring good from evil" (*Enchiridion* 11, *PL* 40.236). So, it belongs to the limitless goodness of God that he permits evils to exist and draws good from them.[3]

For Aquinas, as for Augustine, evil does not negate God's goodness because God brings good out of evil. The question for theology, of course, is whether or not the ensuing good justifies God's permission of evil. Theodicy, as the rational attempt to reconcile the reality of God with the reality of evil, employs various configurations of Aquinas's cost-benefit analysis.

In Aquinas, then, we find an instructive entry point into a broader reconsideration of the problem of evil and the plurality of theodicies

2. Hans Küng, *On Being a Christian*, trans. Edward Quinn (Garden City, NY: Doubleday, 1976), 431: "'Why do I suffer? This is the rock of atheism. The slightest throb of pain, even if it stirs merely in an atom, makes a rent in creation from top to bottom.' Georg Büchner, in his play *Danton's Death*, attributes these sentiments to Thomas Paine."
3. Aquinas, *Summa Theologiae* Ia, q.2, a.3, *ad* 1, p. 26.

it evokes. Aquinas classically formulates the problem as a logical tension between God's goodness and the experientially verifiable reality of evil and its existential counterpart, suffering. Moreover, he identifies the high theological stakes of the problem: nothing less than God's existence is on the line. Finally, he offers a blueprint for theodicy, to find, as far as possible, the various ways in which God brings good out of evil. In our exploration of theodicy below we will frequently encounter his basic theological framework.

Hans Küng expresses the personal stakes of the question, beyond the mere logical implications. Suffering calls into question the ultimate meaning of our lives: "In suffering man reaches his extreme limit, the decisive question of his identity, of the sense and nonsense of his life, of reality as a whole."[4] Suffering cuts to the core of faith, calling it into question, and creating a spiritual crossroads where some turn away from God, while others turn toward him: "For many a person concrete suffering has been the occasion of his unbelief, for many another the occasion of his faith."[5] Hence, the problem of evil threatens the intellectual viability of Christian theology as well as the personal viability of Christian faith in the face of suffering.

Christian theology has too often dismissed the project of theodicy as unproductive and insoluble. Since we cannot solve the problem of evil, we must abandon it.[6] These hasty dismissals are misguided and dangerous. As I will argue in chapter 2, Christian theodicy does

4. Küng, *On Being Christian*, 431. Theodicy, as I have argued elsewhere, attempts to restore cosmic coherence in the face of the destabilizing reality of evil through a complex process of meaning-making, which I call navigation. See Mark S. M. Scott, *Journey Back to God: Origen on the Problem of Evil* (New York: Oxford University Press, 2012), chapter 1: "Theodicy as Navigation: Toward a Theoretical Paradigm," 8–22.

5. Küng, *On Being Christian*, 431.

6. For a representative example of the rejection of theodicy, see Terrence W. Tilley, *The Evils of Theodicy* (Washington, DC: Georgetown University Press, 1991): "My conclusion is that theodicy as a discourse practice must be abandoned because the practice of theodicy does not solve the problems of evil and does create evils" (5). We will expound on these types of objections in chapter 7.

not search for solutions; it searches theological resources to respond to the problem of evil. A properly chastened theodicy does not audaciously offer exhaustive answers, but only pathways, imperfect and partial ways of interpreting evil within a Christian theological framework. Theodicy honestly acknowledges the mystery of evil, but that acknowledgment does not mark the end of the conversation. If that were so, other Christian doctrines shrouded in mystery—the Trinity, the human and divine nature of Christ, the relationship between providence and free will—would foreclose conversation rather than stimulate it, and the history of theology has shown us otherwise on these controversies. There is too much at stake to walk away from the conversation, and theology has resources to speak to the problem even if it cannot "solve" it. The language of "solution" befits mathematics and the other hard sciences, not Christian theology.

Map of the Book

The book unfolds in three stages. First, we begin with two methodological chapters. Chapter 1 frames the discussion by exploring the nature and problem of evil, shifting the focus from ontology to theology. Chapter 2 examines the definition, modes, questions, and criteria for theodicy, setting the methodological agenda for the subsequent chapters. Second, in chapters 3–5, we examine three constructive models—the free will defense, soul-making theodicy, and process theodicy—and analyze their theological sustainability and relevance. Finally, in chapters 6–8, we discuss important trajectories in theodicy. In chapter 6 we focus on the cross's contribution to the problem of evil, and the possibility of redemptive suffering. In chapter 7 we note the intellectual and moral objections to theodicy and the practical turns they have initiated, and chapter 8 explores how appeals to the afterlife and to mystery inflect theodicy. While the parameters of the study preclude an exhaustive account of every facet of theodicy, we cover enough ground to give the reader secure footing as we chart the inner logic and disputes of each facet.

I do not adopt or promote a particular theodicy in my analysis of the major constructive perspectives on theodicy. Instead, I present them in as fair and sympathetic light as possible, letting them speak on their own terms and from within their own contexts. After detailing their salient features as generously as possible, I invite the reader into conversation in the dialogue section, where I assess their strengths and weaknesses. I do not conclude these chapters with an authoritative pronouncement on the tenability of the particular theodicy, only with the major problems and prospects one must consider before subscribing to it or deploying it. My study seeks to spark conversation rather than foreclose it with prescriptive judgments.

Although I do not advance my own theodicy in this book, I do make several constructive moves. First, I call for theology to reclaim the problem as central to theological reflection, rather than dismiss it as unanswerable or abdicate it to philosophy. I also enumerate several criteria for assessing theodicy. Moreover, I demonstrate the dialogical nature of theodicy, arguing for the insufficiency of any single theodicy. Finally, I recommend an approach to theodicy rather than a particular theodicy in the conclusion. Hopefully my dialogical approach, which tries to give each voice a fair hearing within a theological framework for understanding the task of theodicy, will reinvigorate stalled, sterile debates, and help blaze new pathways forward in theodicy.

Punishment Theodicy

In the backdrop of the theodicies we discuss below lurks the specter of punishment theodicy, which has haunted theological discourse on evil.[7] Punishment theodicy argues that God employs suffering to punish sin.[8] Pain functions as divine discipline, God's cosmic belt that serves multiple purposes: "Defenders of the punishment theodicy have argued that pain can be good for one (or more) of four things: *rehabilitation*, *deterrence*, *societal protection*, and *retribution*."[9] Punishment, then, restores personal, social, and cosmic harmony and justice, which sin upsets. Not all suffering, however, results from wrongdoing, so punishment theodicy does not exhaust the possible explanations for evil. Whether taught with malicious or benevolent intent, the simplistic correlation between suffering and punishment causes emotional, psychological, and spiritual distress, and clouds the constructive project of theodicy. Not only does it compound suffering by blaming the victim, it withholds the salutary resources available in Christian theology to ameliorate suffering. Punishment theodicy brings judgment, not comfort, or hope. Unfortunately, it has been the default theodicy throughout the history of Christianity: the uncritical theological reflex for many pastors, priests, chaplains, and theologians.

On the one hand, punishment theodicy has some direct biblical justification. In Deuteronomy 28, for instance, God clearly outlines the covenantal expectations for Israel and the consequences for disobedience. Deuteronomy 30:15-20 expresses the correlation between righteousness and reward on one side and wickedness and

7. Michael J. Murray, "Theodicy," in *The Oxford Handbook of Philosophical Theology*, eds. Thomas P. Flint and Michael C. Rea (New York: Oxford University Press, 2009), 360–62.
8. For an examination of punishment theodicies in the Bible, see James L. Crenshaw, *Defending God: Biblical Responses to the Problem of Evil* (New York: Oxford University Press, 2005), 117–31.
9. Murray, "Theodicy," 360–61.

punishment on the other. Throughout the Old Testament God punishes Israel for its infidelity and individuals for their sins. Similarly, in the New Testament, Jesus sometimes associates suffering with punishment for sin. For example, after healing an invalid, Jesus tells him: "Do not sin anymore, so that nothing worse happens to you" (John 5:14), which suggests a link between his physical and spiritual condition. Moreover, to shift from the biblical to the sociological, we often observe natural consequences for sin, as when addicts suffer from their addiction, or criminals receive a penalty for their crime. These natural consequences might fit within the theological matrix of punishment theodicy, if they are interpreted as part of a cosmic system of restorative justice and remedial rehabilitation.

On the other hand, punishment theodicy tends to overdraw a symmetrical correspondence between sin and suffering, and righteousness and blessing. The Book of Job, the *locus classicus* for reflection on the problem of evil in the Old Testament, problematizes the unnuanced version of the doctrine of retribution. In chapters 3–37, Job's friends attribute Job's egregious sufferings to his wrongdoing, but Job maintains his innocence and God ultimately vindicates him (Job 42:7). In the Gospel of John, when the disciples assume that a congenitally blind man's impairment was the result of sin, Jesus rejects their assumption, and tells them that his blindness served a divine purpose that he did not discover until that moment (John 9:1-3). These texts, and other related passages (see Luke 13:4), subvert the simplistic doctrine of retribution, which mistakenly argues that *all* suffering results from sin, and that the righteous receive their just desserts.

It does not require special insight to see that the wicked often prosper and that the good often suffer. A cursory glance at history and the world around us confirms that conclusion. Punishment theodicy globalizes a theory of evil, applying it to particular cases, to the exclusion of other possible theological perspectives. Ultimately goodness will be rewarded and wickedness will be punished, but not until the afterlife, according to Christian eschatology, so we cannot expect the scales of justice to be balanced in this life. Punishment theodicy, in short, gives an insufficient and potentially harmful account of evil, myopically opting for only one of the many possible explanations for evil. In contradistinction to punishment theodicies, which have a destructive bent when universalized and disconnected from the doctrine of divine grace, our study focuses on constructive perspectives that move beyond simplistic, facile, and trite explanations.

Now that we have framed the core question of theodicy, detailed the stakes of the problem of evil, outlined the map of the book, and identified a hidden interlocutor, we are prepared to embark on the first stage of the journey: evil. What is evil? How does it manifest itself in the world? How has it been portrayed in Christian theology? What are some helpful ways to categorize evil, and to formulate the problem of evil? And, finally, how should theology rethink the classic narratives of the nature and problem of evil? These considerations will set the stage for the task of theodicy, and the constructive perspectives we entertain afterwards.

Questions for Discussion:

1. Why study the problem of evil/theodicy? What do you hope to gain?
2. What theological presuppositions do you bring to the study of theodicy?
3. What is at stake in the problem of evil for you, personally and academically?
4. What are some of the major questions you begin with as you embark on the study?
5. Who will be your dialogue partner(s) throughout your study of theodicy?

1

Rethinking Evil

From Ontology to Theology

"It is in suffering that the whole human question about God arises; for incomprehensible suffering calls the God of men and women into question. The suffering of a single innocent child is an irrefutable rebuttal of the notion of the almighty and kindly God in heaven. For a God who lets the innocent suffer and who permits senseless death is not worthy to be called God at all."[1]

The elusive term *evil* conjures up a vast array of images and emotions. It recalls horrific historical events, natural disasters, and personal losses. It refers to heinous acts of cruelty and violence. It expresses our sense of outrage at the worst that humanity does and the worst that it suffers. Evil, however, resists concrete categorization and simple definition. Despite the pervasiveness of the term in scholarly and colloquial discourse, the concept has different valences in different

1. Jürgen Moltmann, *The Trinity and the Kingdom: The Doctrine of God*, trans. Margaret Kohl (Minneapolis: Fortress Press, 1993), 47.

contexts. Most scholarly treatments of the problem of evil merely restate the standard philosophical formulations of the logical tension between the nature of God and the reality of evil, which calls traditional theism into question. In the first chapter, I rethink the concept of evil and reformulate the problem of evil for Christian theology specifically, rather than for theism generally.

At the outset, then, we will situate the salient questions about evil within a Christian theological matrix. As we reframe the stock philosophical concepts and categories of evil, we will strive to avoid excessive abstraction and generic formulations. I will focus my rethinking of evil on four distinct yet interrelated topics: the nature of evil, the categories of evil, the problems of evil, and paradigmatic evils. Throughout, I recommend a shift from ontology to theology as a way to reclaim the issue for Christian theology and, ultimately, to respond to it utilizing its distinctive theological resources. Theology must take ownership of the problem of evil in order to ensure its intellectual and moral credibility, and to do that, it must speak from within its own traditions.

What Is Evil?

What is the nature of evil?[2] What do we mean when we classify someone or something as evil? Common expressions such as "evildoers," "the axis of evil," "pure evil," and "acts of evil" intensify the question without substantially answering it. Despite widespread theoretical imprecision and ambiguity, the term "evil" permeates our vocabulary. In fact, it is so commonplace that we rarely subject it to careful scrutiny. In the media, film, literature, and the academy, it appears without any consistent definition. In colloquial discourse, evil

2. See Chad Meister, *Evil: A Guide for the Perplexed* (New York: Continuum, 2012) for the basic landscape.

usually signifies egregious immorality or extreme wickedness, something beyond the outer reaches of acceptable human behavior, but it can also signify suffering without any relation to morality. In academic philosophy and theology definitions of evil suffer from the same theoretical imprecision and ambiguity found in ordinary discourse. In his 2003 Gifford Lectures, philosopher Peter van Inwagen defines evil simply as "bad things," which only raises further questions.[3] What do we mean by bad? What criteria do we employ to make that determination? How bad must someone or something be to warrant the designation of evil?[4] For the most part, discussions of evil, in both colloquial and academic discourse, dodge the issues and avoid a critical examination of terminology. Let us commence our rethinking of evil by asking about its nature or ontological reality. What *precisely* is evil?

EVIL: Classically defined as the "absence of the good" (*privatio boni*), evil denotes the depravation, corruption, and perversion of the good of creation. Just as darkness is the absence of light and silence is the absence of sound, so evil is the lack or absence of the good.

3. Peter van Inwagen, *The Problem of Evil* (New York: Oxford University Press, 2006), 4, 12–13, 60. He later explores definitions of evil as "the extreme reaches of moral depravity" (12–13). Van Inwagen explores the conceptual ambiguities of the term evil, especially "radical evil" versus "ordinary evil" (14).
4. "Does the word not bring to mind Sauron and his minions or at any rate Heinrich Himmler and Pol Pot?" (Peter van Inwagen, *The Problem of Evil*, 12).

Biblical Portrayals of Evil

When asked to define the reality of evil, philosophers and theologians reflexively turn to the language of metaphysics, particularly ontology, to engage the question. Evil, they say, denotes the deficiency or distortion of being. It is the privation of the good, the negation of the goodness of creation. Although ontological categories give us conceptual resources for theorizing the nature of evil, they often bypass biblical insights. Methodologically, reflection on the nature of evil ought to begin with scripture as its starting point, not with a preexisting ontological system. Thus, as a corrective, let us *begin* with the secure ground of scripture before we delve into the slippery footing of ontology.[5]

Three qualifications will help forestall potential misconceptions. First, the Bible does not advance a singular notion of evil. We will not discover *the* biblical conception of evil because scripture does not admit of a uniform perspective on its nature or ontological status. Instead, it talks about evil in a plurality of ways and in a variety of contexts. Nor, secondly, does scripture define evil with philosophical precision. We will not encounter the language of negation and privation in the Bible because it does not strive for ontological clarity. Instead, it talks about evil in relation to the nature of God and God's work in creation. Finally, I do not intend to undertake an exhaustive analysis of evil in the Old and New Testament, since that would take us too far afield from our focus. Rather, I will select representative passages and examples to illustrate the multiplicity of biblical perspectives on evil that will then inform our analysis of the standard ontologies and categories of evil below. In particular, we will focus on four central representations of evil in the Bible: evil as chaos, sin, satanic, and suffering. We begin with chaos.

5. Scripture employs multiple ontologies without being driven by any single metaphysical system.

Evil as Chaos

In the Old Testament, chaos signifies the evil and destruction that threatens or impairs creation. God creates the world, in the first place, by subduing chaos, as Genesis implies: "The earth was formless and void and darkness covered the face of the deep, while a wind of God swept over the face of the waters" (Gen. 1:2). The sea or turbulent waters symbolize chaos in the Old Testament, both in Genesis and even more explicitly in other passages, especially Job 38:8-11, where God speaks of creation as victory over chaos. God "shut in the sea with doors" (Job 38:8) and "prescribed bounds for it" (Job 38:10) as part of the divine construction of the universe or cosmos (κόσμος = order) in the exact sense. Similarly, in Ps. 74:13-14, the creation of the world involves God's mastery over the sea and, additionally, the destruction of the Leviathan, a mythical sea monster who personifies chaos, in concert with the symbolism of the sea or turbulent waters.

Talk of dragons and mythical monsters strikes modern readers as archaic and bizarre, but the writers of the Old Testament draw from Ancient Near Eastern creation mythology, not contemporary cosmologies.[6] Theologically, however, the language of the monstrous resonates as much with contemporary audiences as it did with its ancient audience. It expresses the menacing, horrific, destructive nature of evil, as we will discuss below. The Book of Job provides the most vivid depiction of "chaos monsters" in the Old Testament. God affirms his sovereignty over creation through his taming of the land monster Behemoth (Job 40:15) and the sea monster Leviathan (Job 41). On one level, these creatures threaten the safety of mortals because of their great strength; on a deeper level, they represent the threat of chaos against the order of creation. Just

6. For a study of "myth and mythmaking in the Bible" and its utilization of Ancient Near Eastern mythology, see Bernard F. Batto, *Slaying the Dragon: Mythmaking in the Biblical Tradition* (Louisville: Westminster John Knox, 1992), 1.

as God tames these creatures, so God will push back the intrusion of chaos into creation.

Who makes the primordial sea and ancient sea monsters? Put differently, does God create chaos or does God conquer it? Both of these options engender further questions about divine power and goodness. Why would God create chaos rather than order? If God does not create chaos, where does it come from? Does it coexist with God, or does it emerge after creation? These questions allude to the intricate problem of the origin of evil. Mythological imagery does not afford us with straightforward answers. If, on the one hand, you affirm creation out of nothing (*ex nihilo*), then you have to account for the presence of chaos in the world. If, on the other hand, you affirm creation out of chaos, then you must account for the origin of chaos. Either way, creation and chaos stand in fundamental tension in the Old Testament, and God's act of creating and sustaining the cosmos involves the initial and ongoing subduing of chaos.[7]

Notice, however, that chaos does not stay within its divinely prescribed boundaries; it reemerges, even after its initial subjugation. Therefore, God must perpetually keep it at bay as it seeks to undo the threads of creation. But the cosmic battle between God and chaos does not continue indefinitely: God eventually destroys it. We see a hint of this in Isaiah's portrayal of the "day of the Lord" when Leviathan will rear its head no more: "On that day the Lord with his cruel and great and strong sword will punish Leviathan the fleeing serpent, Leviathan the twisting serpent, and he will kill the dragon that is in the sea" (Isa. 27:1). So, in terms of the chaos imagery of the

7. What if, speaking speculatively, chaos metaphorically represents the fallen condition of creation? In that case, God creates the world good, but through the misuse of freedom it degenerates further and further from its created goodness, which God must remedy throughout history and eventually overcome through the renewal of creation at the end of time. Alternatively, or additionally, what if chaos metaphorically represents demonic opposition to God? In that case, God creates the angels, some of whom fall and thereafter strive to subvert God's benevolent and orderly design for creation.

Old Testament, the Leviathan harasses creation until the end of days when, to use Christian imagery, it is caught by the great fishhook of God, the cross, and destroyed forever.

What, then, are we able to glean about the reality of evil from the language and imagery of chaos and chaos monsters in the Old Testament? Chaos invokes a plurality of images: social and political unrest, the effects of natural disasters, the disorderly features of existence. These aptly correspond to the categories of evil we will discuss below (moral, natural, and metaphysical evil). Moreover, the language of the monstrous expresses the horror of evil, its power to frighten and destroy, and its threat to the order of creation. It jeopardizes the harmony of creation in its various manifestations. From the language of chaos and chaos monsters we begin to appreciate the ways in which the order and harmony of our lives and the world around us are constantly assailed by forces inimical to God's good creation.

Evil as Sin

Scripture portrays evil primarily as sin or disobedience against God's law, variously construed and conceived. Sin, in fact, becomes a major motif in the Old and New Testaments, beginning with the primordial sin of Adam and Eve. Their disobedience of the divine command results in their expulsion from the Garden of Eden (Genesis 3). Cain's cold-blooded murder of Abel results in his exile from the lands he polluted with his brother's innocent blood (Genesis 4). In both instances, sin or disobedience creates a relational rupture between God and humanity. Adam and Eve are driven out of Eden (Gen. 3:24), the place of intimate encounter with God (Gen. 3:8), and Cain is sent away from God's presence (Gen. 4:16) as an endangered fugitive. These stories of archetypal disobedience set the stage for the story of the flood, which purges the earth of a hybrid race of humanity that had fallen into decadence and moral decay: "The Lord saw that the wickedness of humankind was great in the earth, and that every inclination of the thoughts of their heart was only evil continually" (Gen. 6:5). The Hebrew word for evil in this verse, רַע (*ra'*), which also occurs in Gen. 8:21, signifies moral depravity and objectionable, displeasing behavior.[8]

If sin or disobedience refers to violations of the divine law, then naturally we must ask: what law? In Genesis, the law referred to God's specific commands to people (such as Adam and Eve) and perhaps a natural law against murder (in the case of Cain) and wickedness. God establishes explicit moral directives for his chosen people, the descendants of Abraham, in the form of the Ten Commandments, thereby giving sharper definition to the divine law. In Exodus 20 and Deuteronomy 5, God discloses the Decalogue, the ten words or commands, which are: (1) Worship of God exclusively; (2) Prohibition against idol worship; (3) Prohibition against misusing the name of God; (4) Keeping the Sabbath; (5) Honor of father and mother; (6) Prohibition against murder; (7) Prohibition against adultery; (8) Prohibition against stealing; (9) Prohibition against lying; (10) Prohibition against coveting. Violations of these divine injunctions, therefore, constitute sin or evil. Importantly, the spectrum of sin encompasses sins of commission, such as stealing, lying, and coveting, and sins of omission, such as failing to keep the Sabbath and honor parents.

In the Book of Deuteronomy, the Ten Commandments are affirmed and expanded in the form of a covenant between God and the Israelites, which operates within a basic system of obligations between the two partners of the covenant, with clear consequences

8. William L. Holladay, *A Concise Hebrew and Aramaic Lexicon of the Old Testament* (Leiden: Brill, 1988), 341.

for fidelity or infidelity. In short, obedience brings blessings, disobedience brings curses. Deuteronomy 28 catalogues the blessings and curses that befall the obedient and disobedient. Deuteronomy 30 outlines the system of rewards and punishments:

> See, I have set before you today life and prosperity, death and adversity. If you obey the commandments of the Lord your God that I am commanding you today, by loving the Lord your God, walking in his ways, and observing his commandments, decrees, and ordinances, then you shall live and become numerous, and the Lord your God will bless you in the land that you are entering to possess. But if your heart turns away and you do not hear, but are led astray to bow down to other gods and serve them, I declare to you today that you shall perish; you shall not live long in the land that you are crossing the Jordan to enter and possess. (Deut. 30:15–18)

The rest of the Old Testament tells the story of Israel's failure to satisfy the demands of the covenant, and the consequences that ensue. For instance, after the death of Joshua, the successor of Moses, the people disobey the covenant: "Then the Israelites did what was evil in the sight of the Lord and worshiped the Baals; and they abandoned the Lord, the God of their ancestors, who had brought them out of the land of Egypt" (Judg. 2:11–12). Similarly, the famous kings of Israel do evil, including Saul, David, and Solomon, and later, after the division between the Northern and Southern tribes, or Israel and Judah, the respective kings and their subjects almost always "did what was evil in the sight of the Lord" (1 Kgs. 14:22 and *passim*). So the narratives of the Old Testament unfold within the moral orientation of divine law, particularly covenantal law. Evil, then, simply refers to disobedience to the divine law, which has various manifestations, but ultimately crystallizes in the Ten Commandants and in the covenant between God and Israel.

In the New Testament, the theme of disobedience continues. Jesus calls the people to repent (Matt. 4:17). He gives extensive moral instruction in the Sermon on the Mount (Matthew 5–7), the most definitive source for Christian ethics, and he enjoins obedience to the covenant (Luke 10:25-28). Jesus confronts the sin of disobedience (John 8:11) and ultimately overcomes sin through his obedience on the cross. Paul contrasts the obedience of Christ with the disobedience of Adam in Rom. 5:12-21. Just as Adam's sin brought death, so Christ's righteousness brings life. For Paul, Christ is the New Adam, the one in whom the pernicious effects of the primordial sin are reversed: "For just as by the one man's disobedience the many were made sinners, so by the one man's obedience the many will be made righteous" (Rom. 5:19). Christ, then, is the paragon of obedience. He taught fidelity to God's commands, followed God's commands, and obeyed God's plan for the salvation of humanity (Mark 14:36) "to the point of death—even death on a cross" (Phil. 2:8), as we will discuss extensively in chapter 6.

The New Testament upholds the basic moral orientation of the Old Testament. It frequently identifies sinful actions as evil and condemns them. It would not suit our purposes to catalogue all the instances of disobedience in the New Testament, but Paul's itemization of the "works of the flesh" aptly summarizes the Christian view of sin. The flesh and Spirit, Paul avers, work at cross-purposes. The Spirit leads to life, the flesh leads to death. Paul details the actions, attitudes, and behaviors that are antithetical to the Spirit: "Now the works of the flesh are obvious: fornication, impurity, licentiousness, idolatry, sorcery, enmities, strife, jealousy, anger, quarrels, dissentions, factions, envy, drunkenness, carousing, and things like these" (Gal. 5:19-21). Paul's index of sin, while not exhaustive, conveys the standard Christian view of evil, which affirms the Old Testament moral grid and situates it within the work of Christ and the life of the Spirit.

How, then, does the biblical language of sin and disobedience illuminate the nature of evil in Christian theology? Most significantly, the Old and New Testament clearly depict evil in moral rather than metaphysical terms. These are not necessarily disjunctive categories, but the accent lies on evil as disobedience of the divine law, manifested in nature, in the covenant, in the teachings of Christ, and in the injunctions of the Spirit. As we will see below, the Bible speaks of evil principally as *moral evil*, rather than as natural or metaphysical evil, although we will see how these might intersect.

Evil as Satanic

The writers of the Old and New Testament take the reality of hostile spiritual forces for granted. In the biblical imagination, evil sometimes denotes the demonic, personified by the Devil or Satan and symbolized by darkness. According to the traditional account, the Devil and his minions were once angels who rebelled against God before the creation of the universe. These malevolent spirits pervert creation and subvert God's benevolent designs for humanity. In today's post-Enlightenment world, it has become theologically unfashionable to talk about evil in terms of pernicious spiritual forces. For disenchanted modern minds, these spiritual categories have lost their heuristic value. Consequently, they are dismissed or ignored in contemporary philosophical and theological theorizing on the nature of evil. Many Christians, however, still take the reality of inimical forces or beings with the utmost seriousness. How might Christian theology interweave these discarded threads into its conceptual tapestry of evil? First, we will outline the biblical portrayal of evil as demonic, and then we will explore several options for retrieving and reimagining these spiritual categories for a contemporary theological context.

Where does the traditional account of the fall of the Devil originate? Contrary to common belief, it does not originate from the serpent in Genesis 3, who only later became identified with Satan, famously in Milton's *Paradise Lost*. Instead, it comes from an allegorical interpretation of several passages in the Old Testament, particularly Isaiah 14:

> How you are fallen from heaven, O Day Star, son of Dawn! How you are cut down to the ground, you who laid the nations low! You said in your heart, "I will ascend to heaven; I will raise my throne above the stars of God; I will sit on the mount of assembly on the heights of Zaphon; I will ascend to the tops of the clouds, I will make myself like the Most High." But you are brought down to Sheol, to the depths of the Pit. (Isa. 14:12-15)

Ostensibly a prophetic taunt against the proud king of Babylon, Christian theologians and exegetes interpreted Isaiah's *metaphorical* description of the Babylonian king's hubris and expulsion from heaven as an *allegorical* allusion to Satan's pride and fall from heaven.

Similarly, Christian theologians interpreted the diatribe against the King of Tyre in Ezek. 28:11-19 as a crypto-allusion to Satan's expulsion from heaven. The allegorical equation of the King of Tyre with Satan created the cosmological landscape for an explanation of the fall of Satan and, concomitantly, the rise of evil in the universe. Originally, then, Satan was good. In fact, he was exemplary. As Ezekiel states, the king of Tyre (=Satan) was "the signet of perfection, full of wisdom and perfect in beauty" (Ezek. 28:12). At first, he was without sin, which safeguards the original goodness of creation: "You were blameless in your ways from the day that you were created, until iniquity was found in you" (Ezek. 28:15). As with the description in Isaiah 14, pride precipitates the fall: "Your heart was proud because of your beauty; you corrupted your wisdom for the sake of your splendor. I cast you to the ground" (Ezek. 28:17).

These later cosmological overlays of historical potentates supplement the paucity of information in the Old Testament about the origin of Satan. They reinforced the theological narrative of the original goodness of creation, the fall of Satan, and his ultimate destruction.[9]

What was implicit and murky in the Old Testament becomes explicit and clear in the New Testament, although not entirely systematic. The Johannine literature in particular symbolically bifurcates the universe into realms of light and darkness, which perhaps recalls and reinterprets the imagery from Gen. 1:3–4. Light and darkness have multivalent meanings. Light symbolizes God, life, truth, and goodness while darkness symbolizes Satan, death, sin, and demonic activity. The New Testament identifies God as light explicitly in 1 John 1:5: "God is light and in him there is no darkness at all." Similarly, the Gospel of John refers to Christ as the "light" who "shines in the darkness" (John 1:5; cf. 1:7–9). Light, then, symbolizes God's nature as the source of life, goodness, and truth. It also, however, symbolically refers to human morality. "Walking in the light" (1 John 1:7) denotes the ethical enactment and embodiment of God's truth and goodness. So light has closely interwoven theological, cosmological, and ethical meanings.

Conversely, darkness signifies the sinfulness of creation (John 1:5) and sin itself (1 John 1:6). The Word enters into a world engulfed in darkness (John 1:5). Humanity, benighted by sin, resists and rejects the Light (Christ) because he exposes their inner darkness: "And this is the judgment, that the light has come into the world, and people

9. Augustine elaborates on the view of the fall of angels and their original goodness in *City of God* XII.1: "Others, however, delighting in their own power, and supposing that they could be their own good, fell from that higher and blessed good which was common to them all and embraced a private good of their own. They preferred the elation of pride to the loftiest dignity of eternity; the sharpness of vanity to the most certain truth; zeal for selfish ends to the uniting force of love. They became proud, false and envious" (Augustine, *The City of God against the Pagans*, trans. and ed. R. W. Dyson [Cambridge: Cambridge University Press, 1998], 498). Cf. *City of God*, XII.6: "And what else is their fault called than pride?" (505).

loved darkness rather than light because their deeds were evil" (John 3:19; cf. Eph. 5:11). As God personifies and originates truth and goodness, so Satan personifies and originates lies and wickedness: "He was a murderer from the beginning and does not stand in the truth, because there is no truth in him. When he lies, he speaks according to his nature, for he is a liar and the father of lies" (John 8:33). God's goodness is "natural" to him just as Satan's evil is "natural" to him in his fallen state. God's benevolent providential care of creation and Satan's malevolent destructive designs for it reflect their character. Darkness, then, also has closely interwoven theological, cosmological, and ethical meanings.

With the Incarnation, the cosmic conflict comes to a head. The two principals, God and Satan, enter into direct confrontation. It begins with the deceit and blood thirst of King Herod, who massacres Bethlehemian infants in his frenzied hunt for Jesus (Matt. 2:1-18). Herod mirrors Satan's attributes of deceit and violence in his effort to prevent the arrival of the Messiah. Satan vigorously attempts to sabotage God's designs by tempting Jesus to abuse or renounce his mission (Matt. 4:1-11). Satan, the "ruler of the demons" (Matt. 9:34) and the "ruler of the world" (John 12:31; 14:30; 16:11; cf. 2 Cor. 4:4; Eph. 2:2), exerts an enormous amount of influence over the fallen world.[10] In the Incarnation, however, God destroys Satan's power, first through his healings and miracles, especially his exorcisms, which signal the arrival of the "kingdom of God" (Luke 11:20),[11] and ultimately and decisively through his death and resurrection. With every restored mind and body, Jesus, the "light of the world" (John 9:5), and, later, his apostles, put Satan and his dark forces to flight (Luke 10:18).

10. For an analysis of "the warfare worldview of the Bible," see Gregory A. Boyd, *Satan and the Problem of Evil: Constructing a Trinitarian Warfare Theodicy* (Downers Grove, IL: IVP Academic, 2001), 29–39.
11. Boyd, *Satan and the Problem of Evil*, 35–37.

The adversarial language of "light" and "darkness" naturally translates into cosmic war imagery. Many first-century Jews envisioned the world as a battleground between good and evil powers. The Dead Sea scrolls, for instance, employ cosmic battle imagery between the Prince of Light and the Angel of Darkness and their respective "children."[12] Similarly, in Ephesians 6, the cosmic scale of the conflict comes into sharp relief. Paul instructs the Ephesians to don "the whole armor of God" in preparation for the conflict with the devil (Eph. 6:11).[13] We must, Paul insists, know our enemy in order to effectively engage in the conflict: "For our struggle is not against enemies of blood and flesh, but against the rulers, against the authorities, against the cosmic powers of this present darkness, against the spiritual forces of evil in the heavenly places" (Eph. 6:12). Christians must adopt a spiritual "war-footing" if they hope to avoid the spiritual casualty list. Here, then, to fight evil means to resist the devil and his demonic forces.

Evil as Suffering

Finally, the Bible sometimes portrays evil as suffering or misfortune. For instance, Job, after losing his wealth, children, and health, asserts

12. For instance, the "Community Rule" employs the metaphor of light and darkness to evoke the cosmic battle between the forces of truth and the forces of injustice: "Those born of truth spring from a fountain of light, but those born of injustice spring from a source of darkness. All the children of righteousness are ruled by the Prince of Light and walk in the ways of light, but all the children of injustice are ruled by the Angel of Darkness and walk in the ways of darkness" (1QS III). See Geza Vermes, trans. and ed., *The Complete Dead Sea Scrolls in English* (New York: Allen Lane/Penguin, 1997), 101. On the "theology of early Essenism," see Martin Hengel, *Judaism and Hellenism: Studies in Their Encounter in Palestine during the Early Hellenistic Period*, vol. 1 (Philadelphia: Fortress Press, 1974), 218–24.
13. The debate over the authorship of Ephesians need not detain us here. For contrasting viewpoints, see Luke Timothy Johnson, *The Writings of the New Testament: An Interpretation* (Minneapolis: Fortress Press, 2010), 359–74 and Bart D. Ehrman, *The New Testament: A Historical Introduction to the Early Christian Writings* (New York: Oxford University Press, 2008), 389–93.

in response to his wife's rebuke: "Shall we receive the good at the hand of God, and not receive the bad?" (Job 2:10). The Psalms frequently bemoan the troubles that accompany us throughout life: "The days of our life are seventy years, or perhaps eighty, if we are strong; even then their span is only toil and trouble; they are soon gone, and we fly away" (Ps. 90:10; cf. 91:10). In the Lord's Prayer, Jesus prays for deliverance from "evil" (πονηρός) or "the evil one" (Matt. 6:13).[14] Thus, evil sometimes refers to our experiences of misfortune, not to chaos or sin or Satan. Sometimes evil seems to come from God, sometimes from Satan, and sometimes from nature. The Bible is not always clear about causation, and that eventuates in the thorny question of the origin of evil, which we will address below.

Interestingly, the view of evil as suffering shows the intersection of these portrayals. Suffering sometimes results from sin, which Deuteronomy 28 promises. Sometimes Satan causes suffering or misfortune, such as the illnesses Jesus heals in the New Testament. Furthermore, chaos and chaos monsters can symbolize Satan and his work, or they can refer to impersonal destructive forces in nature, which sometimes cause suffering. The complex interplay between chaos, sin, Satan, and suffering in the Bible demonstrates both their multivalence and their opaque interrelationships. Part of the point of the Book of Job and John 9, as we will discuss below, is that not all suffering (evil) results from sin (evil). Similarly, their complex interplay intimates potential correlations between moral, natural, and metaphysical evil insofar as the Bible interweaves chaos, sin, and Satan, even as it problematizes simple or universal correspondences between them.

14. Warren C. Trenchard, *A Concise Dictionary of New Testament Greek* (Cambridge: Cambridge University Press, 2003), 129.

From our sketch of biblical conceptions of evil we may draw several preliminary conclusions. First, and perhaps most importantly, the Bible does not admit of a singular perspective on evil. We will search in vain for *the* biblical perspective on evil. Instead, we encounter a plurality of perspectives. The biblical authors, writing in disparate historical and theological contexts, portray evil in a wide variety of ways, some overlapping, and some in tension. For example, sometimes it is strongly associated with human sin, and at other times it is identified with Satan and his work. Sometimes it is cosmic, sometimes it is personal. Sometimes it is linked to actions, sometimes to attitudes. The collage of images that emerge from the Bible gives ample opportunity for diverse metaphysical speculations and categorizations.

Second, biblical portrayals of evil tend to avoid ontology. We do not encounter the privation language that pervades later theological and philosophical theories. In the Bible, evil tends to be moral, not metaphysical: it appears as a moral condition, both human and angelic, not as a metaphysical concept. Moreover, it tends to be spiritual, not syllogistic: it appears as part of a cosmic battle rather than as a logical problem. Consequently, it requires moral and spiritual remedies, not rational or logical solutions. It is not that the Bible does not address the logical problem of evil: an entire book of the Bible is devoted to an ancient version of the logical problem of evil. It is simply that the Bible operates within a cosmic, moral, and spiritual landscape rather than within a rational, abstract, ontological landscape. Its complex of symbols, then, has more in common with mythology and theology than philosophy *per se*. Later theologians and philosophers would transpose these diverse biblical concepts into ontological categories.

In a post-Enlightenment, disenchanted world, talk of the Satanic and demonic seems archaic, part of an outmoded, pre-scientific worldview. The cognitive dissonance between the biblical cosmology and contemporary science engenders interpretive issues. Rather than debate the cogency of the biblical worldview in light of modern physics and astronomy, readers might allegorize Satan, demons, and dark spiritual forces as symbols of the darkest recesses of human nature. If they take that exegetical and theological route, evil spiritual forces in the New Testament become metaphors for the evil latent in the human heart and mind. Herod's infanticide, then, would be "evil" not in the sense that it was inspired by dark spiritual powers, but only that it reflected the worst of human potentiality. While the psychological approach to evil has much to recommend it, especially its emphasis on human responsibility, it lacks heuristic value in other ways. Some people (Hitler, Stalin, serial killers) and some actions (genocide, torture, rape) are so heinous, so intrinsically warped, that they defy the categories of human psychology. They seem so utterly foreign to human nature, theologically conceived, that it suggests that something sinister, something truly demonic, inspires these people and actions. That viewpoint, however, might seem not only scientifically naïve, but also morally evasive.

What constructive value do the biblical portrayals of evil have for contemporary readers? How might they contribute to our comprehension of the elusive nature of evil? Despite the archaic valences of some of the depictions, the Bible nonetheless presents powerful ways to envision evil. For instance, the concept of chaos and chaos monsters, while scientifically outmoded, remains existentially relevant. It captures our sense of evil as "monstrous," as something beyond the bounds of the ordinary, as horrific. Similarly, as mentioned above, the concept of Satan and the demonic, while theologically passé for some, remains theologically vital to many others. For the latter, the most conspicuous acts of evil, both personal and collective, call for deeper explanations beyond twisted human motives. But even if you reject the concept of transhistorical, supranatural evil, it might still have theological value as a metaphor for or symbol of the foreign, destructive, and odious quality of evil. To call someone or something monstrous or demonic or satanic would merely convey its complete departure from and perversion of recognizably human behavior. There are many ways, then, to retrieve and redeploy the biblical language for evil, and future work in theodicy ought to meditate more deeply and systematically on its latent possibilities, rather than bypass and ignore it in an effort to work within more familiar but often theologically sterile philosophical locutions.

Theological Portrayals of Evil

As Christianity evolved over the centuries, it translated its biblical imaginaries into new philosophical contexts. As a result, theologians pivoted from the biblical language of evil as chaos, sin, Satanic, and suffering to the language of evil as the privation of the good (*privatio boni*). Origen represents the transition well, especially in his *Commentary on John*, where he shifts from the biblical language of God's noncreation of "nothing" to the philosophical language of evil as privation.[15] In this section, we will examine the privative theory of evil in the thought of Augustine, Thomas Aquinas, John Calvin, and Karl Barth in order to illustrate the shift from the biblical to the philosophical in theological engagement with the question of the nature of evil. All of these theologians, in different ways, wrestle with the paradoxical nature of evil.

15. Mark S. M. Scott, *Journey Back to God: Origen on the Problem of Evil* (New York: Oxford University Press, 2012), 24–25.

Augustine

Augustine (354–430 c.e.) popularizes the conception of evil as the privation of the good rather than as an independent metaphysical reality.[16] Even as a young man, evil troubled his astute mind and sensitive conscience. In fact, the dualistic solution advanced by the Manichees, though he denounced it later in life, was probably its chief intellectual appeal. Ultimately, he rejects their position in favor of the more metaphysically sophisticated view of the Neoplatonists, which resonated with his Christian belief in God's goodness and the innate goodness of creation, which has been corrupted by sin.

In the *Confessions* Augustine anticipates his later view of evil as privation as he discusses his early Manichean errors: "I did not know evil is nothing but the diminishment of good to the point where nothing at all is left."[17] Borrowing from Neoplatonic ontology, Augustine argues that evil does not exist *per se*, that is, it has no independent ontological existence. He grounds his ontology in theology, particularly the identification of God's existence and goodness. Since God creates, all creation, insofar as it exists at all, shares in God's inviolable goodness. Augustine's identification of existence with goodness entails that all substances participate in God's goodness, albeit finitely. Evil, then, exists as a metaphysical parasite on the good of creation: "Everything that exists is good, then; and so evil, the source of which I was seeking, cannot be a substance, because if it were, it would be good."[18] Evil is a distortion, perversion, or lack of the good.[19] Good, then, supplies the metaphysical footing

16. For an extensive treatment of the problem of evil in Augustine, see G. R. Evans, *Augustine on Evil* (Cambridge: Cambridge University Press, 1982). On the reception of Augustine's views, see Charles Matthewes, *Evil and the Augustinian Tradition* (Cambridge: Cambridge University Press, 2007).
17. Augustine, *Confessions* III.7.12, trans. Maria Boulding (New York: New City Press, 2001), 83.
18. Augustine, *Confessions* VII.12.18, p. 174.

of evil, which exists only insofar as it deforms and twists created goodness into shadows of itself.

Later, in the *City of God*, Augustine expands on his metaphysical viewpoint. Since God creates everything good, he does not create evil, either in the human or angelic realm. When the fallen angels turn away from God, they step out of the "eternal Light" into the darkness of divine absence. Hence, they do not assume a new "evil" nature; they simply severely diminish their created nature, becoming evil by subtraction, not addition: "For evil has no nature of its own. Rather, it is the absence of good which has received the name 'evil.'"[20] God, the supreme goodness, cannot create evil. Rather, it steals in surreptitiously in the backdoor of creation through the misuse of freedom.

> It is not permissible for us to doubt that the contrasting appetites of the good and bad angels have arisen not from a difference in their nature and origin—for God, the good Author and Creator of all substances, created them both—but from a difference in their wills and desires.[21]

Augustine insists that the fault lies not in the will, which is good, but in its misdirection: "Let no one, then, seek an efficient cause of an evil will. For its cause is not efficient, but deficient, because the evil will itself is not an effect of something, but a defect."[22] God, as the source of being, gives being to all creation. When it deviates from its created goodness, it strays from its true essence, and ventures toward nonbeing, called evil.[23] Consequently, evil only exists derivatively and privatively, not originally and essentially. Interestingly, his

19. Augustine, *Confessions* VII.13.19, p. 174: "For you [God] evil has no being at all, and this is true not of yourself only but of everything you have created, since apart from you there is nothing that could burst in and disrupt the order you have imposed on it."
20. Augustine, *City of God*, XI.9, p. 461.
21. Augustine, *City of God*, XII.1, p. 498.
22. Augustine, *City of God*, XII.7, p. 507.
23. Augustine, *City of God*, XII.2–3, pp. 500–501.

metaphysics precludes the possibility of "pure evil," since evil does not have any independent reality apart from the created goodness it corrupts. Without being to vitiate, evil simply fades into nonexistence: "In some cases, therefore, there can exist things which are wholly good; but there can never be things which are wholly evil."[24] His insight on the impossibility of pure or unalloyed evil illuminates its ontological status as always derivative, parasitic, and dependent on the created reality it corrupts and impairs.

These, then, are the basic contours of Augustine's ontology of evil. It rests on his doctrine of God, particularly divine goodness and immutability, and on his definition of sin as the misuse of freedom. His doctrine of creation *ex nihilo* and his nascent free will defense will reappear in chapter 3. For now, it is important to note how Augustine's theorization of evil sets the stage for later theological reflection on the privative status of evil, and that in Augustine we see a shift from biblical categories of evil to philosophical categories, which would continue in the subsequent centuries, as we will see. Moreover, it raises problems about the cause of evil, its original impulse, which Augustine finds insoluble: "Now to seek the causes of these defections, which are, as I have said, not efficient causes, but deficient, is like wishing to see darkness or hear silence."[25]

Thomas Aquinas

Thomas Aquinas (c. 1225–1274), the prolific Angelic Doctor, takes up the question of the ontological status of evil in *De Malo* (*On Evil*). At the outset, he asks: "Whether evil is something?"[26] Following the

24. Augustine, *City of God*, XII.3, p. 502.
25. Augustine, *City of God*, XII.7, p. 508.
26. Thomas Aquinas, *On Evil*, trans. John A. Oesterle and Jean T. Oesterle (Notre Dame, IN: University of Notre Dame Press, 1995), q.1, a.1, p. 1. See also Herbert McCabe, *God and Evil in the Theology of St Thomas Aquinas*, ed. Brian Davies (New York: Continuum, 2010).

method of disputation, he begins by marshaling twenty ultimately faulty arguments for its "somethingness" before siding with Augustine on the privative status of evil: "On the contrary, Augustine says that evil has no positive nature, but the lack of good has received this name."[27] Furthermore, citing Augustine's theological exegesis of John 1:3, Aquinas argues that evil is "nothing," outside of the "all things" that God creates.[28] Like Augustine, Aquinas associates evil with sin, arguing that sin corrupts creation and so does not belong to its original created goodness.

Confusion arises, Aquinas continues, when we conflate the subject of evil with evil itself.[29] Thus, we call someone evil when they act contrary to the goodness of their nature. Evil, in this sense, refers to their action, not their essence, which remains good insofar as they exist but becomes evil to the extent that they compromise their created goodness with sin. Evil, as the defection of created goodness, "inheres" in being without constituting being, for three reasons. First, God, as the "first and universal good," creates only particular goods. God's nature precludes the possibility of evil, so God could not originate evil.[30] Second, creation naturally strives for its particular form of goodness. Rational agents direct their actions toward beneficial or salutary ends, real or perceived. Evil represents the misdirection of their striving, whereas evil itself has no end or desire in itself, it is simply negation.[31] Third, the principle of self-preservation, whereby beings instinctively protect themselves against harm, demonstrates the inherent desirability or goodness of being. Evil, however, is defined by its opposition to goodness, which entails

27. Aquinas, *De Malo*, q.1, a.1, *sed contra* 1, p. 4.
28. Aquinas, *De Malo*, q.1, a.1, *sed contra* 2–3, p. 4.
29. Aquinas, *De Malo*, q.1, a.1, *respondeo*, pp. 4–5.
30. Aquinas, *De Malo*, q.1, a.1, *respondeo*, p. 5.
31. Aquinas, *De Malo*, q.1, a.1, *respondeo*, pp. 5–6.

its opposition to being, and thus cannot exist, because being cannot oppose itself.[32]

On the basis of these ontological arguments, Aquinas defines evil as the privation of the good: "Consequently I say that evil is not a thing; but that to which evil happens is a thing, inasmuch as evil deprives of only some particular good; thus for instance, blindness is not a thing, but that to which blindness happens is a thing."[33] Like Augustine, Aquinas wrestles with its paradoxical ontological status. Although evil does not have its own existence, it does exist as the defection of created being.[34] Similarly, although evil does not exist in reality, it does exist in the mind as a concept.[35] So evil both exists and does not exist. It exists insofar as it impacts creation and therefore becomes the object of experience and reflection, but it does not exist insofar as it has no independent reality.

Aquinas, then, continues the legacy of Augustine on the question of evil, with some key differences. Whereas Augustine's ontology was influenced primarily by Plotinus and Neoplatonism, Aquinas's ontology was influenced primarily by Aristotle. As a result, Aquinas's mode of argumentation shades more toward the concrete and empirical, even as it reproduces Augustine's privative theory. Both are left with unsolved questions about the ultimate origin of evil in creation. Evil, Aquinas says, cannot have a "*per se* cause," although its accidental cause is goodness, without which it would not exist in any sense.[36]

32. Aquinas, *De Malo*, q.1, a.1, *respondeo*, p. 6.
33. Aquinas, *De Malo*, q.1, a.1, *respondeo*, p. 6.
34. Aquinas, *De Malo*, q.1, a.1, *ad* 19, p. 10.
35. Aquinas, *De Malo*, q.1, a.1, *ad* 20, p. 10.
36. Aquinas, *De Malo*, q.1, a.3, *respondeo*, pp. 20–23.

John Calvin

In his book, *Calvin's* Theodicy *and the Hiddenness of God*, Paolo de Petris explores the origin, structure, and strategies of John Calvin's (1509–1564) defense of divine providence.[37] His study helpfully summarizes Calvin's conception of the nature of evil.[38] First, Calvin defines evil primarily as moral evil, or sin.[39] Second, he argues that God does not author evil directly, which shifts the blame from God to humanity.[40] Third, as an extension of his doctrine of double-predestination, he argues that God ordains evil.[41] Calvin situates his ontology of evil within the cosmic drama where evil complicates the plot until the dénouement, when the hidden narrative arc of providence becomes revealed to all, to their delight.

Calvin casts the question of the nature of evil within the context of divine providence. God creates and exercises providence over his creation, which means that he bears some responsibility for the existence of sin or evil. Calvin does not reject Augustine's privative theory of evil; he integrates it into his broader strategy: "He deemed that the privative conception of evil, right in itself, could not be an exhaustive defense of God's Justice."[42] God's providential arrangement of the universe entails the positive function of evil: it is not simply a negation. It must further God's mysterious plan for creation in ways that elude us, as the Book of Job illustrates. Thus, Calvin sees Augustine as a starting point for reflection on evil, not an end point: "Calvin entirely shared the Augustinian perspective

37. Paolo de Petris, *Calvin's* Theodicy *and the Hiddenness of God: Calvin's* Sermons on the Book of Job (New York: Peter Lang, 2012).
38. See also John Hick, *Evil and the God of Love* (New York: Palgrave Macmillan, 2007), 117–21.
39. De Petris, *Calvin's* Theodicy *and the Hiddenness of God*, 213.
40. De Petris, *Calvin's* Theodicy *and the Hiddenness of God*, 228.
41. De Petris, *Calvin's* Theodicy *and the Hiddenness of God*, 239. Calvin summarizes his position: "Man falls by the providential ordinance of God Himself, yet he falls by his own fault" (CO [*Calvini Opera*] 2:705).
42. De Petris, *Calvin's* Theodicy *and the Hiddenness of God*, 211.

of evil as a *privatio boni* and of sin as an *actus*. It is also worth noting that Calvin, even assuming some basic tenets of Augustinian theology, did not share the speculative and neoplatonic aspects of his thought."[43] Calvin, like Augustine, affirms the original goodness of creation, including the Devil and fallen angels before their fall, and attributes the fall to their misuse of freedom, and believes that God ultimately brings good out of evil. Unlike Augustine, Calvin rooted his conceptions in the Bible and focused on God's providential employment of evil, not its paradoxical ontology.[44]

Like Aquinas and Augustine before him, Calvin was unable to answer the question of the ultimate origin of evil: How does it arise in the first place, given its original goodness? Calvin seemed disinterested in the question, perhaps because it intrudes on the mystery of providence, or perhaps because it distracts from more pressing theological concerns about divine and human culpability for evil.[45] He employs the distinction between the "remote" and "proximate" cause of evil (the theological equivalent to Aquinas's "accidental vs. *per se*" philosophical notion of causation), assigning the divine will to the former and the human will to the latter.[46] These two affirmations, the divine permission (or, more precisely, ordaining) of evil and human culpability, are, in his view, ineffable.[47] Divine sovereignty and human freedom stand in uneasy tension in his theodicy.

Whereas Aquinas transposes Augustine's privative conception of evil into an Aristotelian matrix, Calvin transposes it into a providential matrix. Like Augustine and Aquinas, Calvin clears God from moral culpability, assigning blame to creation, particularly to

43. De Petris, *Calvin's* Theodicy *and the Hiddenness of God*, 213.
44. De Petris, *Calvin's* Theodicy *and the Hiddenness of God*, 281.
45. De Petris, *Calvin's* Theodicy *and the Hiddenness of God*, 212.
46. De Petris, *Calvin's* Theodicy *and the Hiddenness of God*, 230–31.
47. De Petris, *Calvin's* Theodicy *and the Hiddenness of God*, 231.

the misuse of freedom. Unlike Augustine and Aquinas, however, Calvin does not focus on God's permission of evil as much as on his co-option of evil to further his mysterious providential ends. God is not the victim of his own creation, like a failed cosmic experiment. Evil does not take God by surprise or thwart his inscrutable sovereign will. God has not, Calvin insists, lost control of the universe.[48] Rather, evil fits within God's larger designs for creation, and so expresses the divine will even as it resists it. Calvin's paradoxical stance on providence and evil reflects his Augustinian heritage and his commitment to God's omnipotent sovereignty over the universe.

Karl Barth

Karl Barth (1886–1968) takes up the question of the relationship between God and evil in *Church Dogmatics* III/3: The Doctrine of Creation.[49] In §50 he speaks of evil as *das Nichtige*, or "nothingness." Divine providence encounters "resistance" to "God's world-domination": "There is amongst the objects of God's providence an alien factor."[50] In section four Barth discusses "The Reality of Nothingness," where he searches for ways to express its paradoxical "existence." Nothingness, he says, is not mere negation—it does not *not* exist: "Nothingness is not nothing."[51] Nor does it simply signify what is not God (viz., creation), since creation's nondivinity, as the necessary horizon of its existence, belongs to the perfection of God's creation. Nothingness does not have a "nature" or "existence" and

48. De Petris, *Calvin's* Theodicy *and the Hiddenness of God*, 198–201.
49. R. Scott Rodin, *Evil and Theodicy in the Theology of Karl Barth* (New York: Peter Lang, 1997). See also Hick, *Evil and the God of Love*, 126–44.
50. Karl Barth, *Church Dogmatics* III/3, trans. G. W. Bromiley and R. J. Ehrlich, ed. G. W. Bromiley and T. F. Torrance (Edinburgh: T. & T. Clark, 1960), 289. Later Barth explicitly identifies *das Nichtige* with evil: "The character of nothingness derives from its ontic peculiarity. It is evil" (353); "It is only an echo, a shadow" of created reality (367).
51. Barth, *Church Dogmatics* III/3, 349.

thus remains outside the reach of natural human knowledge. God reveals its elusive reality to us in his rejection of it in salvation history.

So while Barth affirms the reality of nothingness, he firmly denies its existence. Its reality stems from the resistance to divine providence that humanity encounters. God's work in creation, then, provides the "ontic context" of nothingness, particularly his "jealousy, wrath, and judgment": "Nothingness is that from which God separates himself and in face of which He asserts Himself and exerts His positive will."[52] Barth's description of nothingness as the negative afterimage of divine providence situates evil in the reality of God's election: "God elects, and therefore rejects what he does not elect. God wills, and therefore opposes what He does not will. He says Yes, and therefore says No to that which He has not said Yes."[53] Nothingness, then, has no reality outside of God's sovereign activity in creation, which engenders, he notes, an ontological paradox:

> It "is" problematically because it is only on the left hand of God under His No, the object of His jealousy, wrath and judgment. It "is," not as God and His creation are, but only in its own improper way, as inherent contradiction, as impossible possibility. Yet because it is on the left hand of God, it really "is" in this paradoxical manner.[54]

Barth's concept of nothingness moves beyond the ontological emptiness of the privative theory of evil to a more theologically and existentially grounded reflection on the paradoxical reality of evil. It strains the limits of language and thought to articulate the "impossible possibility" of evil, that is, to ascribe substance to insubstantial reality. Nevertheless, it unflinchingly situates the ontological discussion about the nature of evil within the broader matrix of God's providential work in creation, which serves as an instructive

52. Barth, *Church Dogmatics* III/3, 351.
53. Barth, *Church Dogmatics* III/3, 351.
54. Barth, *Church Dogmatics* III/3, 351.

paradigm of how to think about evil beyond metaphysical abstractions.[55]

Theologians and philosophers appeal to analogies from the physical realm to illustrate the concept of the privative status of evil. Darkness, for instance, has no ontological or substantial existence: it is the absence of light. Similarly, silence has no positive existence: it is merely the absence of sound. There is no "sound of silence," despite artistic intimations to the contrary. Darkness and silence signify in the physical realm what evil signifies in the metaphysical realm: the privation of a positive quality. Barth talks about nothingness in similar terms: as an "echo" and a "shadow."[56]

The commonplace definition of evil as the privation of the good, which we have encountered in various forms in all four theologians, raises some significant conceptual difficulties. First, evil exists paradoxically, that is, it both does and does not exist. Technically, it does not exist on its own but denotes the defacement or depravation of existence. And yet, once it negates the good, it attains some level of existence, albeit parasitically. So, in the first place, it is deeply problematic to talk about the existence or reality of evil. What does it mean to say that evil "is" in any meaningful sense? When does someone or something *become* evil rather than simply being *diminished* by evil? It requires a degree of nuance and qualification not attained in most discussions of evil.

Second, it is difficult to account for the origin of evil in the traditional theistic accounts of evil as privation. If God does not create evil, from whence does it derive? How can something exist that God does not create, given the belief in God as Creator (irrespective

55. Barth, *Church Dogmatics* III/3, 366: "Here we ourselves have tried to avoid this abstraction. We have not sought to apprehend the relationship between Creator and creature philosophically and therefore from without, but theologically and therefore from within."

56. Barth, *Church Dogmatics* III/3, 367: "It [nothingness] is only an echo, a shadow, of what it was but is no longer, of what it could do but can do no longer."

of the means of creation)? The traditional answer is that evil arose from the misuse of freedom. But who is *ultimately* responsible for it? Did the Devil usher evil into creation with his primal sin of pride, or was it Adam and Eve's disobedience, or is it each of us when we choose against the good or opt for a lesser good over a greater good? Moreover, how does the impulse and possibility of sin arise in a perfect creation? And why would God give us free will if God presumably knew we would misuse it? These are some of the questions that complicate the traditional answer to the origin of evil.

Lastly, the philosophical and theological definition of evil as privation potentially attenuates the experiential reality of evil. By definition, evil is unreal, ontologically speaking. But it is very real—devastatingly real—to those who encounter it in their lives. To say that evil does not properly exist to the victim of abuse or disease or loss fails to capture the reality of their experience or to offer any meaningful apparatus to interpret their experience. Evil is not an abstract category for most people: it is a profoundly concrete experience. Thus, the privative theory of evil, without additional refinements, potentially minimizes or trivializes the reality of evil. It is difficult to define evil without negations. The classic definition accurately conveys its antithetical relation to God and divine goodness, but we need to enrich it by expressing its experiential reality even as we deny its ontological reality as a thing in itself, independent of God's good creation.

As a preliminary step in theodicy, then, theologians must carefully parse their ontology of evil. How does evil warp being, and how does it simultaneously exist and not exist? Moreover, as a next step, they must address the murky problem of the origin of evil. Whence comes evil into the world and to whom do we assign blame for its existence? God? The Devil? Adam? Eve? You? Me? Perhaps more appositely, what are the levels or degrees of moral culpability for evil?

And, finally, how do we define evil privatively without minimizing its impact? What are some alternative definitions or refinements that would capture the experiential reality of evil and its relation to God as Creator? These are just some of the salient ancillary questions we would have to address in order to provide a cogent response to the primary theoretical question: What is evil?

As we have seen, discourse on evil quickly shifts from the mythical and moral register of the Bible to the metaphysical register of philosophy. While I appreciate the heuristic value of ontological categories, I recommend the retrieval and redeployment of biblical imagery for evil. First, methodologically, it would situate the problem within its internal theological matrix, rather than subtly transposing it into an external philosophical matrix. Second, it would inject vibrancy and relevance into an issue obscured by onerous ontological oxymora and aporia. Talk of chaos, sin, Satan, and suffering, though controversial and problematic, rings truer to human experience than talk of nonbeing. Third, it correlates better with the resources available in theology to speak to problems of evil in the world. Privative definitions of evil, though helpful, take us too far afield from the theater of redemption, from the language of salvation, and from the biblical deposit.

Typology of Evil

The standard typology of evil also engenders conceptual difficulties for theodicy. Traditionally, theologians and philosophers have distinguished between three different types of evil: moral, natural, and metaphysical evil.[57] Moral evil signifies the sin and suffering that

57. See Gottfried Wilhelm Leibniz, *Theodicy: Essays on the Goodness of God, the Freedom of Man, and the Origin of Evil* (Chicago: Open Court Classics, 1998). See Chad Meister, *Evil: A Guide for the Perplexed*, 3–4. Hick, *Evil and the God of Love*, "The Kinds of Evil," 12–14.

result from the culpable misuse of freedom: murder, violence, abuse, and all the other ways we damage and diminish ourselves and others.[58] It is the most intuitive, accessible, straightforward category. Natural evil signifies the pain and suffering that arise from natural events. It refers to the death, injury, and destruction caused by nature, apart from free will: earthquakes, tsunamis, famine, tornados, and other destructive natural events.[59] Lastly, metaphysical evil signifies the imperfections and limitations of the universe, which create the possibility for moral and natural evil.[60] It refers to the finite, flawed conditions of the cosmos. Occasionally, metaphysical evil denotes the dark spiritual forces of the world, such as Satan. This type is the most elusive of the three.

TYPOLOGY OF EVIL: Scholars distinguish between three categories of evil: moral, natural, and metaphysical evil. Moral evil signifies suffering caused by human agency. Natural evil signifies suffering caused by natural forces. Metaphysical evil signifies the underlying cosmic structures that cause evil.

58. For a recent study of four models of moral evil, see Andrew Michael Flesher, *Moral Evil* (Washington, DC: Georgetown University Press, 2013). He summarizes his classifications as follows: "The first is evil as the presence of badness (i.e., evil as substantively and radically separate from the good—Manicheanism). The second is evil as the presence of goodness (i.e., evil as tantamount to the good—theodicy). The third is evil as the absence of badness (i.e., evil as an invention, a designated contrast to the good—thorough-going perspectivalism). The fourth is evil as the absence of goodness (i.e., evil as what occurs in lieu of the good—privation or Augustinianism)" (10).
59. Hick, *Evil and the God of Love*, 12.
60. Hick, *Evil and the God of Love*, 13. "This phrase refers to the basic fact of finitude and limitation within the created universe."

These standard classifications of evil are problematic for several reasons. First, the third category, metaphysical evil, lacks conceptual utility. It either shades into moral or natural evil or it fades into abstraction. Since it has no stable, consistent concrete referent, it loses its heuristic value for theodicy. Moreover, it would have to explain how the conditions of the universe themselves constitute evil, since they seem necessary for the possibility of creation in the first place. If God wishes to create free creatures of finite duration, he seems to have designed a universe suited to that purpose, which the category overlooks. In practice, theologians tend to ignore metaphysical evil in their discussions of the problem of evil. Has it become irrelevant or do we need to redefine or redeploy the category of metaphysical evil?

Second, the line between moral and natural evil sometimes blurs. Occasionally evil involves both, in different respects. For instance, would we classify an oil spill as a moral evil or natural evil? Since it often involves human error and oversight, we might rightly call it moral evil. On the other hand, since it involves a natural substance, oil, we might rightly call it natural evil. Even more pointedly: Does the cancer that someone contracts from drinking contaminated water count as natural evil or moral evil? Cancer is a natural evil, but its contraction was the result of moral evil. Lastly, many theologians have argued that some natural evils are the result of moral evil, a punishment for human or angelic sin. In those cases, the two categories are inextricably linked. We see, then, the imprecision and fluidity of these categories when applied to specific scenarios. It is not always clear-cut, and they are not hermetically sealed types. Nevertheless, I think they remain relevant, so long as we recognize that they are not oppositional or exclusive.

Thirdly, on what basis do we determine an action, person, or event to be evil? What are the theological and philosophical criteria involved? And at what point does an action, person, or event move from being really bad to being evil? Put differently, how do we name evil and how do we determine degrees of evil? In order to do so we must appeal to a conception of goodness. With respect to natural evil, when does an event become evil? Some think only moral evil can be called evil, properly speaking. Moreover, most natural phenomena, even destructive phenomena, serve a necessary natural function. They are part of the natural cycle, so why do we call them evil? Is a hurricane evil only when it results in death and destruction? Furthermore, how much destruction would these events have to cause or how many lives would they have to take to be really evil?

Lastly, the category of moral evil is particularly susceptible to politicization. Politically charged language of the "axis of evil" and "evildoers" implies a dualism between good and evil people or nations. It removes moral evil, and thus moral culpability, away from us, making it something "out there," something "other" than us. But, as Alexander Solzhenitsyn astutely observes, the line between good and evil lies not between us and them, but within each of us: "If only it were all so simple! If only there were evil people somewhere insidiously committing evil deeds, and it were necessary only to separate them from the rest of us and destroy them. But the line dividing good and evil cuts through the heart of every human being."[61] Every person and every nation has the capacity for good and evil. In point of fact, every person and every nation is inextricably involved in both. I do not mean to suggest that there are not people and nations that are more or less evil, I only mean to point out that no person (save one) and no nation can claim immunity from evil. So how do we talk responsibly and coherently about evil in international and interpersonal relationships? What does it mean to call our nation

61. Aleksandr Isayevich Solzhenitsyn, *The Gulag Archipelago 1918–1956 Abridged: An Experiment in Literary Investigation (P.S.)* (New York: Harper Perennial Modern Classic, 2007), 168.

or another nation evil? What does it mean to call ourselves or others evil? What do we risk in these assessments? These, then, are a few of the questions that we must address when appealing to the tripartite division of evil into moral, natural, and metaphysical.

The Problem of Evil

Reflection on the ontological status of evil and the categories of evil naturally issue in the theological question of the relationship between the nature of God and the reality of evil. The problem of evil, in its classic formulation, draws out the apparent contradiction between God and evil.[62] The classic logical problem of evil poses the problem as an inconsistent set of propositions: (1) If God is good, God would want to prevent evil; (2) If God is omnipotent, God would be able to prevent evil; (3) Evil exists. Therefore, according to the logic of the argument, either God does not exist or God is not good and/or omnipotent or there must be some morally sufficient reason for God's permission of evil. These three propositions are, at least *prima facie*, incompatible.[63] Recently,

PROBLEM OF EVIL: In theology and philosophy, the problem of evil refers to the logical tension between belief in divine omnipotence and goodness and the reality of evil. If God is almighty, he would be able to prevent evil, and if God is good, he would be willing to prevent evil. Whence, then, is evil?

62. Michael W. Hickson, "A brief history of the problems of evil," in *The Blackwell Companion to the Problem of Evil*, ed. Justin P. McBrayer and Daniel Howard-Snyder (Malden, MA: Wiley Blackwell, 2013), 3–18.

however, the ground has shifted away from the logical tension between these propositions to the evidential argument from evil, which argues that the breadth and depth of evil supplies strong evidence against God's existence, even if it does not constitute a logical contradiction.[64] Although the problem of evil typically refers to the logical problem of evil, it is not limited to that version. There are, in fact, multiple ways to parse the problem. These broadly divide into theoretical and practical versions, and subdivide further into several different related conceptual branches of the problem.[65] In reality, then, the "problem of evil" refers to "this family of problems collectively," and our response to any one of them will have implications for all of them.[66]

Marilyn McCord Adams has pioneered reflection on the plurality of the problems of evil. In addition to the logical and evidential problems, she enumerates others. For instance, she says that "the entrenchment of evils in our world poses a *practical* problem for living things generally."[67] At a basic biological level, evil threatens our existence, so one aspect of the problem of evil involves survival. At a higher emotional, psychological, and intellectual level, evil threatens our sense of meaningfulness: "Human beings, moreover, all face the *existential* problem of whether and how a life laced with suffering and

63. This is the famous "trilemma" of evil. See Ronald M. Green, "Theodicy," *The Encyclopedia of Religion*, 2nd edition, vol. 13, ed. Lindsay Jones (Detroit: Macmillan Reference USA, 2005), 9112.
64. On the evidential argument, see Daniel Howard-Snyder, ed., *The Evidential Argument from Evil* (Bloomington: Indiana University Press, 1996). There are a plethora of alternative terms for this approach: "Many philosophers distinguish between the 'logical' argument from evil (on the one hand) and the 'evidential' or 'inductive' or 'epistemic' or 'probabilistic' argument from evil (on the other)" (Peter van Inwagen, *The Problem of Evil*, 8).
65. See Michael L. Peterson, "Introduction," in *The Problem of Evil: Selected Readings*, ed. Michael L. Peterson (Notre Dame, IN: University of Notre Dame Press, 1992), 3–4.
66. Van Inwagen, *The Problem of Evil*, 4. "[T]he many problems of evil, for all they are distinct, do form a family and are intimately related to one another. . . . In practice, in concrete cases, they run into one another; they so to speak raise one another" (10).
67. Marilyn McCord Adams, "Introduction," in *The Problem of Evil*, ed. Marilyn McCord Adams and Robert Merrihew Adams (New York: Oxford University Press, 1990), 1.

punctuated by death can have any positive meaning."[68] So, according to Adams, there are at least four problems of evil: logical, evidential, practical, and existential.[69] Van Inwagen employs a similar taxonomy of the problem, which, while not identical to Adams, shares similar broad strokes: theoretical (doctrinal and apologetic) and practical (personal and pastoral).[70] Adams also notes that scholars approach these problems either atheologically (i.e., to disprove God's existence) or aporetically (i.e., as a challenge or puzzle to faith that invites deeper analysis).[71]

Adams's work signals the need to broaden our construal of the problem of evil, that is, to expand the ways we conceptualize it. We could suggest further options. For instance, we could focus on the *social* problem of evil, that is, the problems of poverty, abuse, and violence in society and the systemic evils of unjust power relations between individuals and various institutions of power. Or we could analyze the *spiritual* problem of evil, which poses the problem in terms of our personal struggle with sin and perhaps dark spiritual forces. Or, finally, we could focus on the *pastoral* problem of evil, which explores clerical engagements with the problem of evil in their spheres of influence. The options are as endless as the contexts in which we encounter evil. When talking about the problem of evil, then, we should always remember that there are several ways to parse the problem and that the way we formulate it will inevitably shape our theodicy.

68. Adams, "Introduction," *The Problem of Evil*, 1.
69. See also her related discussion in Marilyn McCord Adams, *Horrendous Evils and the Goodness of God* (Ithaca, NY: Cornell University Press, 1999), 7–16.
70. Van Inwagen, *The Problem of Evil*, 4–5. Van Inwagen further subdivides personal problems of evil into subjective and objective (suffering directly experienced versus suffering observed) and further subdivides apologetic problems of evil into internal and external (prompted from within or without).
71. Adams, "Introduction," *The Problem of Evil*, 2–3.

Despite these expansions on the traditional formulation of the problem of evil, we must not dispense with the global, abstract, logical problem of evil.[72] The logical tension between the reality of evil and the existence of God still exerts an enormous intellectual force that we must confront with various theological and philosophical resources. Nevertheless, it is also instructive to move from the macro to the micro level of analysis when examining the problem of evil. In addition to the global, abstract, and logical problem of evil, we should also attend to the particular, concrete, existential problems that confront individuals. The problem of evil surfaces in various ways, then, and we should examine them in their irreducible particularity, but not at the expense of the broader problem that impacts all of humanity. We will discuss possibilities for practical turns in theodicy extensively in chapter 7.

Lastly, the common allusion to "the problem of evil" is problematic in another sense. We have already discussed the theoretical problem with its implied singularity: there is not one *problem* of evil, there are many *problems* of evil. In addition, the term *problem* naturally implies its analytic counterpart: *solution*. But the problem of evil does not admit of a single solution or any intellectual solution at all. Few claim to have "solved" the problem of evil. It is not like a mathematical equation. Theodicy responds to the problem of evil with plausible reasons why God allows evil. It develops a coherent theological approach, but it does not, strictly speaking, solve it. To claim otherwise outstrips the capacity of human reason and underestimates the intractability of the problem. Some questions are never fully answered; some aspects of life remain a mystery. This does not mean that we should abandon the project. It simply means that

72. Van Inwagen argues that the distinction between the global and local arguments from evil is more important than the distinction between the logical and evidential versions of the problem of evil (Peter van Inwagen, *The Problem of Evil*, 8).

once we have exhausted our intellectual and imaginative resources we arrive at the horizon of mystery where we must, in Hamlet's final words, leave the rest to silence.

We have explored various configurations of the problem of evil: theoretical (logical, evidential, doctrinal, apologetic) and practical (biological, existential, personal, and pastoral). What do these all have in common? From a sociological and philosophical perspective, evil, in all its manifestations, undermines our constructions of reality: "Evil threatens meaning. Evil threatens our ability to regard the world in which we find ourselves as comprehensible."[73] From a specifically theological standpoint, evil calls God's existence into question. In most classic theistic formulations of the problem of evil, God is conceived of as omnipotent (which includes omniscience, omnipresence, and immutability) and goodness (which includes justice, mercy, and love).[74] Moreover, these divine attributes are believed to inhere in the divine life in perfect harmony, which begs the question of theodicy: Why does God, conceived thus, permit evil?

Paradigmatic Evils

Finally, let us briefly discuss paradigmatic evils.[75] Paradigmatic evils are those events in history that illustrate the problem of evil. Evil, in varying degrees of severity, occurs daily. It always has, and it always

73. Van Inwagen, *The Problem of Evil*, 15.

74. Van Inwagen argues that "omnipotence and moral perfection" are "non-negotiable components of the idea of God" (*The Problem of Evil*, 62–63). Process theodicy, as we will discuss extensively in chapter 5, denies the first of God's non-negotiable divine attributes.

75. Sarah Pinnock notes the contextual nature of paradigmatic evils, or what she calls, borrowing from Marilyn McCord Adams, "paradigmatic horrors," which include the Holocaust, colonization, slavery, violence, and disease. These are viewed as paradigmatic "depending on a person's national, social, geographical, and political situation." See Sarah K. Pinnock, *Beyond Theodicy: Jewish and Christian Continental Thinkers Respond to the Holocaust* (Albany: State University of New York Press, 2002), 2.

will. Paradigmatic evils refer to those events that shock us by their heinousness, pervasiveness, and senselessness. They do not merely exemplify the problem of evil, they embody it. In every generation, atrocities and misfortunes occur that bring the problem of evil into sharp relief. They become the focal points of the dilemma and the touchstones of theodicy. In our generation, the terrorist attacks of September 11, 2001, the tsunami in South East Asia, and, recently, the massacre of twenty schoolchildren in Newton, Connecticut, all serve as paradigmatic evils. Some evils, however, transcend their historical particularity. Historically, the Lisbon earthquake, the bubonic plague, and the two world wars functioned as paradigmatic evils.[76] Above all, the Holocaust stands out as the paradigmatic evil *par excellence* to which theodicy constantly refers.[77]

Two problems beset the concept of paradigmatic evil. First, the global, historical dimension of paradigmatic evils potentially overshadows individual encounters with evil. While everyone is affected by the Holocaust in the sense that it illustrates the depths of human malice and the problem of unjust suffering, it is more often than not our personal experiences of evil and suffering that become definitive for us. While I do not suggest that we should ignore global or historical examples of injustice and suffering, we should also explore the paradigmatic evils that impact individuals today. At some point, everyone has a crisis or agonizing experience that calls God's justice, or God's very existence, into question. These can be fruitful entry points into discussions of the problem of evil, but they need not overshadow the significance of shared or collective evils.

Second, the particularity and singularity of paradigmatic evils potentially cause us to overlook other important instances. For

76. In Luke 13:4, Jesus mentions the death of eighteen people "when the tower of Siloam fell on them," which strikes me as a contemporary "paradigmatic evil" for Jesus.

77. Stephen T. Davis, "Introduction," *Encountering Evil: Live Options in Theodicy*, ed. Stephen T. Davis (Louisville: Westminster John Knox, 2001), xiii.

example, the constant reference to the Holocaust as the paradigmatic evil might cause a moral myopia where we fail to address other historical and contemporary instances of evil. The terrorist attacks of 9/11, for example, have become a paradigmatic evil. Recent earthquakes and tsunamis also bring the problem of evil into focus. So while the Holocaust remains a unique and indelible instance of paradigmatic evil, we should also look for recent examples and we should also recognize that just as individuals experience their own distinctive paradigmatic evils, so nations and different groups experience their own distinctive paradigmatic evils. The events of 9/11 impacted the world, but they impacted America in a particular way. The tsunami that devastated Japan impacted the world, but it has particular relevance and resonance for the Japanese. In short, global paradigmatic evils should not eclipse individual and national examples of paradigmatic evils. Just as there are many problems of evil, so there are many paradigmatic evils, even though some, such as the Holocaust, remain decisive.

Conclusion

My task has not been to give definitive answers to these interlocking questions about the reality of evil and its theological implications. Instead, I have pursued a more modest agenda: to clarify and refine the questions and suggest productive ways to engage them. Three themes have emerged. First, we must not lose sight of the biblical grounding or experiential reality of evil in our discussions of its ontological status. Second, we must explore the plurality of ways to formulate the problem of evil and to connect it to contemporary intellectual and experiential contexts. Finally, Christian reflections on evil gain traction when they shift from ontology to theology, which situates the problem within the broader question of the relationship between divine providence and human experience. Karl Barth's concept of *nothingness* provides an instructive example of how to configure the reality of evil within a distinctive theological matrix. Hopefully these prolegomena will facilitate further discussions and research on the variety of ways evil continues to impinge on creation and inform optimal strategies for crafting a coherent response. Before we analyze some of these strategies, let us explore the task of theodicy itself.

Questions for Discussion:

1. What is the privative theory of evil? How would you define evil?
2. Which biblical portrayal of evil do you find most helpful and least helpful?
3. Which theological portrayal of evil do you find most helpful and least helpful?
4. What is the most urgent or instructive way to configure the problem of evil?
5. What events would you identify as paradigmatic evils, either personally or historically?

2

Redefining Theodicy

Expanding the Boundaries

"That to the height of this great argument
I may assert eternal providence,
And justify the ways of God to men."[1]

The term *theodicy* has been prone to misapprehension and misinterpretation. Some see it as empty technical jargon: a word reserved for specialists, disconnected from real life, which reinforces the perceived disjunction between the academy and the real world. Whatever theodicy might mean, it is something elusive and abstract, a topic for think tanks in ivory towers, not for the average person. For others, particularly experts on the subject, theodicy has a precise purpose and purview: it refers to the logical attempt to reconcile God's nature with the reality of evil. It operates in an amorphous

1. John Milton, *Paradise Lost*, 1.24–26, ed. Stephen Orgel and Jonathan Goldberg, Oxford World's Classics (New York: Oxford University Press, 2008), 4.

theistic zone between theology and philosophy. Most people, academics and nonacademics alike, define theodicy as a narrow, technical, specialized area of scholarly inquiry.

These impressions, however, misperceive the simplicity of the project at its core: to make sense of suffering.[2] Although the *term* itself might mystify and stratify, it merely signifies an intellectual process that happens all the time in all segments of society. We all encounter troubles and hardships. We all observe the suffering that besets the world, where each new day evil manifests itself in new ways. The task of theodicy is to interpret the reality of evil: to situate it within a meaningful theological matrix. Theodicy simply tries to explain evil. These explanations vary in intellectual sophistication, as Peter Berger aptly observes in *The Sacred Canopy*, but they all have the same basic objective, viz., to comprehend and thereby domesticate and defuse the ubiquitous reality of evil, injustice, and misfortune.[3] In this chapter I propose that we expand the narrow definition of theodicy that has dominated the theological and philosophical landscape since the eighteenth century to include the plurality of encounters and engagements with evil that we find in "real life."

Furthermore, theodicy has been situated primarily within the field of philosophy. The term itself was developed by a philosopher, and most scholarly treatments of it occur in books and courses on philosophy, the philosophy of religion, philosophical theology, and the like. Theodicy, however, belongs *primarily* to theology and only *secondarily* to philosophy, in my view. Questions about God's goodness and justice, which the term denotes, fall within theology's purview, but theology has often been content to abdicate them to its

2. For a detailed examination of the theoretical task of theodicy, see Mark S. M. Scott, *Journey Back to God: Origen on the Problem of Evil* (New York: Oxford University Press, 2012), 8–22.
3. Peter Berger, *The Sacred Canopy: Elements of a Sociological Theory of Religion* (New York: Anchor, 1990), 53.

nearest disciplinary neighbor: philosophy.[4] Theology, then, ought to reclaim theodicy for itself by shaping the discourse with its distinctive methodologies and theorists. To be clear: I do not repudiate philosophy's involvement with theodicy. In fact, theodicy benefits from the conceptual nuance and precision that philosophy brings to the question. Furthermore, overlap between theology and philosophy engenders productive interdisciplinary dialogue. Philosophy need not renounce its legitimate claim on theodicy; rather, theology needs to reassert its claim on the question and revisit its responses.[5]

What Is Theodicy?

Let us begin with the traditional definition of theodicy. *Theodicy* itself is a neologism, that is, an invented term. It fuses two Greek nouns: θεός (God) and δίκη (justice).[6] At the beginning of the eighteenth century, G. W. Leibniz transliterated them into the French word *théodicée* (German: *Theodizee*) in his book on the subject: *Essais de Théodicée sur la bonté de Dieu, la liberté de l'homme et l'origine du mal*. So the term itself was invented by a philosopher to describe a philosophical enterprise. It has retained its original sense of the vindication of divine justice, as Immanuel Kant's definition illustrates: "By 'theodicy' we understand the defense of the highest wisdom of the creator [providence] against the charge which reason brings against it for whatever is counterpurposive (*das Zweckwidrige*) in the

4. Tensions often arise between near neighbors, both because of their familiarity and the desire to clearly demarcate the boundaries between them. Theology and philosophy have a long history of cooperation and tension. Despite their similarities, both with respect to their major theorists and the types of questions they address, they often strain to differentiate themselves, not unlike, to switch metaphors, close siblings.
5. René van Woudenberg, "A brief history of theodicy," in *The Blackwell Companion to the Problem of Evil*, ed. Justin P. McBrayer and Daniel Howard-Snyder (Malden, MA: Wiley Blackwell, 2013), 177–91.
6. Sarah K. Pinnock, *Beyond Theodicy: Jewish and Christian Continental Thinkers Respond to the Holocaust* (Albany: State University of New York Press, 2002), 2–3.

world."[7] Theodicy, in its narrow, classic, technical sense, explores logical strategies to vindicate God from moral culpability for evil. In short, theodicy seeks to "justify the ways of God to men."[8] It does not simply refute the accusation of injustice, it demonstrates God's justice: "A theodicy is not simply an attempt to meet the charge that God's ways are unjust: it is an attempt to exhibit the justice of his ways."[9] Theodicy tells a "story" about how God and evil logically coexist.[10]

THEODICY: The technical term *theodicy* signifies the defense of divine justice in the face of evil. It employs logical strategies to "justify the ways of God to men," that is, to vindicate God from moral culpability. More broadly, theodicy denotes the attempt to explain or make sense of suffering.

As we saw earlier, the logical problem of evil has a syllogistic structure: If God is good, he would be *willing* to prevent evil. If God is omnipotent, he would be *able* to prevent evil. Evil exists. God, therefore, does not exist, at least not in the standard theistic sense. David Hume famously encapsulates the logical problem of evil: "Is he [i.e., God] willing to prevent evil, but not able? Then he is impotent. Is he able, but not willing? Then he is malevolent. Is he both able and willing? Whence then is evil (*unde malum*)?"[11]

7. Immanuel Kant, "On the miscarriage of all philosophical trials in theodicy," in *Religion within the Boundaries of Mere Reason and Other Writings*, trans. and ed. Allen Wood and George Di Giovanni (Cambridge: Cambridge University Press, 1998 [2003]), 17. Later he describes the task of theodicy as "the vindication of the moral wisdom of the world-government against the doubts raised against it on the basis of what the experience of this world teaches" (23). And also: "All theodicy should truly be an *interpretation* of nature insofar as God announces his will through it" (24).
8. Milton, *Paradise Lost*, 1.24–26, p. 4.
9. Peter van Inwagen, *The Problem of Evil* (New York: Oxford University Press, 2006), 6.
10. Van Inwagen, *The Problem of Evil*, 7, 65.

Theodicy confronts this logical "trilemma": (a) God is good; (b) God is omnipotent; (c) Evil exists. Through highly nuanced and complex—almost mathematical—calculations, it endeavors to affirm divine goodness and omnipotence in the face of evil. These reflections, often undertaken by philosophers and philosophical theologians, try to prove the compatibility between God and evil. Although they address a perennial problem that affects all humanity, they strike many readers as cold, dispassionate, and overly abstract.

Traditional theodicy defends theism from the intellectual threat of the logical problem of evil. It is, therefore, fundamentally defensive: it responds to the intellectual and existential force of the problem of evil. Where is God? Why does God permit suffering? Why does God not intervene to stop the wicked and to help the innocent? God sits in the dock of the cosmic courtroom, as it were, on trial for the misfortunes and miseries of the world.[12] A cursory glance at the evidence suggests that God, the Creator of the cosmos, is morally culpable for evil. The prosecution makes their case against God: the depth and breadth of evil in the world problematizes, or undermines, theistic beliefs. The defense gives exculpatory reasons why God allows evil. Afterwards, the jury must render a verdict. At stake in the theological and philosophical trial, therefore, are the credibility of the traditional theistic doctrine of God and, thus, the viability of faith.

11. David Hume, *Dialogues Concerning Natural Religion*, Part X, ed. Martin Bell (New York: Penguin, 1990), 108–9.
12. Kant, "On the miscarriage of all philosophical trials in theodicy," 17: "The author of a theodicy agrees, therefore, that this juridical process be instituted before the tribunal of reason; he further consents to represent the accused side as advocate through the formal refutation of all the plaintiff's complaints."

Expanding the Definition

Why expand the boundaries of theodicy? How does it advance the project of theodicy? First, it follows as a natural corollary to the expansion of the problem of evil beyond the strictly logical problem of evil. If the problems have expanded, so must theodicy. Theodicy must find new ways to speak to these new formulations of the problem of evil. That does not entail abandoning traditional theodicies any more than the new formulations of the problem of evil entail the abandonment of the logical problem of evil. It remains in full force, as do the theodicies that have arisen to neutralize it.

Second, we must expand the definition of theodicy in response to contemporary critiques of traditional theodicies.[13] As we will discuss in chapter 7, recent work in theodicy has leveled serious criticisms against traditional theodicy, which run along two lines. First, they believe that the classic problem of evil cannot be solved. Second, they argue that traditional approaches fail to attend to the experiential reality of suffering. Critics of traditional theodicy call for a rejection or reconfiguration of theodicy. They recommend a transition from the theoretical to the practical, from the abstract to the concrete, from the global to the particular. Suffering, they say, poses an existential problem *before* it poses an intellectual problem, and traditional theodicy has lost sight of the human experience of suffering in their rarefied ruminations on the reality of evil.

These criticisms of traditional theodicy, combined with the multifaceted nature of the problem, engender the necessity of redefinition. Theodicy, in an expanded sense, moves beyond syllogistic, rationalistic, philosophical solutions to the logical problem

13. See, as representative examples, Sarah K. Pinnock, *Beyond Theodicy: Jewish and Christian Continental Thinkers Respond to the Holocaust*, Terrence Tilley, *The Evils of Theodicy* (Washington, DC: Georgetown University Press, 1991), and Kenneth Surin, *Theology and the Problem of Evil* (Eugene, OR: Wipf & Stock, 1986 [2004]).

of evil to creative, diverse, experientially grounded analyses of the many problems of evil. It invites new methodologies, especially from Christian theology. More specifically, it draws from the often-untapped insights of systematic, historical, practical, pastoral, and moral theology, as well as other disciplinary lenses, to enrich and enhance the study of theodicy. These subfields intersect and overlap in several ways, but they all open new vistas for reimagining the task of theodicy to meet contemporary theological concerns.

Redefining theodicy in experiential, practical directions does not negate the utility or urgency of traditional theodicies, however. Contrary to many antitheodicists, I do not reject classic theistic treatments of the logical problem of evil, nor do I think that they are universally guilty of detached intellectualization. Traditional theistic theodicies remain vital to academic discourse on theodicy, particularly in philosophy and religious studies. Rather than reject them, theology should interface them with more theologically grounded theodicies that respond to the experiential reality of suffering. Interfacing traditional theistic models with theologically and experientially grounded models would be mutually beneficial. Traditional theodicy would benefit from the practical slant of the new perspectives in theodicy, while these new perspectives, especially in theology, would benefit from the history and logical rigor of traditional theistic approaches.

Expanding theodicy in these directions gives it a distinctly ethical edge. Theodicy no longer simply explains evil, its key theoretical function; it also strives to overcome and transform it through various practical responses. It identifies instances of violence, oppression, and exploitation in society and works to ameliorate those conditions. So theodicy in this redefined sense shades into the realm of ethics. Ethics, then, becomes a new frontier of theodicy, but it need not abandon its traditional location in theology and philosophy. These diverse approaches to theodicy are complementary, not antithetical.

We see the results of expanded versions of theodicy at work already. Practical theology and philosophy have already begun to move in this direction. Pastoral theology has long recognized the need to connect theodicy to real-life experiences of suffering. Examples of theodicy in an expanded sense include what I call "theodicy at the margins," which attends to the oppression of the marginalized, such as women, the poor, and ethnic minorities.[14] Theodicies at the margins, exemplified by feminist, liberation, and black theology, have a practical, particular, experiential focus. Theodicy, then, is slowly migrating from the exclusive realm of philosophy to the realm of real life. The task of theology is to chart new pathways forward in theodicy that unite philosophical treatments with concrete experiences within a clearly defined theological matrix. These pathways will move in different directions and at different paces, but they will have the same theological grounding, as we will discuss in the final chapter.

Modes of Theodicy

Thus far, we have defined theodicy and explored constructive ways to expand the definition. Now, to further refine the task of theodicy, let us examine the different modes or ways of doing theodicy. Theodicy involves intellectual engagement with the problem of evil, but it happens in strikingly different ways and in drastically different contexts. These distinctions, though not mutually exclusive, reveal the diverse pathways traversed in theodicy, which frequently have

14. Mark S. M. Scott, "Theodicy at the Margins: New Trajectories for the Problem of Evil," *Theology Today* 68, no. 2 (2011): 149–52.

distinct methodologies, presuppositions, objectives, strategies, interlocutors, and audiences.

First, theodicy typically takes place in the academy. Academic theodicies explore the problem of evil from within clearly defined disciplinary boundaries, employing their distinctive theories and methods to illuminate the problem. Academic research on theodicy occurs in several sectors of the social sciences and humanities. It may even take place in the hard sciences. Most commonly, academic theodicies are found in philosophy, religious studies, and theology. Let us explore its various manifestations in each of these.

Philosophy departments have been the most common location for research on theodicy in the academy. Within philosophy, theodicy might be examined from the standpoint of logic, the philosophy of religion, the history of philosophy, or constructive proposals. These are not mutually exclusive lenses, but research has become increasingly specialized. Philosophy explores theodicy as a matter of intellectual history and coherence, utilizing the insights of its major thinkers, such as G. W. Leibniz, David Hume, Immanuel Kant, and, more recently, John Hick, Alvin Plantinga, and others.

Religion departments also explore theodicy from multiple vantage points. Religious Studies might explore the theory of theodicy, that is, how it functions in religion generally, or it might examine the theodicy of a particular religion in a particular thinker or text. Alternatively, it might take a comparative approach, interfacing theodicies from different religious traditions, tracing significant points of convergence and divergence. Subfields of Religious Studies interested in theodicy include religious studies theory, philosophy of religion, history of Christianity, and comparative religion.

Finally, academic theology (in contrast to confessional theology) obviously takes a keen interest in theodicy. It might research the theodicy of a particular theologian in his or her historical context, such as the Apostle Paul, Irenaeus, Perpetua, Clement of Alexandria, Origen, Augustine, Anselm, Thomas Aquinas, Julian of Norwich, Martin Luther, John Calvin, Friedrich Schleiermacher, Karl Rahner, Karl Barth, Dorothee Sölle, or Jürgen Moltmann. We would classify this as historical theology. Alternatively, academic theology might explore how theodicy intersects with and impacts the major tenets of Christian faith. We would classify this as systematic theology. Or, finally, academic theology might critically engage or craft constructive proposals in dialogue with major thinkers and themes in theodicy. We would classify this as constructive theology. These, again, are not necessarily mutually exclusive categories (this book utilizes all three), but they are distinct points of entry.

Next, theodicy also takes place in the realm of apologetics. Apology here does not mean the expression of remorse and regret; it refers to the defense of Christian faith. Apologists defend Christianity against intellectual threats, so naturally it takes an interest in the problem of evil. Apologetic theodicies are theologically invested, confessional, and evangelical in the sense that they seek to uphold the integrity of the gospel through the profession of the coherence of faith.[15] Apologetic theodicies have varying levels of intellectual sophistication, but the intent remains the same. They have many atheistic counterparts, which seek to undermine faith by exploiting the problem of evil.[16]

Recent work in theodicy examines pastoral perspectives on the problem of evil.[17] Clergy are on the front lines of theodicy. They provide comfort, hope, and succor to their parishioners as they

15. See, for example, N. T. Wright, *Evil and the Justice of God* (Downers Grove, IL: IVP, 2006); Os Guinness, *Unspeakable: Facing Up to the Challenge of Evil* (New York: HarperOne, 2006); John G. Stackhouse Jr., *Can God Be Trusted? Faith and the Challenge of Evil* (New York: Oxford University Press, 1998); C. S. Lewis, *The Problem of Pain* (New York: HarperOne, 2001 [1940]).

16. For instance, Bart D. Ehrman, *God's Problem: How the Bible Fails to Answer Our Most Important Question—Why We Suffer* (New York: HarperOne, 2008) as well as most books by the New Atheists.

undergo traumatic life experiences, such as illness, abuse, loss, and other forms of suffering. They are called to preach on the problem of evil and to guide their parishioners through times of crises. Moreover, chaplains at hospitals, in the military, and in other venues directly encounter the problem of evil on a routine basis. For clergy of all descriptions, evil represents an intellectual, experiential, and spiritual dilemma that they confront daily. Pastoral perspectives look at the ways some clergy have failed to speak wisdom in these moments of suffering and how they might draw from the resources of theology to preach, counsel, and write on the problem of evil and suffering with more compassion, theological sophistication, and practical relevance.

Theodicy also takes place at the personal level, as the existential effort to make sense of suffering in one's own life. People strive to situate their experiences of suffering within a coherent personal narrative. These self-rationalizations or self-theodicies occur at mental, verbal, or written levels, but they all involve the integration of painful experiences into a meaningful framework. These theodicies might never be spoken or written, but they still operate invisibly in the person's innermost thoughts. We most frequently encounter these personal theodicies in our interactions with people in crisis and in autobiographies where the person recounts their suffering and explains how they ultimately came to terms with their pain, confusion, and despair. Personal theodicies rarely rely on academic theodicies. More often than not, they draw on the spiritual resources of their tradition, perhaps as taught by their clergy or respected friends.

Personal theodicies might take the form of artistic expression. Perhaps looking for theodicy in the arts pushes the boundaries of

17. For two examples, see Thomas G. Long, *What Shall We Say? Evil, Suffering, and the Crisis of Faith* (Grand Rapids, MI: Eerdmans, 2011), and John Swinton, *Raging with Compassion: Pastoral Responses to the Problem of Evil* (Grand Rapids, MI: Eerdmans, 2007).

theodicy too far. But what if theodicy ranged beyond the purely logical engagement with the problem of evil? What if theodicy, which always tries to make sense of suffering, utilized artistry instead of argumentation? What might this look like? In point of fact, it already exists. We find theodicy in music, literature, art, TV, film, and other artistic mediums. These give expression to theodicy artistically, and through their artistry they find new pathways to interpret experiences of evil and to integrate them into a broader meaningful matrix. The problem with pastoral, personal, and artistic theodicies, however, is that they are prone to become overly subjective and therapeutic, which strays too far from theodicy's logical, rationalistic roots.

Questions of Theodicy

Theodicy explores several interrelated theological and philosophical questions about evil. Theodical models or systems address all of them, to varying degrees, in different ways. Theodical themes or trajectories, on the other hand, address only a few of them, and are found in virtually all theodical models as component parts. The next three chapters explore major models of theodicy, while the final three address key themes or trajectories in theodicy. These are the five essential questions of theodicy.

1. Origin of evil: How does evil originate? Who is responsible?
2. Nature of evil: What is the ontology of evil? How does it exist?
3. Problem of evil: How does evil pose a problem for theology?
4. Reason for evil: Why does God permit evil? What is the morally sufficient reason?
5. End of evil: How will God end evil and/or ultimately bring good out of evil?

Theodicy need not address these questions sequentially, nor does it need to have definitive positions on them, especially since the origin and end of evil are inherently speculative. Nevertheless, a complete theodicy will respond to all five questions.

QUESTIONS OF THEODICY: Theodicy explores five interrelated theological-philosophical questions: (1) the origin of evil; (2) the nature of evil; (3) the problem of evil; (4) the reason for evil; and (5) the end of evil. These questions often overlap in the development of theodicies.

Criteria for Theodicy

In the dialogue section of every chapter we will assess the strengths and weaknesses of the theodical model and trend we investigate. At the outset, therefore, let us establish an explicit set of criteria that will function as our rational, practical, and theological litmus test for theodicy. These are our five criteria for a sound *Christian* theodicy.[18]

18. John Hick enumerates two primary criteria for theodicy: "The two main demands upon a theodicy hypothesis are that it be (1) internally coherent, and (2) consistent with the data both of the religious tradition on which it is based, and of the world, in respect both of the latter's general character as revealed by scientific enquiry and of the specific facts of moral and natural evil" (John Hick, "An Irenaean Theodicy," in *Encountering Evil: Live Options in Theodicy*, ed. Stephen T. Davis [Louisville: Westminster John Knox, 2001], 38). These correspond, roughly, to my first three criteria. Similarly, Sarah Pinnock proposes four "guidelines" for theodicy from the perspective of practical theology or ethics: (1) epistemic humility, (2) moral sensitivity, (3) religious practice, and (4) narrative memory" (Pinnock, *Beyond Theodicy*, 139). Her guidelines correspond, roughly, to my first, third, and fifth criteria.

CRITERIA FOR THEODICY: In order to assess the cogency and credibility of theodicy, we must delineate explicit criteria. To facilitate our analysis in the dialogue section of each chapter, then, we will utilize five criteria: (1) Fidelity; (2) Coherence; (3) Relevance; (4) Creativity; and (5) Humility.

1. Fidelity: Does it utilize the sources of theology, especially scripture and tradition?
2. Coherence. Does it make sense logically? Is it internally consistent?
3. Relevance. Does it speak to contemporary experiences of evil?
4. Creativity. Does it creatively engage the problem of evil?
5. Humility: Does it recognize and respect the limits of theodicy?

These five criteria are not equally weighted. Some count more decisively than others in determining the overall effectiveness and cogency of the theodicy. They are listed (roughly) in order of importance. To assign a relative value to the criteria (1=40%, 2=30%, 3–5=10% each, for instance), however, would be artificial and arbitrary. There is no precise theological algorithm for theodicy. Nevertheless, the first and second criteria are primary, while the latter three are secondary, which does not diminish their value; it simply subordinates them to the definitive criteria of fidelity and coherence. All five will factor into our analysis of the viability of theodicial models and trends.

Conclusion

Evil shatters lives and theoretical systems in a single blow. Theodicy tries to put the pieces back together through plausible explanations of why God permits evil.[19] Why redefine theodicy? First, the expansion of the *problems* of evil necessitates a corresponding expansion of theodicy to respond to new configurations of the problem. Second, expanding the definition in experiential and practical directions addresses the perennial critique that theodicy intellectualizes an existential problem; in other words, that it does not sufficiently attend to the experiential reality of suffering. Third, we must expand the narrow formulation of theodicy, typical in philosophical circles, to make room for new methodologies, new insights, and new voices, particularly in theology.

Academic theodicy has been primarily the trade of philosophy for far too long. The time has come for theology to reclaim the problem of evil for itself and to draw from its own diverse intellectual heritage to speak to it in new ways and with new voices. Theology's reclamation of theodicy does not mean the dismissal of generic theistic theodicies or its isolation from philosophical engagements with the problem of evil. Quite the contrary: theology would be wise to appropriate and utilize the insights of philosophy as it breaks new ground in theodicy, clearing its own *theological* pathways forward. Discussion of theodicy should not transpire in hermetically sealed intellectual silos. Disciplinary insularity stultifies work in theodicy. Instead, theology should promote and welcome vibrant, dynamic, respectful, interdisciplinary dialogue. Before theology can contribute

19. Nicholas Wolterstorff, *Lament for a Son* (Grand Rapids, MI: Eerdmans, 2001). Wolterstorff poignantly expresses the shattering experience of evil and the task of theodicy to somehow put the pieces back together: "I cannot fit it together at all. I can only, with Job, endure. I do not know why God did not prevent Eric's death. To live without the answer is precarious. It's hard to keep one's footing . . . I have no explanation. I can do nothing else than endure in the face of this deepest and most painful of mysteries. I believe in God the Father Almighty, maker of heaven and earth and resurrecter of Jesus Christ. I also believe that my son's life was cut off in its prime. I cannot fit these pieces together. I am at a loss. I have read the theodicies produced to justify the ways of God to man. I find them unconvincing. To the most agonized question I have ever asked I do not know the answer. I do not know why God would watch him fall. I do not know why God would watch me wounded. I cannot even guess" (67–68).

to these discussions, however, it must find its own voice, or, rather, *voices*.[20]

Questions for Discussion:

1. Does theodicy belong to theology or philosophy or both, and why, in your view?
2. What are the risks and rewards of expanding the traditional definition of theodicy?
3. Which mode of theodicy most interests you and why?
4. Which question of theodicy strikes you as the most important and why?
5. Which criterion of theodicy strikes you as the most important and why?

20. "There is no single uniform appropriate faith response to suffering and evil, nor should there be. Responses to evil and suffering take on different configurations appropriate to different religious communities, given the complex dynamic of coping with evil" (Pinnock, *Beyond Theodicy*, 144).

3

Free Will Defense

Playing the Blame Game

> "Here that problem raises itself, which is often brought up with murmurings and mutterings: men are ready to accuse anything else for their sins rather than themselves."[1]

Theodicy travels along two parallel tracks: it deflects blame for evil from God and redirects it elsewhere. These positive and negative functions operate simultaneously to diffuse the atheological force of the question: "Whence evil?," which Epicurus and, later, Hume, effectively pressed.[2] The search for origins doubles as the search for culpability: it implicitly links causal and moral responsibility. Discover the origin of evil, and you will discover the culprit. So, when translated from metaphysical to moral terms, the question

1. Augustine, *The Problem of Free Choice*, III.19.53, trans. Dom Mark Pontifex, Ancient Christian Writers 22 (New York: Newman Press, 1955), 194.
2. Alvin Plantinga, "Supralapsarianism, or 'O Felix Culpa,'" in *Christian Faith and the Problem of Evil*, ed. Peter van Inwagen (Grand Rapids, MI: Eerdmans, 2004), 3.

"whence evil" really asks "who is to blame for evil"? According to the logical problem of evil, the blame rests squarely with God, at least if we accept the traditional theistic premises of divine goodness and omnipotence. God, who creates and sustains the universe, must take ownership of its imperfections and miseries. The free will defense (hereafter FWD), exemplified by Augustine[3] in ancient times and Alvin Plantinga in modern, disputes that deduction.[4] Instead, it transfers blame from God to humanity. Whence evil? Who is to blame? According to the FWD, *we* are to blame, not God.[5]

Shifting culpability from God to humanity has been the basic instinct and trademark maneuver of Christian theodicy for centuries.[6] It remains the "first line of defense" in debates on the problem of evil. It has several permutations, but they all identify freedom, with all the possibilities—both good and evil—it entails, as the morally sufficient reason why God permits evil. Humanity's misuse of freedom exacts an enormous toll on the universe. Is the cosmic benefit of freedom worth the cost? Does it get God "off the hook"? In this chapter we will explore the background, structure, coherence, vulnerabilities, and viability of the FWD.

3. For the authoritative treatment of Augustine's perspective on the problem of evil, which covers all the relevant themes and complexities, see G. R. Evans, *Augustine on Evil* (Cambridge: Cambridge University Press, 1982).
4. R. Douglas Geivett, "Augustine and the Problem of Evil," in *God and Evil: The Case for God in a World Filled with Pain*, ed. Chad Meister and James K. Dew Jr. (Downers Grove, IL: InterVarsity, 2013), 65.
5. Stephen T. Davis, "Free Will and Evil," in *Encountering Evil: Live Options in Theodicy* (Louisville: Westminster John Knox, 2001), 75: "Unfortunately, human beings did just this: they fell into sin. So God is not to be blamed for the existence of moral evil. We are."
6. Evans, *Augustine on Evil*, viii–ix: "Augustine's solution to the problem of evil is a *tour de force*. Whether we regard it as still helpful, or as interesting principally because of the influence it has had upon Western thought for fifteen hundred years, it cannot but be striking in its scale and magnificence, its essential boldness and simplicity and in the patient working out of its details."

Theo-Biblical Narrative: The Drama of the Creation, Fall, and Redemption of Humanity

The story of the creation and fall of humanity in Genesis 1–3 frames the FWD. It begins at *the* beginning, with creation: "In the beginning when God created the heavens and the earth, the earth was a formless void and darkness covered the face of the deep" (Gen. 1:1-2). For the purposes of the FWD, the precise means and mechanism of creation are secondary to the fundamental theological point that God creates the universe, which has two key implications. First, whatever exists in the universe must ultimately derive from God, a fact that will complicate its account of the origin of evil. Second, the FWD posits the original goodness of creation, which God deems "good" (Gen. 1:25) and "very good" (Gen. 1:31) because it reflects God's goodness.[7] Its doctrine of creation, then, positively predisposes the FWD to the universe as the site of God's omnipotent and omnibenevolent providential work, theological assumptions that inflect its hermeneutical and philosophical account of the origin, status, problem, function, and end of evil.

The narrative, however, quickly pivots from paradisal delight to primordial disaster: the Fall.[8] Adam and Eve play a major role in the FWD. They have the distinction of being created in the image of God: "So God created humankind in his image, in the image of God he created them; male and female he created them" (Gen. 1:27).[9] Their privileged place in paradise comes with great promise and great peril. God gives them free reign in the Garden of Eden with only one minor provision: they are forbidden to eat from "the tree of

7. For the Neoplatonic undercurrents of his doctrine of the goodness of creation, see John Hick, *Evil and the God of Love* (New York: Palgrave Macmillan, 2007), 43–45. "Here, then, is a central theme of Augustine's thought: the whole creation is good. . . . So Augustine rejects the ancient Platonic, Neo-Platonic, Gnostic, and Manichaean prejudice against matter" (45).
8. Evans, *Augustine on Evil*, 94–95.
9. Augustine, *City of God*, XII.24.

the knowledge of good and evil" (Gen. 2:17). The crafty serpent, traditionally identified with Satan,[10] tempts Eve, who eats, and then Adam follows in turn (Gen. 3:1-6). As a result of their disobedience to the divine decree, however minor it might seem, they are expelled from the Garden of Eden and forced to endure severe hardships, both them and their progeny: "In the first man, therefore, there existed the whole human race which was to pass through the woman into her progeny when that conjugal pair received the divine sentence of its own damnation."[11] Augustine interjects into the biblical accounts of the fall the notion of original sin whereby Adam and Eve biologically transmit "sin and death" to their progeny, thus implicating the entire human race in their original sin.[12]

The theo-biblical narrative of the typical FWD has textual and theological complications that are often overlooked. It begins with theological assumptions about divine goodness and power. It adopts a mythological view of creation, often without any attempt to correlate it with contemporary scientific theories. It harmonizes different parts of the creation stories in Genesis 1–2. Finally, it imports vital theological assumptions into its reading of Genesis, including the identification of the serpent and Satan, the inordinate culpability of Eve for the primordial sin, its association with sexuality, and, finally, the notion that Adam and Eve's "original" sin transmits biologically to future generations of humanity. Creation and the Fall in the FWD, then, have resonances and assumptions that reflect its theological sensibilities.

The third element of the theo-biblical narrative is the redemption of fallen humanity through the life, death, and resurrection of Christ.

10. Augustine, *The Problem of Free Choice*, III.25.75.

11. Augustine, *City of God*, XIII.3.

12. Evans, *Augustine on Evil*, 170. "When Adam fell, the whole race of men who were to come from Adam was condemned with him; it became a *massa damnata*. Human nature itself was changed, so that the human will could not in practice choose the good any longer without assistance."

Despite its self-inflicted state of perdition, God, out of mercy, elects to save some of humanity. God's election of these saints occurs before the fall of Adam, which results in a strict doctrine of predestination. So God the Son becomes man to redeem or save them, which makes it possible for them not to sin, whereas in their fallen state they were unable not to sin. Ironically, then, the primordial sin of Adam and Evil is the "happy fault" that paves the way for the incarnation.

Despite its exegetical liberties and theological assumptions, the theo-biblical storyline of the creation and fall of humanity remains at the heart of the FWD. It gives scriptural grounding for its fundamental move: to shift the blame for evil from God to humanity. While God created the universe good, humanity flagrantly transgressed the divine command, which ushered evil into the world and corrupted creation. Henceforth humanity must contend with its sinful disposition and creation must contend with its vitiated state. The narrative pinpoints the blame for the disaster that befell creation: free will. Adam and Eve's misuse of their freedom, despite its triviality and inexplicability to many modern readers, corrupts human nature and mars creation.

In the background of the FWD's theo-biblical narrative looms Augustine, whose theological hermeneutics shapes its contours.[13] John Hick classifies the FWD as the "Augustinian Type of Theodicy," which becomes the majority view in Christianity.[14] We will distinguish between the free will defense and the free will theodicy momentarily, but for now it is sufficient to note the centrality of the primordial couple to the narrative that underwrites both. Adam and Eve embody prelapsarian perfection, an "idealized" state of immortality, morality, and spiritual equanimity.[15] Augustine

13. Hick, *Evil and the God of Love*, 37. For an interesting counterview, which also surveys Augustine's mature theodicy, see Jesse Couenhoven, "Augustine's Rejection of the Free-Will Defence: An Overview of the Late Augustine's Theodicy," *Religious Studies* 43 (2007): 279–98.
14. Hick, *Evil and the God of Love*, 36.

AUGUSTINE: Augustine (354–430 C.E.), Bishop of Hippo and the most influential church father in the West, wrote voluminously, including the *Confessions*, *City of God*, and *De Trinitate*. His account of the fall of humanity through the misuse of freedom would shape the development of the FWD.

extols the perfection of our pre-fallen state partly to underscore the severity of the fall and partly to protect God's character as the creator of a universe that has gone awry. Augustine's narrative of the fall safeguards God's integrity by affirming original perfection and placing the blame on Adam and Eve at the very beginning of creation. Otherwise, if humanity were faulty or sinful from the outset, the blame would rest with God, not humanity. We will explore the criticisms of the FWD leveled by soul-making and process theodicy in the subsequent two chapters.

The Free Will Defense

The logical problem of evil argues that the affirmation of divine goodness and omnipotence is logically inconsistent with the reality of evil. In his famous article "Evil and Omnipotence," J. L. Mackie distilled the problem to three propositions that form an internal contradiction:

15. Augustine, *City of God*, XII.22; XIV.10. "We must, then, confess that the first human beings were so constituted that, had they not sinned, they would not have experienced any kind of death" (XIII.3). John Hick, *Evil and the God of Love*, 64–65.

(1) God is omnipotent;
(2) God is wholly good;
(3) Evil exists.

For Mackie, these three affirmations are logically incompatible: "There seems to be some contradiction between these three propositions, so that if any two of them were true the third would be false."[16] So, you can logically affirm divine goodness and evil if you deny divine omnipotence. Likewise, you can logically affirm divine omnipotence and evil if you deny divine goodness. Finally, you can logically affirm divine omnipotence and goodness if you deny the reality of evil. What you *cannot* logically affirm, however, is that divine omnipotence and goodness are compatible with the existence of evil. And yet, Mackie argues, "ordinary theists" embrace the triad despite its inconsistency because of their theological commitments.[17]

FREE WILL DEFENSE: The Free Will Defense (FWD) transfers moral culpability for evil from God to humanity by attributing its origin to the misuse of free will. Freedom is the morally sufficient reason why God permits evil, since the ability to exercise meaningful agency requires the possibility of evil.

The task of the FWD is to neutralize the seemingly inexorable logical force of the atheological argument from evil. As a starting point, free will defenders distinguish between a defense and a

16. J. L. Mackie, "Evil and Omnipotence," *The Problem of Evil: Selected Readings*, ed. Michael L. Peterson (Notre Dame, IN: University of Notre Dame Press, 1992), 89–90.
17. Mackie, "Evil and Omnipotence," 90.

theodicy. According to Plantinga, theodicy *answers* the question "Whence evil?" or "Why does God permit evil?"[18] While the theist might wish to know God's reasons for permitting evil, his or her inability to produce a viable theodicy does not entail the success of the atheological argument. Just because the theist does not know why God allows evil does not imply logical defeat. There might be any number of reasons why we cannot know the answer, Plantinga argues. "Why suppose that if God does have a good reason for permitting evil, the theist would be the first to know? Perhaps God has a good reason, but that reason is too complicated for us to understand. Or perhaps He has not revealed it for some other reason."[19] We do not need a theodicy to combat the logical problem of evil; we simply need a defense against the claim that divine omnipotence and goodness preclude the possibility of evil.

ALVIN PLANTINGA (1932–). An American analytic philosopher and Emeritus Professor of Philosophy at the University of Notre Dame, Plantinga has been an influential proponent of the Free Will Defense, which he delineates famously in *God, Freedom, and Evil* (1974).

Plantinga carefully distinguishes between a "Free Will Theodicy" (FWT) and a "Free Will Defense" (FWD). The former positively affirms the reason for God's permission of evil, while the latter simply suggests a potential reason, without any formal justification. Augustine's approach might be seen as a FWT, since Augustine specifies the reason God allows evil: free will, which requires the

18. Alvin C. Plantinga, *God, Freedom, and Evil* (Grand Rapids, MI: Eerdmans, 1974), 10.

19. Plantinga, *God, Freedom, and Evil*, 10. "The theist believes that God has a reason for permitting evil; he doesn't know what that reason is. But why should that mean that his belief is improper or irrational?" (11).

possibility of moral evil, was necessary for the perfection of the world. The FWD, conversely, does not seek to "justify the ways of God to man," as Milton describes it, but, more modestly, to subvert the atheistic argument that God and evil cannot logically coexist: "A theodicist, then, attempts to tell us why God permits evil. Quite distinct from a Free Will Theodicy is what I shall call a Free Will Defense. Here the aim is not to say what God's reason *is*, but at most what God's reason might *possibly be*."[20] In other words, theodicy speaks in the indicative mode, while defenses speak in the subjunctive. Van Inwagen makes a similar distinction:

> A defense is not necessarily different from a theodicy in content. Indeed, a defense and a theodicy may well be verbally identical. Each is, formally speaking, a story according to which both God and evil exist. The difference between a defense and a theodicy lies not in their content but in their purposes. A theodicy is a story that is told as the real truth of the matter; a defense is a story that, according to the teller, may or may not be true, but which, the teller maintains, has some desirable feature that does not entail truth—perhaps (depending on the context) logical consistency or epistemic possibility (truth-for-all-anyone-knows).[21]

The FWD, then, speculates that God permits evil for the sake of freedom, argues that freedom constitutes a morally sufficient reason for God's permission of evil, but, crucially, does not assert its truth, only its possibility. A defense does not make categorical metaphysical assertions; it raises logical possibilities that undermine the atheological force of the argument from evil.

By shifting from theodicy to defense, the FWD circumvents the criticism that it has not unlocked the mystery of suffering. The FWD, in its basic form, does not masquerade as a theodicy. It does not

20. Plantinga, *God, Freedom, and Evil*, 28.
21. Peter van Inwagen, *The Problem of Evil* (New York: Oxford University Press, 2006), 7. "I employ the free-will defense as just precisely a defense, a story that includes both God and evil and, given that there is a God, is true for all anyone knows" (70).

pretend to know why God permits evil. It does not claim to have any final answers: "God has his reasons for permitting evil, but the epistemic distance between him and us is such that we can't really hope to know what those reasons are, or why they require him to permit the evil we see."[22] In short, it is far less ambitious than a theodicy. Strategically, it gives the theists surer ground against the atheist by limiting its scope. Rather than positively state why God permits evil, it simply states that the atheist has not demonstrated an internal logical contradiction in theism. It is far easier to refute an argument than prove one.

At bottom, then, the FWD posits the logical possibility of reconciling divine goodness and omnipotence with the reality of evil through the concept of a greater good that God might possibly bring out of evil. In other words, it argues that if we are able to identify a reasonable morally sufficient reason why God allows evil, it would defuse the logical problem of evil. Plantinga summarizes the aim of the FWD: "The Free Will Defense can be looked upon as an effort to show that there may be a very different kind of good that God can't bring about without permitting evil."[23] Predictably, the morally sufficient reason for evil, the greater good that ultimately justifies it, is free will.

The argument turns on the nature of freedom. Freedom presupposes the ability to choose between genuine moral alternatives: "The possibility of doing evil is the inevitable companion of the possibility of doing good."[24] The faculty of freedom relates, in the FWD, not to mundane or trivial choices—whether to wear black or white socks—but morally significant choices. Nothing significant hinges on the color of your socks, except perhaps your reputation

22. Plantinga, "Supralapsarianism, or 'O Felix Culpa,'" 4.
23. Plantinga, *God, Freedom, and Evil*, 29.
24. Davis, "Free Will and Evil," 75.

for being fashionable. Morally significant actions, however, shape our identity and give us a sense of self-determination. The FWD says that the capacity to make morally significant choices brings about a greater good that justifies the evil that arises as an unfortunate but necessary byproduct.

The cosmic value of freedom underwrites the FWD: "A world containing creatures who are significantly free (and freely perform more good than evil actions) is more valuable, all else being equal, than a world containing no free creatures at all."[25] In the cosmic moral calculus of the FWD, a world with free creatures who choose the good is better than a world with automata who are preprogrammed to choose the good. God does not create robots; God creates agents who exercise their God-given freedom. Genesis 1:26-27 states that God creates humanity in the image of God. Humanity, therefore, reflects the divine life in a finite, mutable way, which means that our freedom, our ability to make morally significant choices, becomes a point of contact between our life and God's, enabling us to realize our innate capacity for divine likeness.

Moreover, God desires humanity to freely respond to God's love. God demonstrates his love through the creation and redemption of humanity. If we automatically entered into a relationship with God as preprogrammed divine companions, it would be less reciprocal and less meaningful than if we entered into it on our own volition. Human freedom creates the condition for the possibility of intimacy with God. Without it true mutuality would be impossible. It would be a relationship between an "I" and "It" rather than an "I" and a "Thou," to state it in Buberian terms.

But surely, objects the atheist, an omnipotent God would be able to create creatures with unfailing freedom, that is, with sinless freedom.

25. Plantinga, *God, Freedom, and Evil*, 30.

An all-powerful God could create the type of freedom that does not and cannot go astray because it does not have any sinful options to choose from, only beneficent and benign alternatives, or because it has the wisdom and resolve to avoid sinful alternatives in every instance. The FWD says that freedom without the possibility of error would not be real freedom.[26] It would be the illusion of freedom. God does not give us an illusory freedom; he gives the capacity for moral good or moral evil. True, authentic, genuine freedom, then, requires the ability to opt for moral evil. It does not, according to Plantinga, "count against" divine omnipotence and goodness, since it was necessary to realize the greater good of a universe that allowed intimacy with God.[27]

God's inability to create harmless freedom does not count against divine omnipotence because omnipotence does not mean the ability to do *absolutely* anything. God cannot create a married bachelor or a square circle not because of any limitation on his part, but because they are incoherent, illogical concepts. In short, they are not real. God, as the source of existence, as Reality itself, only trades in the real. Omnipotence means that God can do anything consistent with his nature. Similarly, God cannot create freedom without consequences not because of a lack of power or imagination, but because it would not be real freedom. God's inability to do what is morally or logically inconsistent with his nature manifests God's power; it does not undercut it.

So, according to the FWD narrative, the greater good of freedom constitutes the morally sufficient reason why God might permit evil, which diffuses the threat of the logical problem of evil: "God's decision will turn out wise because the good that will in the end result from it will outweigh the evil that will in the end result from it."[28]

26. Davis, "Free Will and Evil," 77.
27. Plantinga, *God, Freedom, and Evil*, 30.

Before we discuss how a FWD naturally transmutes into a FWT, let us raise two questions that we will explore at the conclusion of the chapter. First, the value of freedom warrants a cost-benefit analysis. Put simply, is the value of freedom worth the cost to humanity, both individually and collectively? Might a world of automata without rape, torture, and murder be, on the whole, better? Second, granting that freedom presupposes genuine alternatives, might it not be possible to allow for humanity to choose some moral evil, but not all? In other words, the depth and breadth of evil seems excessive for the logical and moral requirements of freedom. We will discuss these below.

From Defense to Theodicy

Although the FWD carefully differentiates itself from a theodicy, it ultimately exists on a continuum with it. On its own, it does not answer the core questions of theodicy, but it does supply a conceptual framework for justifying God's permission of evil, at least hypothetically. Even in its restricted form, it operates as a theodicy insofar as it seeks to make sense of suffering. It fits the criteria for theodicy in its expanded sense, not in the classical sense. Nevertheless, I would argue that the FWD is functionally equivalent to a theodicy, though rhetorically distinct.[29] It may not claim to know why God permits evil, but by positing freedom as the morally sufficient reason

28. Davis, "Free Will and Evil," 75.

29. Jerry L. Walls argues that Plantinga's FWD presupposes "libertarian freedom" (in contrast to "compatibilist freedom"), which forces him to move from a FWD to a FWT: "And if we are so free [in the libertarian sense], then it naturally follows that God must think that freedom and its related good outweigh the evil in our world. And with this commitment in hand, Plantinga must move out of the relatively modest realm of defense into the bolder arena of theodicy" ("Why Plantinga Must Move from Defense to Theodicy," in *The Problem of Evil*, ed. Michael L. Peterson, 333). Plantinga disagrees that his FWD commits him to "libertarian freedom" (Plantinga, "(Plantinga, *Ad Walls*, 337). Ad Walls," *Philosophy and Phenomenological Research* 51, no. 3 [September 1991]: 621).

why God could possibly permit evil, it enters into the territory of theodicy, albeit on tip-toe.

What steps would the FWD have to take to traverse the ground from a defense to a theodicy? As a necessary first step, it would have to pivot from the negative task of nullifying the logical problem of evil to the positive task of explaining why God permits evil. The next steps would involve explicit engagement with the five essential questions of theodicy: the origin, nature, problem, reason, and end of evil. These would have to supplement the conceptual framework of the FWD. Plantinga identifies Augustine as the face the FWT: "Augustine's kind of theodicy might be called a Free Will Theodicy, since the idea of rational creatures with free will plays such a prominent role in it."[30] Augustine's theodicy has been amply treated elsewhere.[31] For our purposes, we will simply flesh out the FWT by showing how Augustine addresses these five questions, without undertaking a full-scale analysis of his theodicy.

First, the question of the origin of evil puzzled Augustine for many years. He ultimately rejected the Manichean attribution of evil to materiality, and assigned the proximate origin of evil to the misuse of freedom.[32] Despite concerted conceptual efforts, however, he was unable to perceive the ultimate origin of evil.[33] Where does the impulse to deviate from the divine will, to turn our will against the will of God, originate? To say, "from the Devil," only pushes the question back a step,[34] since the Devil was also created good, so we would have to account for where the impulse and possibility of rebellion arises from in a creation devoid of evil. Augustine raises

30. Plantinga, *God, Freedom, and Evil*, 27.

31. G. R. Evans, *Augustine on Evil* and Charles T. Matthewes, *Evil and the Augustinian Tradition.*

32. Augustine, *City of God*, XIV.13.

33. Augustine, *Confessions*, VII.3.5.

34. Hick, *Evil and the God of Love*, 60. Hick calls the turning of the will to the self or to an exterior good apart from God a "self-originating act, and is as such not explicable in terms of causes that are distinguishable from the agent himself."

the question "What made the first evil will evil?"[35] in the *City of God*, only to dismiss it shortly thereafter as unknowable because of the privative nature of evil, akin to "wishing to see darkness or hear silence."[36] We will take up this problem later in the dialogue section.[37]

The mystery of the ultimate origin of evil notwithstanding,[38] Augustine famously locates the proximate origin of evil to the misuse of freedom, or sin: "Perverted will, then, is the cause of all evil."[39] It does not arise from innately good or evil natures, which would compromise divine justice, but from the misdirection of our wills.[40] The option of a lesser good over a greater good, or the disproportional and inordinate love of a lesser good at the expense of a greater good, brings about evil: "It is a turning away from that which has supreme being and towards that which has less."[41] We naturally want to shift the blame for evil away from us. We shift the blame to our progenitors or circumstances, Adam shifts it implicitly to God and explicitly to Eve, Eve shifts it to the serpent, and the serpent no doubt would shift it to God. While we can trace the cosmic origin of evil back to Adam and Eve and to the Devil, Augustine argues, we cannot circumvent our personal culpability for the evil we engender through our ignorance and our actions.[42]

35. Augustine, *City of God*, XII.6.
36. Augustine, *City of God*, XII.6. "Let no one, then, seek an efficient cause of an evil will. For its cause is not efficient, but deficient, because the evil will itself is not an effect of something, but a defect."
37. Augustine, *Confessions*, VII.3.5.
38. Hick, *Evil and the God of Love*, 61. "Thus the origin of evil lies forever hidden within the mystery of finite freedom; for 'what cause of willing can there be which is prior to willing?' (FW III.xvii.49)."
39. Augustine, *The Problem of Free Choice*, III.17.48. Hick, *Evil and the God of Love*, 59. "Rejecting the Neo-Platonic view that evil is a metaphysical necessity, inevitably appearing where being runs out into non-being, Augustine attributes all evil, both moral and natural, directly or indirectly to the wrong choices of free rational beings."
40. Augustine, *City of God*, XII.3.
41. Augustine, *City of God*, XII.8.
42. Augustine, *The Problem of Free Choice*, III.19.53.

Second, Augustine defines evil as the privation of the good.[43] During his Manichean phase,[44] he defined evil in corporeal terms. Evil, he thought, "was not only a substance, but even a bodily substance."[45] Typical of Manichean dualism, he saw God and evil as antithetical corporeal realities. Later in his spiritual journey, under the influence of Platonic philosophy, particularly Plotinus, he shifts his view of evil from the material to the immaterial: "Everything that exists is good, then; and so evil, the source of which I was seeking, cannot be a substance, because if it were, it would be good."[46] His new ontology of evil follows from his new cosmology: it is the outcome of his rejection of Manichean duality and his absorption of Neoplatonic, particularly Plotinian, metaphysics.[47] No longer was the world the battleground between hostile corporeality and transcendent corporeality. Instead, God creates the world good, which equates goodness and being. Once Augustine perceives the goodness of created reality, he begins to see evil as the privation of original created goodness: "For you [i.e., God] evil has no being at all, and this is true not of yourself only but of everything you have created."[48]

Evil as privation, then, has strong philosophical resonances.[49] It is, according to John Hick, "adapted" rather than "adopted" from

43. Evans, *Augustine on Evil*, 1–2. "In a sentence (his 'conversion' moment, when the final shadow of doubt was dispelled by the light of faith, *Confessions* VII.12.29) he gives us the principle which solved for him the problem of evil. Where light shines there cannot be darkness. When light comes, darkness proves to have been simply the absence of light. Where there is good, evil is driven out; it proves to have been simply an absence of good."

44. Evans, *Augustine on Evil*, 11–16.

45. Augustine, *Confessions*, V.20.

46. Augustine, *Confessions*, VII.12.18.

47. Hick, *Evil and the God of Love*, 40–43.

48. Augustine, *Confessions*, VII.13.19.

49. Hick, *Evil and the God of Love*, 41: "Here we meet a very old and tenacious conception, which is to reappear again and again in the course of Christian reflection upon the problem of evil. Evil is non-being; it is a lack, a privation and a non-entity; it comes from the *Ungrund*; as *das Nichtige* it opposes God Himself."

Plotinus.[50] It argues that evil does not have any independent ontological reality, any positive metaphysical qualities, or any nature of its own. Rather, as we discussed in the chapter on the problem of evil, it is the corruption, distortion, and defection of God's good creation: "Evil is essentially the malfunctioning of something that in itself is good."[51] It is fundamentally "privative and parasitic" on creation, whereby an entity somehow loses its proper function and being.[52] Otherwise, if it had substantiality, it would redound back to God directly, which is precisely what Augustine rejects.[53] The privative theory of evil, then, distances God from ontological and thus moral accountability for its existence.

Third, Augustine reflected on the problem of evil his entire life.[54] It was a major intellectual preoccupation for him, which he confronted with rigor and honesty.[55] The crux of the problem, for Augustine, was the viability of divine justice in light of evil.[56] On the surface, it seems as though God creates evil and bears moral responsibility, but, upon deeper reflection, Augustine assigns blame to humanity's misuse of freedom. The problem of evil perplexed Augustine, particularly in his younger years.[57] The specious plausibility of dualistic theodicy prompted his nine-year detour into Manicheism. The Manicheans exploited his uncertainty on the origin of evil[58] until

50. Hick, *Evil and the God of Love*, 46. B. A. G. Fuller, *Plotinus and the Problem of Evil* (Cambridge: Cambridge University Press, 1912), 259. Evans, *Augustine on Evil*, 2, 34–35.
51. Hick, *Evil and the God of Love*, 46.
52. Hick, *Evil and the God of Love*, 47.
53. R. Douglas Geivett, "Augustine and the Problem of Evil," 74.
54. Hick, *Evil and the God of Love*, 37: "From his earliest to his latest writings Augustine was continually turning to the problem of evil."
55. Hick, *Evil and the God of Love*, 39: "His formulation of the philosophical *problem* of evil is as tough-minded as that of any sceptic."
56. Augustine, *The Problem of Free Choice*, I.1.1.
57. "You [Evodius] are inquiring into a problem which deeply interested me when I was quite a young man; it troubled me so much that I was worn out and driven right into heresy" (Augustine, *The Problem of Free Choice*, I.2.4).
58. Augustine, *Confessions*, III.7.12.

he came to realize the vacuity of their view and the veracity of the Christian view of God as the author of goodness, and created beings as the authors of evil.

Fourth, God permits evil to enable human freedom. If God prevented evil by thwarting human agency, freedom would cease to exist. God values human freedom enough to allow the deleterious cosmic consequences that ensue from our capacity to turn toward or away from God. God could have created automata that would never sin or stray, but instead God desires our free response to divine grace. Freedom, then, functions as the necessary existential precondition for our union and communion with God. Without human agency, we could not realize our capacity for divine likeness. Precisely why God values freedom so highly, and whether freedom is cost-effective for creaturely happiness, will be taken up in the dialogue section.

Fifth, evil ends at the final judgment, when God's justice will be revealed.[59] Admittedly, on earth, God's justice does not always manifest itself clearly or openly. Quite the contrary: injustice, not justice, characterizes human life: "As it is, however, there are good men who suffer evils and evil men who enjoy good things, which seems unjust."[60] Augustine enumerates some of the endless examples of injustice that call God's justice into question, only to argue that, in the afterlife, on the Day of Judgment, God's justice will be vindicated. The justice of God, hidden from us now, will be fully revealed, silencing the doubts and recriminations of the skeptics.

The end of evil also entails postmortem rewards and punishments. Augustine categorically affirms the reality of heaven and hell, without which the FWD would collapse because choices must have consequences.[61] Once the Devil, demons, the wicked, and sin itself

59. Davis, "Free Will and Evil," 88.
60. Augustine, *City of God*, XX.2.
61. Augustine, *City of God*, XXI.9; XXII.3.

are destroyed, evil will cease to exist, never to rear its ugly head again. Conversely, the righteous will enjoy eternal felicity, devoid of evil and suffering: "How great that felicity will be, where there will be no evil, where no good thing will be lacking, and where we shall be free to give ourselves up to the praise of God, Who will be all in all!"[62] In that redeemed state, we will no longer be able to sin, thereby safeguarding the eternity of heavenly bliss.[63]

Dialogue

What are some of the problems and prospects of the FWD and its expanded version, the FWT? All the theodicies we will examine have conceptual strengths and weaknesses, insights and blind spots, assets and liabilities. In our assessment of their cogency, beginning with the FWD, we will apply the five criteria for theodicy we outlined earlier: fidelity, coherence, relevance, creativity, and humility. The point of the dialogue section is not to rule for or against a particular theodicy, but to highlight the salient theological and conceptual issues to facilitate further discussion.

Strengths

First, the FWD draws explicitly from Christian sources of authority, both scripture and tradition. It relies heavily on the creation and fall stories in Genesis 1–3 to construct a theological framework for theodicy. God creates humanity in the divine image, humanity falls, and evil ensues. Augustine expands the basic framework with notions of the fall of angels, original sin, the nature of evil as privation, and cosmic judgment. Theists like Alvin Plantinga redeploy these

62. Augustine, *City of God*, XXII.30.
63. Augustine, *City of God*, XXII.30.

theological principles to contemporary philosophical debates on the problem of evil, staying close to the biblical narrative and its Augustinian theological interpretation. We will see that the FWD's fidelity to the Bible and tradition counts against it in the determination of some.

Second, the FWD has empirical validation and intuitive plausibility insofar as human action routinely engenders evil in our experience. To be sure, there is not always a direct correlation between sin and suffering, but there are many instances where the misuse of freedom inflicts pain and suffering. Moreover, both the FWD and FWT consistently work within a theological matrix of divine justice and goodness, shifting the blame for evil from God to humanity. The FWD identifies freedom as the morally sufficient reason for why God allows evil, thereby neutralizing the logical problem of evil, at least for those who accept the premises of the defense. The FWD enjoys an internal coherence that justifies its honored place in Christian theodicy.

Third, the FWD meets the latter three criteria—relevance, creativity, and humility—in several ways, which I will only begin to sketch here. First, it speaks to a contemporary situation often devoid of personal and collective accountability. Rather than deny or evade responsibility, we ought to acknowledge our failings and search for ways to remedy them. Second, the FWD creatively redeploys the Genesis narrative to address the problem of evil, particularly through its theological hermeneutics, which draws relevant theological insights from scripture and applies them to contemporary debates on the problem of evil. Part of the critique of the FWD, in fact, has been that it is *too* creative in its interpretation of Genesis and its cosmic vision. Finally, the FWD acknowledges the mystery of the ultimate origin of evil and its ultimate defeat at the eschaton, even as it leans heavily on its eschatology.

Fourth, the FWD promotes ethical empowerment by accenting human responsibility and accountability, both personally and collectively. Empowerment begins with the realization of our moral agency, and the choice to direct our agency toward positive, constructive, ethical ends. We become empowered as we take ownership of our choices and keep ourselves accountable to our ideals for ourselves and society. The FWD posits the potency of freedom to corrupt or to create, to destroy or to build. It stresses the dire consequences of its misuse and, inversely, the salutary possibilities of its proper deployment. Advocacy initiatives, charitable endeavors, community projects, vocational roles, and many other social and political enterprises presuppose the reality of freedom and the moral imperative to direct it rightly. The doctrine of predestination, which often accompanies the FWD, obviously complicates the presupposition, as we will see below.

Finally, the FWD fits into the wider narrative of the gospel of Christ's redemption of fallen humanity. The fall becomes the "happy fault" that leads to the incarnation of Christ and the salvation of the elect, consummated in the eschaton, through the person and work of Christ. It naturally, if not always seamlessly, interconnects with Christology, soteriology, and eschatology. While these systematic correlations raise further problems beyond the scope of our discussion, the internal continuity of the FWD with the principal points of theology counts in its favor.

Weaknesses

There are several problems with the FWD, particularly at the level of coherence and relevance. First, the FWD does not adequately explain the origin of evil. Hick poses the problem well: "The basic and inevitable criticism is that the idea of an unqualifiedly good creature committing sin is self-contradictory and unintelligible."[64] If creatures were "finitely perfect" in any real sense, they would not fall prey to pride, so the fact that they fell suggests a deficiency in creation.[65] To attribute it to the misuse of freedom only defers and deflects the theological problem, since both the capacity to choose and the range of possibilities open to freedom ultimately come from God.[66] The basic move of the FWD, then, does not conclusively exonerate God, who still bears at least causal culpability for the creation of the world, humanity, and the options available to human agency. The attempt to locate an ultimate origin of evil, to find its transcendental or existential impulse, has been the Achilles heel of the FWD. Put differently, if God is good, omnipotent, and omniscient, why would God allow even the possibility of sin and evil in the first place?

Second, the FWD argues that freedom constitutes the morally sufficient reason why God might permit evil without compromising divine goodness and omnipotence. That argument, however, requires a cost-benefit analysis, since the cost of freedom might outweigh its value, depending on our criteria. At least on the surface, the bloodshed and heartache of history, where "the life of man" has been "poor, nasty, brutish, and short,"[67] calls into question the value of our ability to realize divine likeness and enter into an eternal relationship with God, especially if the vast majority of people never attain the desired end of their existence.[68] If freedom results in egregious suffering, both personally and collectively, we must ask ourselves: Is it worth it? If not, what are the alternatives to human happiness? If so, how do we account for all the waste?

64. Hick, *Evil and the God of Love*, 62–63.
65. Hick, *Evil and the God of Love*, 63.
66. Hick, *Evil and the God of Love*, 69.
67. Thomas Hobbes, *Leviathan*, ed. Edwin Curley (Indianapolis: Hackett, 1994), I.xiii.9.
68. Augustine, *City of God*, XXI.12: "But many more are left under punishment than are redeemed from it."

Another critique leveled against the FWD by John Hick and other contemporary critics is that its literal interpretation of the Genesis creation narrative is out of step with contemporary science.[69] Its theological edifice depends, he argues, on an outmoded cosmology, which undercuts its plausibility and relevance. Without the concept of the primordial couple and the fall, as well as the later overlays of original sin, the FWD collapses. Conversely, Hick and others employ metaphorical interpretations of Genesis 1–3, a hermeneutical move that allows the FWD to retain its emphasis on freedom as the origin of evil without the historical and scientific overlays that have been the subject of repeated attack. Thus, one could subscribe to the FWD without its traditional scientific presuppositions by shifting the ground from the historical origin and transmission of sin and evil to its biological, social, and psychological origin and transmission. New studies on theodicy and evolution explore the intersection of science and the problem of evil and situate the classic dilemma into a contemporary scientific context.[70]

Theologically, the FWD has been impugned for its portrayal of God as punitive. God's response to Adam and Eve's trespass seems disproportional to the crime, and the emphasis on the just divine judgment of sin has been thought to obscure divine goodness and the reality of grace. Does the primeval sin of Adam and Eve really merit the disastrous consequences it engendered? Does God's exacting punishment of human sin overlook human frailty and God's responsibility as the creator? The God of the FWD strikes many as unjust, and the apparent imbalance between justice and mercy leaves many contemporary philosophers and theologians dissatisfied.

69. Hick, *Evil and the God of Love*, 245–53.

70. See, for example, Cornelius G. Hunter, *Darwin's God: Evolution and the Problem of Evil* (Grand Rapids, MI: Brazos Press, 2001), Richard W. Kropf, *Evil and Evolution: A Theodicy* (Eugene, OR: Wipf & Stock, 2004), and Christopher Southgate, *The Groaning of Creation: God, Evolution, and the Problem of Evil* (Louisville: Westminster John Knox Press, 2008).

Adherents to the FWD might retort, with Augustine, that humans receive what they deserve, whether or not we deem it equitable, and that God's just punishment of sin does not negate divine mercy, which saves some when all deserve damnation.

David Ray Griffin argues that the FWD rests on irreconcilable theological assertions. On the one hand, it affirms divine omnipotence, omniscience, infallibility, and immutability. On the other hand, it says that God endows humanity with freedom and justly punishes their misuse of it. Griffin argues that the God of the FWD would *foreknow* and thus *determine* human actions, since they could not deviate from God's immutable foreknowledge of them: "If this being knows infallibly that next year I will do A, instead of B or C, then it is necessary that I will do A. It may seem to me then as if I make a real choice among genuine alternatives, but this will be illusory."[71] So, if we are not really free, Griffin thinks God would be unjust to punish human sin.

Griffin's critique highlights the tension between divine omnipotence and human freedom endemic to the FWD. There are various ways to construe the problem, but they all point out the ways that the reality of one limits or negates the reality of the other. Does authentic freedom necessarily limit the range of possibilities open to God? Does God, in essence, tie the hands of providence? Or, alternatively, does freedom operate within God's larger providential designs and, if so, does that preserve the integrity of both freedom and omnipotence? These questions reflect larger soteriological debates on the nature of predestination and election, but, for our purposes, they underscore a theological vulnerability, or at least complexity, of the FWD.

71. David Ray Griffin, *God, Power, and Evil: A Process Theodicy*, 61.

Finally, the FWD rests on the presumption that genuine freedom requires the ability to sin. Contra J. L. Mackie, who argues that an omnipotent God could create free beings who never sin,[72] the FWD argues that true freedom must have the ability to sin, otherwise it would be counterfeit. A complication arises when we consider the fact that, for Augustine at least, in heaven we will not be able to sin, and yet we will be genuinely free. The inability to sin does not negate human freedom, Augustine says, it perfects it. If God has the ability to give us that kind of freedom in heaven, why could we not have that kind of freedom from the start?[73] On the one hand, then, the FWD insists that real freedom requires the ability to sin; on the other hand, in the afterlife, freedom involves the inability to sin without in any way diminishing its reality.

Conclusion

The FWD has been a mainstay of Christian theodicy. Its longevity corroborates, or at least suggests, its enduring heuristic value for reflection on evil, even as its detractors, both ancient and modern, expose its vulnerabilities and limitations. In its various versions, the FWD redirects blame for the misfortunes of the world away from God and toward humanity. It identifies human freedom as the morally sufficient reason why God permits evil, sees suffering as the natural consequence for sin, and posits the vindication of divine

72. J. L. Mackie, "Evil and Omnipotence," 97: "I should ask this: if God has made men such that in their free choices they sometimes prefer what is good and sometimes what is evil, why could he not have made men such that they always freely choose the good?"

73. Augustine, *City of God*, XXII.30: "Also, they will then no longer be able to take delight in sin. This does not mean, however, that they will have no free will. On the contrary, it will be all the more free, because set free from delight in sinning to take delight in not sinning. For when man was created righteous, the first freedom of will that he was given consisted in an ability not to sin, but also in an ability to sin. But this last freedom of will will be greater, in that it will consist in not being able to sin."

justice in the afterlife, when God will balance the cosmic ledger. While it leaves many questions unanswered, it supplies crucial insights into the puzzle of evil. Dissatisfaction with the FWD, however, has prompted an alternative perspective that rejects key premises of the FWD: soul-making theodicy. We turn to that next.

Questions for Discussion:

1. Who is responsible for evil? How would you assign blame/apportion moral culpability?
2. Are we free? What might impair our freedom, and how would that impact the FWD?
3. Could an omnipotent God create "significantly free" creatures who would never sin?
4. Is freedom worth the cost (viz., evil)? In other words, is the cost of freedom too high?
5. Is God's response to humanity's misuse of freedom (the fall) fair? Why or why not?

4

Soul-Making Theodicy

No Pain, No Gain

> "Rather, this world must be a place of soul-making. And its value is to be judged, not primarily by the quantity of pleasure and pain occurring in it at any particular moment, but by its fitness for its primary purpose, the purpose of soul-making."[1]

For centuries, the FWD enjoyed almost universal acceptance in Christian theology. It was the central prism through which theologians reflected on the problem of evil. In 1966, however, John Hick published a sweeping study on evil that would prove to be a game-changer. *Evil and the God of Love* developed a new paradigm that would fundamentally reshape the conversation for decades. In her Foreword to the 2007 reissue, Marilyn McCord Adams characterizes Hick's study as a "framework-setting, discussion-shifting" reappraisal of Christian theodicy.[2] With scholarly depth

1. John Hick, *Evil and the God of Love* (New York: Palgrave Macmillan, 2007 [1966]), 259.

and theological ingenuity, Hick analyzes traditional perspectives on theodicy, subjects them to critical analysis, and constructs his own proposal in dialogue with scripture and tradition. His "soul-making theodicy," a phrase drawn from John Keats, contends, at bottom, that pain and suffering are necessary for moral, spiritual, and intellectual growth.[3] Evil, then, has constructive, productive, and positive value: it enables our development into divine likeness. In this chapter, we analyze the formation and theological logic of Hick's soul-making theodicy (hereafter SMT).

Deconstruction of the Free Will Defense

Hick proposes his SMT in explicit contradistinction to the "creation-fall myth" of the FWD.[4] Before he constructs his counterproposal, he clears the field of the deeply "entrenched" worldview of the FWD: the creation of Adam and Eve in the Garden of Eden, their fall into sin, and its cosmic repercussions: "According to this conception in its developed form, man was created finitely perfect, but in his freedom he rebelled against God and has existed ever since under the righteous wrath and just condemnation of his Maker."[5] Since the traditional view conflicts with contemporary science and intellectual sensibilities, Hick calls for a repudiation of the traditional paradigm on evil. Rather than reject theodicy, however, he offers an alternative anchored in a theological undercurrent that has flowed beneath the mainstream of the FWD. We will first outline Hick's critique of the

2. Marilyn McCord Adams, Foreword to *Evil and the God of Love*, xviii.
3. Quoted by Hick, *Evil and the God of Love*, 259, fn. 1: "Call the world if you Please 'The vale of Soul-Making.'" Interestingly, in *The Problem of Pain*, published in 1940, C. S. Lewis employs the phrase "vale of soul-making" to characterize his theodicy, twenty-six years before Hick adopts it as the trademark slogan of his theodicy (Mark S. M. Scott, "C. S. Lewis and John Hick: An Interface on Theodicy," *Journal of Inklings Studies* 4, no. 1 [2014]: 26).
4. Hick, *Evil and the God of Love*, 248.
5. Hick, *Evil and the God of Love*, 201.

FWD as expressed in the classic Augustinian theodicy, then chart his constructive proposal, and, finally, assess its strengths and weaknesses.

According to Hick, there are two major types or paradigms of theodicy in Christian theology: the Augustinian type and the Irenaean type. Over the centuries, the Augustinian type has dominated the theological landscape, becoming the "majority report." Despite its dominance, the Irenaean type has persisted at a subterranean level as a "minority report."[6] For Hick, the Augustinian viewpoint pervaded Christian reflection on the problem of evil, and thus rarely encountered critical scrutiny. While in the past its central premises have been taken for granted, today they lack scientific, moral, and philosophical credibility, he insists. While not necessarily logically impossible, the FWD appears "radically implausible."[7] For these reasons, Hick rejects the Augustinian type of theodicy as suffering from "profound incoherences and contradictions," clearing the way for the minority report to surface as the long-lost alternative to save the day.[8]

JOHN HICK: John Hick (1922–2012) was a British philosopher of religion and perhaps the most influential theodicist of the twentieth century. His groundbreaking book, *Evil and the God of Love* (1966), details his soul-making theodicy (SMT), which revolutionized discourse on the problem of evil.

6. Hick, *Evil and the God of Love*, 253. Cf. John Hick, "An Irenaean Theodicy," in *Encountering Evil: Live Options in Theodicy*, ed. Stephen T. Davis (Louisville: Westminster John Knox, 2001), 39.
7. Hick, "An Irenaean Theodicy," 40.
8. Hick, *Evil and the God of Love*, 249.

What are Hick's three major objections to the Augustinian type? First, it relies on an ancient cosmology and mythology at odds with contemporary science, which diminishes its intellectual plausibility in the modern world. According to the FWD narrative, Adam and Eve violated the divine command and their "original" sin tarnished creation and transmitted it biologically to humanity, like a spiritual contagion, infecting every person from birth. That mythical narrative, however, has been replaced by the scientific narrative of evolution, which does not trace evil back to a singular event or a primordial couple, but to the ongoing struggle of life, forcing Christians to reexamine traditional doctrines of creation and original sin.[9] Without its cosmological foundations, the FWD loses theological traction, he contends: "Most educated inhabitants of the modern world regard the biblical story of Adam and Eve, and their temptation by the devil, as myth rather than as history," with the result that the FWD, which builds on those presumptions, becomes "fatally lacking plausibility" to a modern audience.[10]

Second, Hick argues against the morality of the FWD. If we accept the historicity of the Augustinian worldview, we are forced to accept that the fault of Adam and Eve results in the corruption of creation and, consequently, the guilt and punishment of subsequent generations. But that theological scenario seems excessive and cruel, beneath the dignity of an omnibenevolent God. Hick appeals to a commonsense conception of human morality: "[T]he policy of punishing the whole succeeding human race for the sin of the first pair is, by the best human moral standards, unjust and does not provide anything that can be recognized by these standards as a theodicy."[11] If a parent punished his or her child and all their

9. Hick, *Evil and the God of Love*, 249.
10. Hick, "An Irenaean Theodicy," 39.
11. Hick, *Evil and the God of Love*, 249.

descendants in perpetuity for a minor fault of their youth, any decent person would be outraged. The punishment would be drastically disproportional to the crime. Why, then, would we accept a worldview where God punishes all of humanity for all time and eternity for a minor youthful infraction? Hick concludes, then, that the FWD is morally indefensible by any contemporary standard.

Finally, Hick identifies a logical problem with the FWD account of the rise of evil in the world. How, he asks, could evil arise in a perfect paradise? It simply defies logic: "The notion that man was at first spiritually and morally good, orientated in love towards his Maker, and free to express his flawless nature without even the hindrance of contrary temptations, and yet that he preferred to be evil and miserable, cannot be saved from the charge of self-contradiction and absurdity."[12] If God created everything perfect, including humanity, evil could not enter the Garden of Eden. Whence the imperfection? Whence the desire, opportunity, and ability to sin? Hick rejects the notion that evil could arise in a perfect paradise as self-contradictory: "It is impossible to conceive of wholly good beings in a wholly good world becoming sinful. To say that they do is to postulate the self-creation of evil *ex nihilo*!"[13] Given these logical complications, Hick denies the plausibility of the FWD's account of the origin of evil.

Individually, these objections count strongly against the FWD. Collectively, Hick sees them as logically insuperable. In the dialogue section of this chapter, we will explore potential counterarguments to Hick's scientific, philosophical, and theological objections, but, for now, they simply form the backdrop to his repudiation of the Augustinian type of theodicy and his opting for the Irenaean type, which he defines and develops as a viable theological alternative.

12. Hick, *Evil and the God of Love*, 69.
13. Hick, *Evil and the God of Love*, 250.

Construction of the Soul-Making Theodicy

In contrast to the FWD, which he rightly classifies as an Augustinian type of theodicy, Hick proposes his groundbreaking soul-making theodicy, which he wrongly classifies as an Irenaean type of theodicy. In short, Hick does not firmly establish the link from Irenaeus's writings and Irenaeus would categorically reject Hick's unorthodox conclusions, particularly his espousal of the doctrine of universalism.[14] I have argued elsewhere that Hick unjustifiably co-opts Irenaeus as the patron saint of *his* SMT, loosely borrowing from Irenaeus when convenient and explicitly aligning his theory with him purely for theological cover, and that scholars of theodicy have subsequently uncritically adopted and perpetuated his classification in the secondary literature.[15] Furthermore, I have suggested that Origen, not Irenaeus, would function better as the patron saint of Hick's SMT because of his speculative theology, explicit interest in the problem of evil, theological metaphors, and willingness to entertain risky theories, such as universalism.[16] I will not rehearse those arguments here, but refer readers to the relevant articles on the topic.[17]

IRENAEUS: Irenaeus (c. 130–200 C.E.) was an influential second-century bishop and apologist in the East. Hick adopts Irenaeus as the patron saint of his SMT, with the result that many call it an Irenaean theodicy. Origen (c. 185–254 C.E.), however, makes a more fitting patron saint for the SMT.

We must, I argue, reject Hick's classification of his SMT as an Irenaean type of theodicy

14. Hick, *Evil and the God of Love*, 253–61. Cf. Hick, "An Irenaean Theodicy," 40.

as a specious and untenable theological ploy, and, instead, carefully delineate the essential plot points of his own theory, which he associates with Irenaeus for political purposes.[18] As a first step, SMT inverts the FWD narrative to make it more palatable to contemporary scientific, philosophical, and theological sensibilities. Rather than beginning as fully formed, spiritually and morally mature adults, we begin as children. Irenaeus speaks of Adam and Eve as children in the process of maturation, and Hick latches onto that picture to construct a rival theological anthropology that comports with evolutionary science.[19] For too long Christians have wistfully pined for an imagined state of perfection that, science tells us, never existed. We never lost paradise, Hick insists, and we cannot return to a fictitious Garden for answers to our identity. Instead, we must look to the future for our perfection, for the paradise that eludes us now. We did not lose paradise in the distant past; rather, we gain it in the distant future, as we will see.

Hick reimagines traditional theological anthropology in light of his evolutionary-Irenaean framework. Creation, he argues, unfolds in two stages: creation in the "image" of God and creation in the

15. Mark S. M. Scott, "Suffering and Soul-Making: Rethinking John Hick's Theodicy," *Journal of Religion* 90, no. 3 (2010): 313–34. Hick's designation of his soul-making theodicy as an "Irenaean theodicy" has become part of the terminological landscape of contemporary treatments of theodicy. See Barry L. Whitney, ed., *Theodicy: An Annotated Bibliography on the Problem of Evil: 1960-1991* (Charlottesville, VA: Bowling Green State University Press, 1998 [1993]), 115; Davis, ed., *Encountering Evil*, 38; Michael L. Peterson, ed., *The Problem of Evil: Selected Readings* (Notre Dame, IN: University of Notre Dame Press, 1992), viii; David Ray Griffin, *God, Power, and Evil: A Process Theodicy* (Philadelphia: Westminster, 2004 [1976]), 174, as well as virtually every introduction to the philosophy of religion, philosophical theology, and the problem of evil.
16. Scott, "Suffering and Soul-Making," 322–34.
17. In addition to the article above, see Mark S. M. Scott, "Guarding the Mysteries of Salvation: The Pastoral Pedagogy of Origen's Universalism," *Journal of Early Christian Studies* 18, no. 3 (2010): 347–68.
18. For Hick's thoughtful discussion of the "PR" reasons to retain Irenaeus as the patron saint of SMT, despite Origen's closer affinities to it in "several ways," see Scott, "Suffering and Soul-Making," 333, fn. 125.
19. Hick, *Evil and the God of Love*, 212.

"likeness" of God.[20] Hick redeploys Gen. 1:26 to accord with an evolutionary scientific model of the gradual intellectual, social, and religious development of *homo sapiens* and an Irenaean theological model of the gradual intellectual, ethical, and spiritual development of humanity. In other words, God creates humanity with the innate potentiality for "knowledge of and relationship" with God, which constitutes the first stage of God's creative work.[21] The second stage of creation involves the realization of divine likeness through the proper exercise of their freedom. Humanity, then, slowly actualizes their capacity for spiritual felicity. While Hick discusses his two-stage theory of creation at the macro level, it equally applies to the micro level. We move, collectively and individually, from spiritual imperfection to spiritual perfection.

According to Hick, perfection lies in the future, not the past.[22] We must look forward, not backward, for insight into our spiritual nature and destiny: "We cannot speak of a radically better state that *was*; we must speak instead in hope of a radically better state which *will be*."[23] God does not create us in "a finished state."[24] Instead, we are "still in process of creation."[25] We begin at an "epistemic distance" from God, a distance we must traverse throughout our lives and, as we will see, beyond our terrestrial existence, to achieve divine likeness.[26] Put simply, we are works in progress, collectively and individually. Like children, we make mistakes and, if we are wise, learn from them. Like children, we must mature morally, intellectually, and spiritually. Like children, God guides our first faltering steps toward our *telos*. As we try to find our spiritual and moral footing, we inevitably make

20. Hick, "An Irenaean Theodicy," 40.
21. Hick, "An Irenaean Theodicy," 40–41.
22. Griffin, *God, Power, and Evil*, 177–78.
23. Hick, *Evil and the God of Love*, 176.
24. Hick, *Evil and the God of Love*, 253.
25. Hick, *Evil and the God of Love*, 254.
26. Hick, "An Irenaean Theodicy," 42.

several missteps. When we fall, as we all do, God does not punish us like a cosmic judge for the sake of God's slighted justice. Instead, like a parent, God picks us up, dusts us off, and has us continue on the journey toward divine likeness.

Hick radically redefines "the Fall" in light of his revamped theological anthropology. First, he employs a mythological hermeneutic for the Genesis narrative. He denies the historicity of Adam and Eve in the Garden of Eden who tragically forfeit an "ideal state" through their sin.[27] That traditional theological picture depends on an antiquated cosmology that has been supplanted by evolution, he argues. Significantly, Hick does not reject Genesis *in toto*. Its stories still impart insight, but they convey mythological truth, not historical, scientific truth. Unlike the grim Augustinian portrayal of "the Fall," SMT totally recasts "the fall," now with a lower-case "f," in existential terms: "The reality is not a perfect creation that has gone tragically wrong, but a still continuing creative process whose completion lies in the eschaton."[28] The fall signifies the "immense gap" between our present spiritual state and our future spiritual destiny.[29] In other words, it refers to the existential distance between who we are and who God designs us to be, that is, the extent to which we have fallen short of our innate capacity for divine likeness.

Evil, then, bursts into creation not through the sin of the primordial couple but through our missteps and mistakes as we traverse the gap from biological life (*Bios*) to spiritual life (*Zoe*).[30] The point of human existence, both individually and collectively, is to transcend biology to enter into higher forms of reality, a key concept in his later works. Hick defines sin as self-centeredness,

27. Hick, "An Irenaean Theodicy," 41.
28. Hick, "An Irenaean Theodicy," 41.
29. Hick, "An Irenaean Theodicy," 41.
30. Hick, *Evil and the God of Love*, 254.

the natural state of biological life, and the spiritual life as other-centeredness, which Christ exemplifies.[31] In order to achieve our potential for divine likeness, we must evolve beyond our biological instinct for self-preservation and self-advancement to attend to the good of the other, even at one's own expense. Contrary to the Augustinian version of the FWD, Hick does not attribute evil to Adam and Eve or the angelic fall, but to the long, often brutal process of transcending purely biological instincts on the road to realizing our highest spiritual capacity.

SMT posits the origin of evil in the struggle of life to evolve over millions of years.[32] The self-preservation and adaptation of humanity leaves many casualties in its wake. Life arises from the ashes of death and destruction. The ontology of evil, in Hick's philosophical evolutionary framework, focuses on the moral and spiritual distance between our biological life, with its innately selfish instincts, and our spiritual life, with its concern for the other. Evil signifies for Hick not a transhistorical, spiritual force, like Satan, but the ways we fall short of realizing our divine likeness. The problem of evil, however, still remains: Why does God permit the protracted, often pernicious, process of soul-formation? Why did God not create us fully formed, without the capacity to sin, and thereby bypass the soul-making process? These questions take us into the heart of the SMT view of the purpose of creation and the soul-making design of the universe.

God does not create the world for our pleasure, to satisfy our self-indulgent whims and wishes. Contrary to Hume, who thinks the best of all possible worlds would resemble a hedonistic paradise, Hick thinks the best of all possible worlds more closely resembles a classroom.[33] The purpose or goal of creation is to facilitate our

31. Hick, *Evil and the God of Love*, 257.
32. Hick, "An Irenaean Theodicy," 40.
33. Hick, *Evil and the God of Love*, 257–58.

intellectual, moral, and spiritual development, not to maximize our pleasure and minimize our pain. God wants to create the conditions for human growth to enable communion with God. Dangers, obstacles, and difficulties are necessary for our spiritual growth. Without problems and challenges, we would slide into spiritual stagnation, atrophy, and apathy. The question, then, is not, contra common Enlightenment configurations of the problem: "Is this the best of all possible worlds for our physical *enjoyment*?" but "is this the best of all possible worlds for our moral and spiritual *development*?" To interpret suffering as purely detrimental misses its positive import: "But such an assumption overlooks the fact that a world in which there can be no pain or suffering would also be one without moral choice and hence no possibility of moral growth or development."[34]

To underscore his point about the pedagogical function of the world, Hick invites us to imagine a world without suffering.[35] In a pain-free world, crime would never harm, knives would never puncture, bullets would never kill, and cars would automatically stop before hitting children.[36] In a cosmic crib, however, we could not develop compassion, courage, and sacrifice: "It would be a world without need for the virtues of self-sacrifice, care for others, devotion to the public good, courage, perseverance, skill, or honesty."[37] The cultivation of these core human virtues depends on more precarious cosmic conditions: "Such a world requires an environment that offers challenges to be met, problems to be solved, and dangers to be faced, and which accordingly involves real possibilities of hardship, disaster, failure, defeat, and misery as well as of delight and happiness, success, triumph, and achievement."[38] Nor, correspondingly, would

34. Hick, "An Irenaean Theodicy," 47.
35. Hick, *Evil and the God of Love*, 324. Cf. Hick, "An Irenaean Theodicy," 46–47.
36. "If one man tried to murder another, his bullet would melt innocuously into thin air, or the blade of his knife turn into paper" (Hick, *Evil and the God of Love*, 324).
37. Hick, *Evil and the God of Love*, 325.

the higher forms of human cultural achievement arise in a stress-free, pain-free universe: "In a world devoid of dangers to be avoided and rewards to be won, we may assume that virtually no development of the human intellect and imagination would have taken place, and hence no development of the sciences, the arts, human civilization, or culture."[39] God, then, treats us not as pets, whom we spoil, but as children, whom we train, sometimes with painful lessons.[40]

SOUL-MAKING THEODICY: Also (inaptly) referred to as the Irenaean Theodicy, SMT argues that suffering is necessary for our moral, intellectual, and spiritual development. Without suffering, we would not realize our potential for divine likeness. SMT posits that all will eventually be saved (universalism).

Hick's guiding analogy of God as a kind, wise parent, not a malicious, punitive judge, and the world as a schoolroom, not a playroom, for soul-development, gives us the essential contours of his SMT:

> If, then, there is any true analogy between God's purpose for his human creatures, and the purpose of loving and wise parents for their children, we have to recognize that the presence of pleasure and the absence of pain cannot be the supreme and overriding end for which the world exists. Rather, this world must be a place of soul-making. And its value is to be judged, not primarily by the

38. Hick, "An Irenaean Theodicy," 47.
39. Hick, "An Irenaean Theodicy," 46.
40. "Men are not to be thought of on the analogy of animal pets, whose life is to be made as agreeable as possible, but rather on the analogy of human children, who are to grow to adulthood in an environment whose primary and overriding purpose is not immediate pleasure but the realization of the most valuable potentialities of human personality" (Hick, *Evil and the God of Love*, 258).

> quantity of pleasure and pain occurring in it at any particular moment, but by its fitness for its primary purpose, the purpose of soul-making.[41]

Hick interprets suffering as providential, not punitive, as an expression of love, not vengeance. According to Hick, "the long travail of the soul-making process" engenders moral goodness, and goodness that arises from strenuous effort has intrinsic value, and more value than readymade goodness, in the eyes of God.[42] Spiritual transformation begins in the crucible of a world of loss, grief, bodyache, heartache, failed dreams, dashed hopes, injustice, inequity, and constant danger.

Hick does not see the world through Pollyanna lenses, where all suffering brings about some evident goodness. Not all suffering contributes to our development, he admits. Some suffering simply destroys, without any redemptive or constructive value: "But too often we see the opposite of this [good coming from evil] in wickedness multiplying and in the disintegration of personalities under the impact of suffering: we see good turned to evil, kindness to bitterness, hope to despair."[43] Hick denies any direct or simple correlation between suffering and spiritual growth. As we know from even a cursory glance at history and the world around us, suffering destroys at least as often as it builds. So Hick's SMT does not lose sight of the grim reality of suffering as it develops the theory of the constructive potential of pain for human growth.

Hick refers to the "surplus" of evil, that is, excessive, pointless, and destructive suffering, as "dysteleological evil."[44] Ivan Karamazov's litany of brutal suffering and bestial behavior illustrates the concept well. To single out only one of his deeply disturbing examples,

41. Hick, *Evil and the God of Love*, 259.
42. Hick, *Evil and the God of Love*, 256.
43. Hick, *Evil and the God of Love*, 339.
44. Hick, *Evil and the God of Love*, 327, 333–36. Griffin, *God, Power, and Evil*, 189–90.

the story of the soldiers "tossing babies up in the air and catching them on the points of their bayonets before their mother's eyes" exemplifies dysteleological evil, since the baby does not benefit from the experience, nor does its mother, nor, incidentally, do the soldiers who commit the heinous act for their perverse amusement.[45] It represents senseless, soulless, excessive, and meaningless suffering. Nevertheless, indiscriminate, disproportional suffering—what Hick calls the "mystery of evil"—still contributes to the soul-making design of the universe at a macro level, since it cultivates compassion and elicits sympathy for those who suffer unfairly, and since it causes us to strive for the good for its own sake, without any promise of reward for good behavior.[46]

The macro-function of dysteleological evil, however, affords little comfort to the victims of horrendous evils, to use Marilyn Adams's term. What of the baby and the mother and the soldiers who have been destroyed by the experience? Hick argues that the soul-making process extends beyond our terrestrial existence: "If there is any eventual resolution of the interplay between good and evil, any decisive bringing of good out of evil, it must lie beyond this world and beyond the enigma of death."[47] Most of us depart from the earth with unfinished lives: "We have not become fully human by the time we die."[48] Moreover, many suffer excessively, and without the chance to grow as they might have under more favorable conditions. Hick extends the time frame for our maturation and perfection, appealing to postmortem existence.

45. Fyodor Dostoevsky, "Rebellion," in *The Problem of Evil*, ed. Michael L. Peterson, 59.

46. Hick, *Evil and the God of Love*, 333–36. Griffin recoils at Hick's suggestion that dysteleological evil contributes to the soul-making design of the world: "I personally find Hick's suggested justification of excessive evils appalling, and cannot accept the goodness of the God he is attempting to defend" (Griffin, *God, Power, and Evil*, 190).

47. Hick, *Evil and the God of Love*, 340.

48. Hick, *Evil and the God of Love*, 347.

For Hick, belief in the afterlife is "crucial for theodicy,"[49] and his theory leans heavily on the future accomplishment of God's soul-making design of the world: "Theodicy cannot be content to look to the past, seeking an explanation of evil in its origins, but must look toward the future, expecting a triumphant resolution in the eventual perfect fulfillment of God's good purpose."[50] After death, Hick speculates, humans enter an "intermediate state" where they continue in their journey toward divine likeness, a position "not far from the traditional Roman Catholic notion of purgatorial experiences."[51] Sanctification through suffering occurs on the earth and continues after death, "its extent and duration being determined by the degree of *un*sanctification" we exhibit at death.[52] Hick is, by necessity, imprecise in his description of the afterlife and its part in our soul-making. And yet, it plays a crucial role in his theodicy.

Despite the suspicions of "secular naturalism,"[53] Hick affirms the reality of life after death as a theological imperative: "But for historic Christian faith, the expectation of a life after death is a part of the total organism of Christian belief."[54] Moreover, the success of his SMT, and of theodicy in general, depends on the reality of heaven: "Would it not contradict God's love for the creatures made in His image if He caused them to pass out of existence whilst His purpose for them was still so largely unfulfilled?"[55] Heaven, Hick declares, will "justify retrospectively" and "render worthwhile" all the pain, misery, and injustice of human history and human existence: "And Christian theodicy must point forward to that final blessedness, and claim that this infinite future good will render worth while all the

49. Hick, *Evil and the God of Love*, 338.
50. Hick, *Evil and the God of Love*, 340.
51. Hick, *Evil and the God of Love*, 346–47.
52. Hick, *Evil and the God of Love*, 347.
53. Hick, *Evil and the God of Love*, 337.
54. Hick, *Evil and the God of Love*, 338.
55. Hick, *Evil and the God of Love*, 338.

pain and travail and wickedness that has occurred on the way to it."[56] Without the reality of heaven, Hick bluntly avers, SMT would fail, since it would leave evil unredeemed, which would mean the failure of God's benevolent, soul-making plan of the universe: "Without such an eschatological fulfillment, this theodicy would collapse."[57] Heaven completes the soul-making process and vindicates God, as we will see.

Even more pointedly, and problematically, Hick argues that in order to justify the violence, bloodshed, and suffering of history, a wonderful, even unexpected, good must result. Only if *all* humanity undergoes spiritual transformation, attaining divine likeness and enjoying the beatific vision, will SMT succeed, as Hick proclaims: "Only if it includes the entire human race can it justify the sins and sufferings of the entire human race throughout all history."[58] Hick elaborates further, specifying the theological stakes of his view: "We must thus affirm in faith that there will in the final accounting be no personal life that is unperfected and no suffering that has not eventually become a phase in the fulfillment of God's good purpose. Only so, I suggest, is it possible to believe both in the perfect goodness of God and in His unlimited capacity to perform His will. For if there are finally wasted lives and finally unredeemed sufferings, either God is not perfect in love or He is not sovereign in rule over creation."[59] At stake in the salvation of all, Hick states in no uncertain terms, is the credibility of divine goodness and omnipotence.

So, for Hick, not a single soul can be left behind, not a single life can be ultimately wasted and destroyed, and no suffering can be

56. Hick, *Evil and the God of Love*, 340.
57. Hick, "An Irenaean Theodicy," 51. "Hick believes a doctrine of an afterlife is essential, since God's purposes for human life so often fail in this life (252–55, 372)" (Griffin, *God, Power, and Evil*, 177).
58. Hick, "An Irenaean Theodicy," in Davis, ed., *Encountering Evil*, 52.
59. Hick, *Evil and the God of Love*, 340. "Hick believes the doctrines of God's love and his sovereignty imply that all persons will be eventually saved" (Griffin, *God, Power, and Evil*, 177).

left unredeemed. Heaven must be for all or for no one because we could never enjoy it without the presence of all our loved ones, and even our enemies, after their transformation. Hick thinks the Bible offers hints of universalism, especially in the writings of Paul, and that Jesus' explicit warnings about hell speak to possibilities that are never actualized because we all ultimately move from self-centeredness to other-centeredness, completing the process in the afterlife.[60] He grounds his doctrine of universalism in the logic of divine love and power: "And it seems to me a reasonable expectation that in the infinite resourcefulness of infinite love working in unlimited time, God will eventually succeed in drawing us all into the divine Kingdom."[61] Hick's universalism means that all suffering eventually comes to an end and that all evil will be transformed into good.

Hick's universalism threads the theological needle between providence and free will, stating "God will eventually succeed in His purpose of winning all men to Himself in faith and love."[62] In other words, God desires the salvation of all, and God has the power to fulfill those desires. Does that certainty compromise human freedom? No, Hick asserts. He employs two analogies to illustrate the "compatibility between divine providence and human freedom."[63] First, God's providential care of humanity resembles a cosmic chess match between "a novice and a world master." We are technically free to make our moves, but God never loses. God's total mastery of the board (the universe) and the players (humanity) ensures his victory. Second, God is the "divine Therapist" whose infinite wisdom and love assures our spiritual amelioration.[64] While Hick accepts the theoretical possibility of divine defeat, he nonetheless posits the

60. Hick, *Death and the Afterlife* (Louisville: Westminster John Knox, 1994), 243–47.
61. Hick, "An Irenaean Theodicy," 69. Griffin, *God, Power, and Evil*, 179.
62. Hick, *Evil and the God of Love*, 342.
63. Hick, *Evil and the God of Love*, 344.
64. Hick, *Evil and the God of Love*, 345.

"practical certainty" that God accomplishes his beneficent designs for the universe.[65]

Dialogue

As with all the theodicies we examine, SMT has its own distinctive strengths and weaknesses. Anytime you stake out a position as clearly and controversially as Hick, you are bound to attract impassioned allies and adversaries. Hick's theory begins, as we discussed previously, with the repudiation of the FWD and with the corollary rejection of punishment theodicies that argue that suffering functions as punishment for sin. Not surprisingly, then, the positive and negative assessments of SMT focus on his central claim that pain and suffering serve a necessary soteriological function: it creates the conditions for our spiritual growth, which is the purpose of the universe. What, then, are the prospects and problems of that assertion?

Strengths

On the criterion of creativity, Hick scores high marks. His theory brilliantly applies evolutionary science to our spiritual transformation, spelling out its theological and philosophical implications. It also ingenuously, albeit misguidedly, utilizes Irenaeus and applies the "minority report" he represents to other theologians, such as F. W. D. Schleiermacher. Moreover, it reinterprets Genesis, the Gospels, and Paul in an effort to align scripture with its cosmological and soteriological scheme. Thus, it tries to bring tradition into

65. Hick, *Evil and the God of Love*, 345. An allusion to Augustine's famous summary of theological anthropology: "[Y]ou have made and drawn us to yourself, and our heart is unquiet until it rests in you" (*Confessions* I.1.1).

conformity with the modern world. Similarly, on the criterion of relevance, Hick also scores in the upper bracket of the grading curve. SMT attempts to update theodicy, to adapt it to contemporary scientific, philosophical, and theological sensibilities. It argues that the FWD has lost relevance in light of modern science and attempts to fill the vacuum with its alternative account of creation, the fall, and redemption. On these two criteria, creativity and relevance, SMT comes through with flying colors.

It is also internally consistent, although not totally devoid of conceptual difficulties. SMT offers an optimistic view of the world and the human quest for self-improvement. Likewise, it offers a positive view of suffering as constructive rather than destructive or punitive, which has intuitive and experiential plausibility. We often see people we know personally grow from their painful experiences, and we know that growth in any area of life often comes at a cost. Moreover, Hick's universalism addresses the problem of dysteleological evil, and offers a hopeful eschatological vision of the harmony of all humanity and the eradication of all evil and suffering. Finally, Hick grounds his SMT in a positive view of God as a parent who guides humanity through the rigors of spiritual transformation, always with our best interests in mind.

Furthermore, the constructive potential of SMT branches in several directions. Three stand out as particularly promising. First, there is an implicit spirituality in Hick's SMT that touches on the spiritual value of suffering. If it were developed theologically, it could link naturally with *imitatio Christi* spiritualities, and with monastic spiritualities of self-renunciation and the careful cultivation of the soul. Second, there is an implicit pluralism in SMT that naturally adapts to different religious contexts. His core principle of the constructive spiritual value of suffering could be retrofitted to other religions.[66] Moreover, his affirmation of the universal salvation of all humanity immediately opens doors to interreligious dialogue.

SMT also promotes constructive dialogue between theology, philosophy, and science. In contrast to the FWD, which stands in uneasy tension with these contemporary sensibilities, SMT builds conceptual bridges. These bridges facilitate interdisciplinary interaction and creative engagement on shared questions, which forges common ground for discussion to move forward. SMT demonstrates the possibility of productive collaborations between disciplines, in contrast to the mutual hostility that too often characterizes conversations between science and theology, and the suspicion that too often characterizes conversations between philosophy and theology.

Finally, despite its departure from traditional theology, SMT tries valiantly to stay tethered to Christian history and theology. Hick takes great pains to ground SMT in the Christian tradition, albeit a minority report, and to demonstrate its consistency, or at least noncontradiction, with scripture. His results seem strained to the point of breaking at times, but not through lack of effort and ingenuity to correlate his theory with Christian sources, which reflects his second criterion of theodicy: internal theological consistency with the religious tradition.[67]

Weaknesses

On the criterion of fidelity to the sources of theology, however, Hick's SMT does not fare as well. Hick fails to establish convincingly a rival patron saint to Augustine. Instead, he reads Irenaeus into his own intellectual framework, and presupposes greater theological and

66. Hick, *Evil and the God of Love*, xvi.
67. Hick, "An Irenaean Theodicy," 38.

exegetical disparity than exists between the two thinkers. Hick also employs problematic hermeneutical sleights of hand, especially on the question of universalism. Rather than reading scripture with tradition to determine the most probable meaning, Hick eisegetically reads his personal theological sensibilities into scripture. For those committed to the priority of scripture, and sound exegesis in theological discourse, his conclusions seem artificial and forced. For those committed to the priority of the fathers, especially Augustine, his superficial appeal to Irenaeus, and his facile contrast between Irenaeus and Augustine, will appear theologically tenuous and unsustainable.

Though internally consistent, several conceptual and theological problems plague SMT. First, as Griffin points out, Hick seems to deny the reality of "genuine" (as opposed to apparent) evil when he adopts "the principle of 'O felix culpa,'" which means that sin arises as the "happy fault" that God foresaw and foreordained would lead to Christ.[68] Second, SMT shades into an instrumentalist view of evil when it claims that suffering serves a necessary function. If evil is divinely ordained, and if it is morally and spiritually necessary, on what grounds do we classify and condemn it as evil, rather than good? SMT's positive valuation of suffering risks justifying and instrumentalizing evil.[69] Third, as a result, it tends to downplay the destructive reality of evil. John Roth objects that Hick "sees the world too much as a schoolroom when it is actually more like a dangerous ally."[70] In reality, suffering destroys more often than it builds, which means that Hick's theory must lean too heavily on its eschatology, which leads to the final problem: Hick's eschatological imprecision. He never fully explicates the postmortem conditions that facilitate

68. Griffin, *God, Power, and Evil*, 198–99.

69. "Hick even brings 'dysteleological' evil within the framework of those things that contribute to soul-making, thereby finally seeing them as teleologically (i.e., instrumentally) good" (Griffin, *God, Power, and Evil*, 200).

70. John Roth, "Critique of 'An Irenaean Theodicy,'" in Davis, ed., *Encountering Evil*, 62.

our growth. Perhaps that simply reflects the imprecise nature of eschatology, but it remains problematic, especially given the weight he assigns to it in determining the success of his theory.

Also, with respect to theological fidelity, Hick's SMT suffers from Christological deficiencies. Christ does not play a central role in Hick's development of his SMT. At best, Christ exemplifies "redemptive suffering," which roughly corresponds to an exemplarist model of Christology.[71] For Hick, Christ embodies other-centeredness, and teaches us the redemptive possibility of suffering, which gives him an important symbolic function, but not much more. Conversely, the classic atonement model, which focuses on the salvific significance of the death and resurrection of Christ, plays a minor, mostly symbolic role. Hick's soteriology inflects his Christology, so his hypothesis of open admittance into heaven attenuates the salvific necessity of Christ. In fact, Hick's Christology illustrates a deeper suspicion that his theodicy is driven more by philosophical concerns than distinctly Christian theological concerns. His later rejection of a specifically Christian viewpoint and adoption of pluralism seems to confirm this suspicion.[72]

Finally, on the question of universal salvation, several problems arise. First, universalism stands in direct tension with both scripture and Christian tradition, at least historically.[73] Hick grounds the doctrine in alternative exegetical and theological streams, but his conclusions strike many as forced and inadequate. As a reaction to older paradigms, his theodicy naturally bypasses scripture and tradition, although he attempts to reconcile them with his theory

71. Hick, *Evil and the God of Love*, 355–56.

72. Hick, *Evil and the God of Love*, xvi.

73. As Stephen Davis remarks, universalism explicitly contradicts scripture, at least *prima facie*. It would be methodologically unsound to base Christian doctrine on emotional and existential grounds: "Let me confess that I would like universalism to be true. . . . But as a matter of theological method, we cannot affirm a doctrine just because we would like it to be true" (Stephen T. Davis, "Critique of 'An Irenaean Theodicy,'" in Davis, ed., *Encountering Evil*, 71).

when possible. Second, his universalism threatens freedom.[74] If all *will* be saved, does that mean all *must* be saved, regardless of their wishes? Hick responds that our innate "Godward bias" drives us toward God, like a spiritual homing beacon, so that God draws us exactly to where we want to go, without any coercion.[75] But the notion of Godward gravitation merely shifts the problem to new ground. Third, Hick does not sufficiently spell out the implications of universalism for divine justice, which undergirds the traditional view. He would retort that the intermediate state of purgatory protects divine justice, since sinners suffer the consequences of their sinfulness, but it does not dispel the suspicion that the most heinous in history literally "get away with murder."

Conclusion

Few developments in theodicy have been as monumental as Hick's SMT. It represents a paradigm shift from the dominance of the FWD and initiates a new, constructive dialogue with modernity. His work in theodicy has become the touchstone for modern treatments of the problem of evil, and new work in theodicy must reckon with his arguments, and position their theories in relation to him. As

74. Griffin objects to Hick's "hybrid free-will defense," which, on the one hand, affirms divine sovereignty at the expense of human freedom, and, on the other hand, posits divine self-limitation to make room for human freedom: "In other words, this view maintains that there is nothing inherently self-contradictory in the idea of God's totally controlling the actions of actual beings, but that God voluntarily relinquishes this control in regard to at least some of the actual creatures in order to make possible the achievement of greater values, ones that are sufficiently great to justify the risk of evil entailed in giving up total control of the universe" (Griffin, *God, Power, and Evil*, 186).
75. Hick, "An Irenaean Theodicy," 52. Hick attempts to balance the postmortem continuation of human freedom with his belief in universalism as the reasonable upshot of divine goodness and omnipotence: "The least that we must say, surely, is that God will never cease to desire and actively to work for the salvation of each created person. He will never abandon any as irredeemably evil. However long an individual may reject his Maker, salvation will remain an open possibility to which God is ever trying to draw him" (Hick, *Evil and the God of Love*, 343).

with any theodicy, his advances come at a price, and it is up to the reader to perform a theological cost-benefit analysis of SMT. For some, it departs too far from core Christian convictions. For others, it strikes the right balance between the past and the present, between theology and science, and between theology and philosophy. For still others, it stays too close to Christian sources when it could be developed independent of them. For all, SMT drives contemporary conversations in theodicy, and interacts with new paradigms, as we will see in the next chapter with the highly inventive and even more controversial process theodicy.

Questions for Discussion:

1. How does suffering build character? Give some examples.
2. How does suffering destroy lives? Give some examples.
3. Do you learn more from pleasure or pain? Explain why.
4. Is the world more like a schoolroom (Hick) or a dangerous ally (Roth)?
5. What is the appeal of universalism? What are the problems with it?

5

Process Theodicy

Denying Divine Omnipotence

"God is the great companion—the fellow-sufferer who understands."[1]

If SMT takes a decisive step away from traditional theism in its effort to explain evil, process theodicy takes a dramatic leap. Process theodicy (hereafter PT) utilizes the cosmology of process philosophy to shed new light on the problem of evil.[2] Alfred North Whitehead (1861–1947), the founder and figurehead of process thought, developed his metaphysical system famously in *Process and Reality* (1929), his *magnum opus*.[3] In a stunning and sweeping synthesis of

1. Alfred North Whitehead, *Process and Reality: An Essay in Cosmology* (New York: Free Press, 1978 [1929]), 351.
2. The two main texts for process theodicy are David Ray Griffin, *God, Power, and Evil: A Process Theodicy* (Philadelphia: Westminster, 2004 [1976]) and its sequel, *Evil Revisited: Responses and Reconsiderations* (Albany: State University of New York Press, 1991), where he addresses objections to his theodicy.
3. David Ray Griffin, "Process Theology," in *A Companion to Philosophy of Religion (Blackwell Companions to Philosophy)*, ed. Philip L. Quinn and Charles Taliaferro (Malden, MA: Blackwell,

philosophy, theology, and science, Whitehead strives "to sound the depths in the nature of things."[4] His cosmology was extended and modified by Charles Hartshorne (1897–2000) and eventually filtered into a theodicy, principally through the work of David Ray Griffin (1939–).[5]

PT stems from the dynamic cosmology of process philosophy, and addresses the major questions of theodicy through the lens of the evolving nature of God and the world, whose destinies are inextricably intertwined. To gain a purchase on PT, we must first sketch its philosophical and theological underpinnings, and then see how its metaphysical maneuvers reconfigure theodicy in crucial ways. Just as John Hick's SMT marked a paradigm shift away from the FWD, so PT marks an even more pronounced shift away from classical theism. Even more than SMT, PT's innovative approach to the problem of evil risks theologically what it gains culturally, a cost-benefit analysis that we will undertake at the conclusion of the chapter.

Process Philosophy

To understand PT, we must acquire some basic facility with the terminology and theoretical orientation of process philosophy. As its starting point, process philosophy rejects the substance metaphysics of Western philosophy, which conceives of reality as static substances

1999), 136. "In Whitehead's usage, 'metaphysics' is the attempt not to describe things that are beyond the possibility of experience but to explain the coherence of *all* things that *are* experienced" (139).

4. Whitehead, *Process and Reality*, xiv.
5. Griffin styles process philosophy as "Whiteheadian-Hartshornean," given its creation by Alfred North Whitehead and modification by Charles Hartshorne (Griffin, *God, Power, and Evil*, 275). Whitehead characterizes his worldview as the "philosophy of organism," while Hartshorne refers to his system as "societal realism" (John B. Cobb Jr. and David Ray Griffin, *Process Theology: An Introductory Exposition* [Philadelphia: Westminster, 1976]), 7.

subject to metaphysical categorization. In its view, reality does not consist of passive matter or ontologically ossified persons and things that enter into various relationships with other persons and things. In short, it dismisses Aristotelian metaphysics, outlined in the *Categories*, which became the pervasive metaphysics of Christian theology after Thomas Aquinas.[6] Moreover, process philosophy denies the bifurcation of reality between organic and inorganic matter as well as human and nonhuman life, as if these were metaphysically unrelated or totally ontologically distinct. Put simply, it discards the ancient metaphysical worldview that sees people and things as constituted by their distinct, independent, static, ontological "stuff" or "thingness."

ALFRED NORTH WHITEHEAD: A famous twentieth-century mathematician and philosopher, A. N. Whitehead (1861–1947) founded process philosophy, a metaphysical system he develops in *Process and Reality* (1929). Whitehead's dynamic cosmology favors flux and interdependence over stasis and substance.

In a "repudiation" of "prevalent habits of thought,"[7] Whitehead develops a "philosophical scheme" titled "the Philosophy of Organism."[8] As an alternative to conventional metaphysical theories, Whitehead posits the evolving nature of reality, and its ontological interdependence: "The positive doctrine of these lectures is concerned with the becoming, the being, and the

6. Whitehead, *Process and Reality*, 209.
7. Whitehead, *Process and Reality*, xiii.
8. Whitehead, *Process and Reality*, xi.

relatedness of 'actual entities.'"[9] Its eclectic philosophical influences include Heraclitus, Plato, Descartes, Locke, Leibniz, Berkeley, Hume, and Hegel.[10] Whitehead transposes the intuition of the pre-Socratic Hellenistic philosopher Heraclitus that "all things flow"[11] into the metaphysical principle of flux within a wider matrix of the ontological interrelatedness of reality.[12] Process philosophy, as it came to be known, privileges "relatedness" over "quality," "flow" over "permanence," inverting Aristotelian metaphysical categories.[13] Two concepts, then, arise as ontologically primary at the outset: flux and interdependence.

Whitehead defines reality as a series of "actual occasions of experience" that encompass all reality, from the biological to the subatomic:[14] "Electrons, molecules, and cells are examples of such enduring things. Likewise the human soul, or stream of experience, is composed of a series of distinct occasions of experience."[15] Each "actual reality" experiences, regardless of its location on the chain of being. Moreover, process metaphysics affirms the nonduality and thus interrelatedness of reality, rather than its ontological isolation or independence: "It is not first something in itself, which only secondarily enters into relations with others. The relations are primary. Whitehead's technical terms for these relations are

9. Whitehead, *Process and Reality*, xiii.
10. Whitehead, *Process and Reality*, xi. Cobb Jr. and Griffin, *Process Theology*, 7.
11. "Upon those who step into the same rivers, different and again different waters flow . . . [It is not possible to step twice into the same river] . . . It scatters and again comes together and approaches and recedes. . . . We step and we do not step into the same rivers" (Heraclitus, in *Readings in Ancient Greek Philosophy: From Thales to Aristotle*, ed. S. Marc Cohen, Patricia Curd, and C. D. C. Reeve [Indianapolis: Hackett, 1995], 30).
12. Whitehead, *Process and Reality*, 208. "[T]he flux of things is one ultimate generalization around which we must weave our philosophical system."
13. Whitehead, *Process and Reality*, xiii.
14. James A. Keller, "Process Theism and Theodicies for the Problems of Evil," in *The Blackwell Companion to the Problem of Evil*, ed. Justin P. McBrayer and Daniel Howard-Snyder (Malden, MA: John Wiley, 2013), 345.
15. Cobb Jr. and Griffin, *Process Theology*, 19.

'prehension' and 'feeling.'"[16] Whitehead calls the process whereby an "actual occasion" becomes a "unified subject" through its integration of previous occasions "concrescence."[17] Afterwards, as it interacts with itself and others, it transmits its data to new occasions of experience, a process called "transition."[18]

All reality, therefore, consists of ever-shifting actualities or "occasions of experience." Two analogies illuminate the basic concept of process metaphysics. First, a wave in the ocean has identifiable features that enable our recognition of it as a wave, such as motion, location, height, length, depth, and cresting. And yet, at any given moment, we cannot capture the full "essence" of the wave, since it constantly shifts as it rolls over the ceiling of the sea. We define the wave by its dynamic motion, not its static substance. Similarly, as a film plays on a screen, it seems continuous when in fact it consists of distinct frames that rapidly shift consecutively and imperceptibly.[19] Reality, similarly, shifts from "actual entities" or "momentary events" that shade seamlessly into subsequent entities, with which they are intimately related at a metaphysical level. The wave and film analogies, then, illustrate the ebb and flow of reality.

Humans perceive reality as unified and static when it is, in fact, fragmentary and fluid. Whereas most experience persons and things as enduring entities, Whitehead sees them as momentary events that subtly transition from one "society" to another.[20] To the untrained eye, a friend or rock seems the same moment-to-moment, with only slight alterations. Upon deeper inspection, however, all existence flows together at the atomic and subatomic level. So, just as the wave, at any given moment, has a reality that links it to its previous

16. Cobb Jr. and Griffin, *Process Theology*, 19.
17. Griffin, *God, Power, and Evil*, 277.
18. Griffin, *God, Power, and Evil*, 277. Whitehead, *Process and Reality*, 210–11.
19. Cobb Jr. and Griffin, *Process Theology*, 14.
20. Cobb Jr. and Griffin, *Process Theology*, 15.

moment, connects it to the next moment, and remains constantly in flux, so all life, sentient and nonsentient, unfolds through a series of interconnected relationships and interactions. Like the wave, all life rolls on in a dynamic dance without clearly demarcated boundaries between "occasions of experiences," which points to the deeper interconnectedness of all reality, amid the apparent individuation.

Finally, given the interdependence of all occasions of experience, it follows that all reality simultaneously influences and is influenced by other occasions of experience. In relation to human subjectivity, that means that humans enjoy the possibility of "creative self-determination" or freedom within the environments that give shape to the self.[21] Humans, then, are empowered to realize ever-higher levels of enjoyment, freedom, and creativity in dynamic interaction with God, others, and the world around them, with which they are intimately related.

Process Theology

Process theology straddles between its religious foundation and philosophical orientation: "Process theology operates on the one side from the perspective of Christian faith and on the other in the metaphysical context provided by process philosophy and its doctrine of God."[22] Naturally, then, its deliberations on God and God's relationship to reality, particularly on the question of evil, involve constant negotiation between two perspectives that are not always or easily compatible. The success or failure of process theology hinges on its ability to retain the integrity of both its religious and philosophical roots within its creative metaphysical synthesis, a

21. Cobb Jr. and Griffin, *Process Theology*, 28.
22. Cobb Jr. and Griffin, *Process Theology*, 41.

delicate and daunting task, given the significant areas of tensions between them.

While process theology retains the term *God*, it jettisons its traditional theological content: "Whitehead and Hartshorne have both used the word 'God' frequently and without embarrassment. However, they have been conscious that what they have meant by the term is philosophically and religiously opposed to much that has been meant by 'God' in metaphysical, theological, and popular tradition."[23] In fact, its radical redefinition of the nature and work of God completely overhauls conventional usage, to the point where the terminology becomes misleading to the uninitiated. Whitehead dismisses traditional theism, particularly the doctrines of impassibility and omnipotence, as imperialistic and philosophically unsustainable.[24] Classic theism portrays God as a cosmic dispassionate potentate—stern and unyielding—rather than a tender lover of humanity: "Love neither rules, nor is it unmoved."[25] His love has two

DAVID RAY GRIFFIN: An American philosopher of religion and founder of the Center for Process Studies at the Claremont School of Theology, Griffin (1939–) develops process theodicy in *God, Power, and Evil: A Process Theodicy* (1976) and *Evil Revisited: Responses and Reconsiderations* (1991).

23. Cobb Jr. and Griffin, *Process Theology*, 8.
24. Whitehead, *Process and Reality*, 342–43.
25. Whitehead, *Process and Reality*, 343.

sides, what Whitehead refers to as the "dipolar"[26] nature of God as both primordial and consequent.

God's primordial nature refers to God's infinite "conceptual realization of the absolute wealth of potentiality," a bottomless well of cosmic possibilities from which all creation flows.[27] God thus grounds the cosmos and directs it toward its highest possible actualization: "In this aspect, he is not *before* all creation, but *with* all creation."[28] God is the "principle of concretion" that gives every finite reality form and direction.[29] God is the basis of creativity and novelty in the world, but it has no consciousness apart from creation. Creativity, in fact, is the central attribute of process theism: "God is the only primordial, omnipresent, all-inclusive embodiment of creativity. And God is the only one who characterizes creativity with perfect love."[30] Creation strives to internalize the creative possibilities God presents to all reality.

God's consequent nature, on the other hand, expresses God's extension in the physical world through the actuality of all reality. It is actual rather than conceptual.[31] All creation derives in part from the values and desires of God's primordial nature, which are imprinted into the world through the subjective aim of each creature. As God realizes God's full potentiality in the cosmos, God arrives at higher states of self-realization. Creation completes God as much as God completes creation: "The completion of God's nature into a fullness of physical feeling is derived from the objectification of the world in God."[32] With the dipolarity of God in mind, let us explore how

26. Whitehead, *Process and Reality*, 345.
27. Whitehead, *Process and Reality*, 343.
28. Whitehead, *Process and Reality*, 343.
29. Whitehead, *Process and Reality*, 344.
30. Griffin, *Evil Revisited*, 23.
31. Whitehead, *Process and Reality*, 345.
32. Whitehead, *Process and Reality*, 345.

process theology takes shape in contrast to specific points of classical theism.

First, in sharp contrast to classical theism, process theology rejects divine omnipotence, that is, the belief in God's all-powerful nature.[33] It raises several objections to it. First, if God were "the Controlling Power,"[34] then nothing could resist God's omnipotent will, which would implicate God for evil, since nothing could arise or occur apart from God.[35] All the evil in history, including the Holocaust, would have to be ascribed to God directly, as part of his omnipotent and inexorable plan. Second, divine omnipotence would compromise human freedom. If God determines all reality, then humans cannot exercise agency in any meaningful sense. Process theology argues, alternatively, that humans have the power of self-determination, even against God, which helps account for the disharmony and disorder of the world.[36]

Second, it recasts God's relationship to creation.[37] God directs reality, but does not determine it.[38] Process theology denies the doctrine of creation *ex nihilo* (out of nothing),[39] which it ties to the faulty belief in God's "monopoly on power."[40] God does not call existence into being from "*absolute* nothingness" because God does

33. "That modification [the denial of divine omnipotence] lies at the heart of process theodicy" (Griffin, *Evil Revisited*, 3).
34. Cobb Jr. and Griffin, *Process Theology*, 9, 52.
35. Griffin, *God, Power, and Evil*, 279.
36. Griffin, *God, Power, and Evil*, 280. Griffin, "Process Theology," 140.
37. Whitehead, *Process and Reality*, 348. For a helpful analysis of the relationship between process cosmology and theodicy, see David Ray Griffin, "Creation out of Nothing, Creation out of Chaos, and the Problem of Evil," in *Encountering Evil: Live Options in Theodicy*, ed. Stephen T. Davis (Louisville: Westminster John Knox, 2001), 108–44.
38. Griffin, "Process Theology," 139: "Process theologians have been able, accordingly, to speak rather straightforwardly of God as creator, in the sense that God accounts for the directionality of the evolutionary process."
39. Griffin, "Process Theology," 139. See, for instance, 2 Macc. 7:28. For supporting passages in the New Testament, see John 1:3, Rom. 4:17, Col. 1:16, and Heb. 11:3 (Griffin, "Creation out of Nothing, Creation out of Chaos, and the Problem of Evil," in *Encountering Evil*, 110).
40. Griffin, *God, Power, and Evil*, 279.

not stand outside creation as the "absolute controller."[41] Instead, God creates the world out of "primeval chaos," conditions of unformed and unrealized potentialities:[42] "Creation is the gradual bringing of order out of chaos."[43] Both Plato and the Old Testament recommend the latter view, where God finds a "formless void" and "begins" to create order from the "low-grade actual occasions happening at random."[44] The doctrine of creation *ex nihilo*, as an extension of the doctrine of divine omnipotence, inadvertently implicates God for the existence of evil, since all reality, including evil, would derive from God alone, without any intermediate factors.[45] According to process theology, God does not exert total control over the cosmos, which means that evil resists God's will. God does not want disease and death and destruction, but God does not have the power to eliminate them.

God and creation exist in a state of perpetual reciprocity, in contrast to the doctrine of divine impassibility and aseity (God's independent reality). "It is as true to say that God creates the World, as that the World creates God."[46] They mutually interpenetrate without remainder. Creation "embodies" God and God "inhabits" creation.[47] God grounds the possibilities of creation and supplies its innate direction. God exists as the primordial unity who subsumes

41. Cobb Jr. and Griffin, *Process Theology*, 65. Griffin, *God, Power, and Evil*, 279.
42. Griffin, "Creation out of Nothing, Creation out of Chaos, and the Problem of Evil," in *Encountering Evil*, 108.
43. Griffin, *Evil Revisited*, 23.
44. Cobb Jr. and Griffin, *Process Theology*, 65. Griffin, "Creation out of Nothing, Creation out of Chaos, and the Problem of Evil," in *Encountering Evil*, 110.
45. "The idea of creation *ex nihilo*, by saying that God is the source of literally everything, including evil, would threaten the perfect goodness of God"; "The history of theodicy would bear out his [Hermogenes'] warning that, if God is said to have created the world out of absolute nothingness, the origin of evil cannot be explained, at least without implying that God's goodness is less than perfect" (Griffin, "Creation out of Nothing, Creation out of Chaos, and the Problem of Evil," in *Encountering Evil*, 112, 114).
46. Whitehead, *Process and Reality*, 348.
47. Whitehead, *Process and Reality*, 348.

the multiplicity of the world, which resolves the problem of the one and the many: "Thus God is to be conceived as one and as many in the converse sense in which the World is to be conceived as many and as one."[48] God's primordial and consequent nature engrafts dipolarity—unity and multiplicity, with all of their conflicting characteristics—into the unity of God's existence.

Process theology denies the power relationship between God and the world implied by the doctrine of divine omnipotence and creation *ex nihilo*, where God exerts total control.[49] It affirms the "shared power" between God and the world, where God, "the supreme embodiment of creativity," influences and is influenced by the events of the world.[50] God relates to the world more as a co-creator than as *the* Creator, which necessitates a shift in theological analogies: "The image of God as the craftsman, the cosmic watchmaker, must be abandoned. God is the husbandman, in the vineyard of the world, fostering and nurturing its continuous evolutionary growth throughout all the ages."[51] These images of God as working in the garden of the cosmos, where weeds (evil) frustrate God's designs for its full flourishing, captures the sense of process theology and cosmology, which unfold together toward an open future of peril and possibility.

So God does not bend creation to the divine will because, in the first place, God cannot. God, as the shaper of creation, remains confined to and within it. God does not coerce creation into submission because, in the second place, God seeks to utilize and

48. Whitehead, *Process and Reality*, 349.
49. "Because power is essentially shared, God's power cannot be thought to be unilateral power. If all creatures essentially have some power to determine themselves and to influence other things, God cannot unilaterally determine any state of affairs" (Griffin, *Evil Revisited*, 23).
50. Griffin, "Creation out of Nothing, Creation out of Chaos, and the Problem of Evil," 22.
51. Lewis Ford, "Divine Persuasion and the Triumph of Good," in *The Problem of Evil: Selected Readings*, ed. Michael L. Peterson (Notre Dame, IN: University of Notre Dame Press, 1992), 249.

maximize human freedom as a fellow-laborer: "[God] is the companion and friend who inspires us to achieve the very best that is within us. God creates by persuading the world to create itself."[52] Coercion would override our freedom. God instead makes us partners in cosmic creation and renewal: "Divine persuasive power maximizes creaturely freedom, respecting the integrity of each creature in the very act of guiding that creature's development toward greater freedom."[53] In contrast to traditional theology, then, God cannot control or determine any events in the universe.[54]

In process theology, divine persuasion supplants divine omnipotence as God's fundamental disposition toward the world: "God's power is persuasive, not controlling."[55] God lures and guides creation toward higher states of actuality and enjoyment: "God's power needs to be reconceived as *evocative* power. By perpetually offering attractive alternatives to creatures' habits, God has gradually brought forth those increasingly complex forms of order that we call atoms, molecules, macromolecules, procaryotic cells, organelles, eucaryotic cells, plants, animals, animals with central nervous systems, animals with conscious souls, and animals with self-conscious souls."[56] God gives all reality, including humans, an "initial aim" that it must strive to actualize within its concrete circumstances.[57] Since persuasion never involves coercion, God does not and cannot force our compliance with the salutary divine *telos* of our existence: "In other words, God seeks to persuade each occasion toward that possibility for its own existence which would be best for it; but God cannot control the finite occasion's self-actualization."[58] God inspires

52. Ford, "Divine Persuasion and the Triumph of Good," 249.
53. Ford, "Divine Persuasion and the Triumph of Good," 249.
54. Griffin, *God, Power, and Evil*, 275: "God not only does not but also in principle *could* not completely control events in the world."
55. Griffin, *God, Power, and Evil*, 276.
56. Griffin, *Evil Revisited*, 23.
57. Griffin, "Process Theology," 139.

all human advances in freedom, creativity, harmony, and intensity of experience.[59]

Why does God desire to help humanity, despite its intransigence to God's beneficent will? Classic theism posits the impassibility of God: God does not suffer, nor does God experience human feelings such as sympathy, compassion, or sorrow, since these would mar the divine perfection. God loves humanity not through feeling, but through action, which the biblical writers translate into emotive terms.[60] Process theology, on the contrary, argues that love must involve sympathy: "Sympathy means feeling the feelings of the other, hurting with the pains of the other, grieving with the grief, rejoicing with the joys."[61] Griffin argues that Whitehead's construal of God as the fellow-sufferer recovers a more intuitive, biblical perspective of divine love, which has been obscured by the misguided importation of Greek philosophy into traditional Christian theology, a charge we will return to in the next chapter in a different context.[62]

Far from the "impassive spectator deity" of traditional theology, process theology asserts God's intimate presence with us throughout the entire spectrum of human experiences: "God suffers with our sufferings, as well as enjoying our enjoyments."[63] God does not stand aloof as the world suffers. God does not spectate on the carnage of history. Rather, God unites with and absorbs human suffering at an ontological level, as the ground of all reality. God does not hover safely above the vicissitudes of human experience, but rather internalizes it in all its complexity: "The divine reality, who not only enjoys all enjoyments but also suffers all sufferings, is an Adventurer,

58. Cobb Jr. and Griffin, *Process Theology*, 53.
59. Griffin, "Creation out of Nothing, Creation out of Chaos, and the Problem of Evil," 122–23.
60. Cobb Jr. and Griffin, *Process Theology*, 44–45.
61. Cobb Jr. and Griffin, *Process Theology*, 44.
62. Cobb Jr. and Griffin, *Process Theology*, 44.
63. Griffin, *God, Power, and Evil*, 309.

choosing the former mode, risking discord in the quest for the various types of perfection that are possible."[64] God does not stand above creation, immune and indifferent to its misery; God shares its risks with us. So God has "skin in the game," as it were.[65]

Finally, with respect to process theology, Whitehead and later process thinkers often employ personal language for God, despite their impersonal conception of God. They refer to God as a friend, companion, and fellow-sufferer, but their anthropomorphic locution does not entail divine personhood. God does not, in their view, have an individual rational consciousness that stands apart from creation, and freely relates to it as "Other." God is a principle, not a person.[66] Process theologians personify the principle "God" in an effort to relate to classic theism, but that does not negate the impersonal nature of the process that lures creation forward to higher states of existence and internalizes all experiences without any independent consciousness, since the totality of reality, with all its experiences, *constitutes* God's existence.

Process Theodicy

Now that we have a sense of its philosophical and theological underpinnings, we are able to discuss PT directly. First, how does PT define evil? In the first place, PT rejects all attempts to downplay the reality of "genuine evil": suffering that has no redemptive value, no positive outcome, and no necessary theological significance.[67] Classic theism ultimately denies its reality through its appeal to "greater

64. Cobb Jr. and Griffin, *Process Theology*, 75.
65. Griffin, "Process Theology," 139. "He does not create the world, he saves it: or, more accurately, he is the poet of the world, with tender patience leading it by his vision of truth, beauty, and goodness" (Whitehead, *Process and Reality*, 346).
66. Ford, "Divine Persuasion and the Triumph of Good," 252.
67. Griffin, *God, Power, and Evil*, 275–76; Griffin, *Evil Revisited*, 79–83; Cobb Jr. and Griffin, *Process Theology*, 69; Griffin, "Process Theology," 140.

good" theories, all of which argue that evil produces greater goods that would have been impossible otherwise. The horrors of the Holocaust exemplify genuine evil,[68] which only wastes and destroys, without remainder and without the prospect of any transmutation into a final harmony.[69] PT takes it as morally imperative to identify and condemn genuine evil, not to justify its existence through specious notions of its instrumentality.

For PT, evil thwarts the "maximal harmonious intensity" of creation, God's desire for enjoyment.[70] "Process entails loss," as Whitehead explains: "The nature of evil is that the characters of things are mutually obstructive."[71] Natural selection destroys even as it overcomes "obstructiveness."[72] The process itself constitutes metaphysical evil, the destructive nature of the cosmos that evolves at a cost. Natural evil signifies the experiential dimension of metaphysical evil, the "discord and *unnecessary*

PROCESS THEODICY: Process theodicy, which emerges from the insights of process philosophy and theology, argues that God is not omnipotent and thus cannot prevent evil. God and humanity must work together to overcome evil and injustice and to realize greater states of freedom, love, and creativity.

68. Griffin, *Revisiting Evil*, 80.

69. Whitehead employs the term "destructive evil," which he defines as "purely self-regarding" (Whitehead, *Process and Reality*, 346).

70. Cobb Jr. and Griffin, *Process Theology*, 70; Griffin, *God, Power, and Evil*, 282.

71. Whitehead, *Process and Reality*, 340: "Selection is at once the measure of evil, and the process of its evasion." Elsewhere, he explains the metaphysical tension between "Evil" and higher realizations of harmony, or "Beauty": "The intermingling of Beauty and Evil arises from the conjoint operation of three metaphysical principles:—(1) That all actualization is finite; (2) That finitude involves the exclusion of alternative possibility; (3) That mental function introduces into realization subjective forms conformal to relevant alternatives excluded from

triviality" that besets all creation.[73] Moral evil consists of the unnecessary *intentional* destruction of the "intrinsic good" of others.[74] Finally, beyond the standard typology of evil, Whitehead identifies the global problem of evil as finitude—the transience of reality, where life blooms for a moment but quickly withers and passes out of existence and memory: "The ultimate evil in the temporal world is deeper than any specific evil. It lies in the fact that the past fades, that time is a 'perpetual perishing.'"[75]

Second, how does evil originate? As we saw with the process doctrine of creation, evil results from the raw material of the universe, a chaos that God shapes into an order, but that constantly resists God's efforts: "The general thesis of the process theodicy which follows is that the possibility of genuine evil is rooted in the metaphysical (i.e., necessary) characteristics of the world."[76] Evil arises as chaos oversteps the divinely proscribed boundaries, and since God only subdues evil partially in creation, it constantly rears its ugly head to subvert God's order. God does not create *ex nihilo* to manufacture a perfect paradise. God creates from cosmic material resistant to divine order, which intrudes in harmful ways despite God's best intentions. The intransigence of chaos as the metaphysical shadow of creativity and humanity's capacity for self-determination over and against God's hopes for creation originates evil in the universe.

the completeness of physical realization" (*Adventures of Ideas* [New York: Macmillan, 1956], 333).

72. Whitehead, *Process and Reality*, 340.

73. Cobb Jr. and Griffin, *Process Theology*, 70: "Discord is evil in an absolute or noncomparative sense. Since discord means some kind of suffering, it is evil in itself, apart from any comparison with that which might have been. . . . Triviality, however, is evil only by comparison, i.e., if an experience is more trivial than it need have been" (Griffin, *God, Power, and Evil*, 284).

74. Griffin, *God, Power, and Evil*, 292. "Evil arises from this capacity not to conform to the divine purpose" (280).

75. Cobb Jr. and Griffin, *Process Theology*, 120.

76. Griffin, *God, Power, and Evil*, 276.

With respect to the problem and reason for evil, two key points follow from its theological and philosophical commitments. First, its denial of divine omnipotence formally neutralizes the problem of evil.[77] It eliminates a central prong of the trilemma, omnipotence, thereby negating the logical problem of evil. Since God is not able to prevent evil, God bears no culpability for its existence: "Evil can occur in the world because God, while influencing all events, fully determines no events."[78] We have no cause, then, to shake an angry fist at God for the state of the world because God does the best that God can under the circumstances: "But God has no monopoly on power, God's power is the creative power to evoke or persuade; it is not the unilateral power to stop, to constrain, to destroy."[79] Griffin spells out the implications of the denial of omnipotence for the problem of evil, specifically the problem of divine culpability: "The obvious point is that, since God is not in complete control of the events of the world, the occurrence of genuine evil is not incompatible with God's beneficence toward all his creatures."[80] Hence, God, while responsible in a qualified sense, is not "indictable" for evil.[81]

Similar to the FWD, PT shifts the blame for evil from God to humanity, but for different reasons. The FWD argues that an omnipotent God creates us free, which results in the fall, while PT says that a limited God, relative to classical theism, helps us realize our freedom, and urges us to deploy it for good. Either way, both the FWD and PT vindicate God from moral culpability

77. "[T]he only possible way to solve the problem of evil is to modify the traditional doctrine of divine power" (Griffin, *Evil Revisited*, 3).
78. Griffin, "Process Theology," 140.
79. Griffin, *Evil Revisited*, 24. Griffin continues: "The reason God does not intervene in nature or human affairs to prevent some of the worst evils is not that God is evil or indifferent, or that to do so would run counter to God's policy, it is simply that God's power is of a different kind."
80. Cobb Jr. and Griffin, *Process Theology*, 53.
81. Cobb Jr. and Griffin, *Process Theology*, 69.

for evil and place the blame on humanity. Despite coming from different starting points, they converge on this classic strategy. For both, God is metaphysically responsible for evil, but not morally culpable.[82] For both, the capacity to realize higher states of goodness involves the corresponding capacity to realize higher states of evil.[83] In PT, God is responsible for evil insofar as God lures creation from primordial chaos into higher states of existence where it could experience "discordant feelings," but that was the cost of enabling higher states of beauty and enjoyment, and endowing it with the power of self and other-determination.[84]

PT does not specify the end of evil. Its cosmic destiny remains an open question, and is "obviously not central" to it.[85] The future is "fully and radically open" because God does not write a cosmic script that history simply plays out to its inexorable and foreknown conclusion.[86] Despite its relegation of eschatology to an appendix (for Griffin, at least), PT crafts an eschatology that redeploys some traditional themes.[87] Personal survival in the afterlife takes the form of our absorption into the collective consciousness of the universe where we fully realize our interconnectedness.[88] Metaphors to describe the end include final unity, final beauty, and, as we will discuss momentarily, the Omega Point.[89] Instead of individual experience of delight or doom, we experience the true collectivity of our existence,

82. Griffin, *God, Power, and Evil*, 276.
83. Griffin, *God, Power, and Evil*, 291.
84. Griffin, *God, Power, and Evil*, 300.
85. Griffin, *God, Power, and Evil*, 311. He sees it as an "optional element" of theodicy (Griffin, *Evil Revisited*, 40). On process eschatology, see Marjorie Hewitt Suchocki, *The End of Evil: Process Eschatology in Historical Context* (Albany: State University of New York Press, 1988).
86. Cobb Jr. and Griffin, *Process Theology*, 112.
87. Griffin, *God, Power, and Evil*, 311–13.
88. Cobb Jr. and Griffin, *Process Theology*, 115. "*My* matter is not a part of the universe that I possess *totaliter*: it is the totality of the Universe possessed by me *partialiter*" (Teilhard de Chardin, *Science and Christ*, 12–13).
89. Cobb Jr. and Griffin, *Process Theology*, 122.

and realize our permanent inscription into the consciousness of God, who takes "tender care that nothing is lost."[90] PT, by necessity, treads softly in eschatology, avoiding categorical statements beyond the principle that God "loses nothing that can be saved"[91] and that existence transcends the "perpetual perishing" of life: "But there remains a profound mystery which even Whitehead's intuition could not penetrate."[92] PT appeals to the concept of mystery in the face of insufficient empirical evidence.[93]

Not content with Whitehead's fog of mystery, Pierre Teilhard de Chardin delineates a more definitive and hopeful vision of the end.[94] All life moves toward the Omega Point of history, a divine consummation of complexity and consciousness where we realize our maximal potential.[95] Teilhard employs the mystical language of union to describe the end: "Like a vast tide, Being will have engulfed the shifting sands of being. Within a now tranquil ocean, each drop of which, nevertheless, will be conscious of remaining itself, the astonishing adventure of the world will have ended."[96] Whether or not we reach the elusive Omega Point, however, remains an open question in PT, despite Teilhard's optimism.[97] God joins us in the cosmic struggle to eliminate evil and to realize higher states of being, but, naturally, there are no guarantees, and the process of constant

90. Cobb Jr. and Griffin, *Process Theology*, 122.
91. Whitehead, *Process and Reality*, 346.
92. Cobb Jr. and Griffin, *Process Theology*, 124.
93. Later, however, Griffin explores the empirical evidence for postmortem existence in more detail and declares: "I found it to be, both qualitatively and quantitatively, surprisingly impressive," but, of course, not definitive (Griffin, *Evil Revisited*, 39).
94. Pierre Teilhard de Chardin, *The Future of Man*, trans. Norman Denny (New York: Harper & Row, 1969), 321–23.
95. Teilhard's vision of an end of history and a consummation, drawn from 1 Corinthians 15, among other sources, stands in tension with process philosophy's principle of constant flux and uncertainty.
96. Teilhard de Chardin, *The Future of Man*, 323.
97. Cobb Jr. and Griffin, *Process Theology*, 117: "Nevertheless, the Whiteheadian, unlike Teilhard, must assert that in this respect too, the future is open. There is no assurance that the human species will move forward."

flux, at any rate, never ends, as it does in Teilhard's description. Consequently, PT does not depend on eschatology, as the FWD and SMT, in different ways, do: "This means that the problem of evil is not solved by images of historical hope."[98] And yet, God's power of persuasive presence in every moment gives grounds for hope: "God's responsive love is the power to overcome the final evil of our temporal existence. Because of God, life has meaning in the face of victorious evil."[99] PT offers no hope of heaven, no hope of cosmic restoration, only the vague poetic hope that "we are always safe with God."[100]

Dialogue

Any assessment of PT must attend to an underlying tension that runs throughout: its metaphysical commitment to process philosophy, and its theological commitment to Christian doctrine, however loose. These two aspects of PT constantly collide on key points, forcing process thinkers to tilt in one direction or another, and to borrow on some points from process metaphysics, and on others from Christian doctrine. The question of our dialogue section, then, is whether or not it successfully balances the two systems in its treatment of the problem of evil. What, then, are the problems and prospects of PT, its strengths and weakness?

Strengths

It should come as no surprise that a theodicy based on an innovative metaphysical system that celebrates the creativity of the universe

98. Cobb Jr. and Griffin, *Process Theology*, 118.
99. Cobb Jr. and Griffin, *Process Theology*, 123.
100. Cobb Jr. and Griffin, *Process Theology*, 123.

should score high points on the criterion of creativity. PT impressively applies the insights of process philosophy and theology to the problem of evil, recasting traditional categories. It completely repositions God's relationship to the universe to account for the genuine evil that traditional theodicies tend to downplay or ignore. Its ability to integrate process cosmology and Christian theology to construct an entirely new approach to the problem of evil requires tremendous creativity, perhaps *too* much creativity, as we will see.

Despite its diverse theoretical background and internal variations, PT comes across as remarkably coherent. It addresses all the major questions of theodicy. It positions itself within the history of Christian thought on the problem of evil, leveling thoughtful critiques against classical theism and traditional theodicies. It neutralizes the logical problem of evil with the denial of one of its core propositions: divine omnipotence. It tells the story of the universe's creation out of chaos, gradual evolution from lower to higher states of consciousness, and God's attempt to lure it toward maximal enjoyment through its realization of greater creativity, freedom, harmony, and love. God experiences all suffering and strives to overcome it as we move ceaselessly together toward a future of countless possibilities. Its overarching vision, though open to dispute, gives a coherent perspective on the question of God's permission of evil.

Moreover, PT applies the insights of contemporary philosophy and science to the problem of evil. It is, therefore, structurally relevant, situating an ancient question within a modern intellectual landscape. It is also theologically relevant, willing to problematize traditional paradigms, especially on the questions of divine omnipotence and impassibility, to align with contemporary theological sensibilities. Instead of a dispassionate despot who controls the future, it affirms a vulnerable God, a great companion, who joins us in our suffering and walks beside us into an unknown future, to share the risks *and* rewards with us. Lastly, it is morally relevant, calling humanity to take responsibility for themselves, others, and the environment, rather than passively rely on an omnipotent God or an afterlife to eliminate the evils of the world. It promotes social justice, environmental responsibility, and personal accountability.

Finally, PT knows it limitations, so it scores well on the criterion of humility. In the first place, it does not think that Christianity provides the exclusive lens through which to interpret the problem of evil. It has an inherently pluralistic, interreligious bent, which allows it to enter into productive interreligious dialogue. Furthermore, with respect to humility, it does not pretend to know the future. It does not espouse a clearly defined vision of the afterlife. Instead, it asks us to trust that we will not fade into oblivion at death, but that we will somehow become "caught up" not in the sky to meet the Lord in the air, but into the consciousness of God, who internalizes all experiences. How that will *feel*, and whether or not we will have an individual consciousness or life, it does not answer. Its humility does not preclude its speculation on the future, however.

Weaknesses

In its effort to craft a creative, coherent, and relevant vision of God's engagement with evil, does PT stay true to its religious moorings? Put differently, does it compromise Christian theology in its attempt to salvage it from incoherence and irrelevance? With respect to the sources of theology, PT employs scripture sparingly and selectively, when it reinforces its metaphysical intuitions. It is more eisegetical than exegetical, more concerned with heuristics than hermeneutics, and more metaphysical than Christological. Moreover, it consistently privileges its philosophical commitments over its theological heritage.

At bottom, process philosophy drives PT, often at the expense of the "mainstream" beliefs of Christianity, which raises the ineluctable question whether or not PT is sufficiently Christian to constitute a Christian theodicy.[101]

To elaborate further, because process metaphysics clearly has the "whip hand" in PT, it remains vulnerable to the critique that it does not operate within a Christian biblical, creedal, or theological worldview. It does at times refer to the traditional language of Christian theology, but usually superficially and artificially, clearly trying to adapt it to a process worldview, rather than *vice versa*. Its denial of traditional theological categories comes at a cost. It seems foreign to many Christian interpreters because it does not clearly position itself within the basic Christian narrative of sin and redemption, where Christ plays the central role. That does not mean that PT must accept traditional theological narratives to remain sufficiently tethered to the faith to speak from within it. It does mean, however, that it would have to explicate more thoroughly and convincingly the significance of Jesus to the human condition to remain recognizably Christian.

Correspondingly, its creativity undercuts its *religious* relevance. Process theology employs personal language for God, which obscures the fact that God exists as a *process*, not a *person*. The God of process theology encounters us ontologically, not relationally. Christians, however, do not pray to a process, they pray to a Person.[102] But since

101. "If process theism is accepted as a framework for solving the problems of evil and more generally for understanding Christianity, some rethinking of what are often taken to be central Christian doctrines will be necessary. . . . It will require a rethinking of Christology, probably eschatology, and perhaps of other Christian doctrines as well. Thus process theism requires a transformation of mainstream Christianity" (Keller, "Process Theism and Theodicies for the Problems of Evil," 347). The transformation, I argue, risks its integrity.

102. On divine personhood in contemporary theology, see Mark S. M. Scott, "God as Person: Karl Barth and Karl Rahner on Divine and Human Personhood," *Religious Studies and Theology* 25, no. 2 (2006): 161–90.

the God of process theology cannot help humanity, prayer would be futile anyway. At the end of the day, Christians do not want God stuck in the ditch with them as much as they want God to pull them out of the ditch. Ideally, they would like both, which, as we will see in the next chapter, is the thrust of cruciform theodicies. A God trapped within the suffering of the world, unable to help or make any guarantees, does not warrant worship, which renders PT religiously irrelevant.[103] Griffin devotes an entire chapter in *Evil Revisited* to address the problem of the religious inadequacy of the God of PT, arguing that we must "live between Gods": the "old God" of traditional theism and the "new God" of PT, who merits worship not for its power, but for its persuasive love.[104]

Lastly, PT does not appeal to belief in the afterlife, and without the hope of heaven, or something "transearthly," Christian theodicy loses coherence and relevance.[105] It denies the necessity of hope for Christian theodicy, as Griffin exclaims at the end of his comprehensive study on theodicy: "I do not consider faith that there actually will be a happy future for humanity in this world [or a transearthly existence] to be essential for theodicy."[106] Without hope, however, we have no grounds for faith in God's promises, or in the promise of the future, where God makes "all things new" (Rev.

103. As John K. Roth says of PT, "A God of such weakness, no matter how much such a God tries to persuade, is rather pathetic. Good though that Platonic God may be, Griffin's God is too small. This God inspires little awe, little sense of holiness" (Response to "Creation out of Nothing, Creation out of Chaos, and the Problem of Evil," 128; cf. Stephen Davis: "I believe Griffin's God is nowhere near powerful enough to merit worship. Could a sick person rationally pray to such a being for healing?" 135).
104. Griffin, *Evil Revisited*, 196–213.
105. Griffin comes to realize this deficiency in PT: "The main change since writing *God, Power, and Evil* can, in fact, be summarized as the realization that a fully adequate theodicy requires an eschatology" (Griffin, *Evil Revisited*, 2).
106. Griffin, *God, Power, and Evil*, 313. On the other hand, he later characterizes the nature of hope in PT as the ultimate preservation of value and meaning, but without sufficient justification: "Good is ultimately victorious in the sense that all value is preserved in the face of the eventual destruction and decay of all worldly structures, so that value and meaning, not destruction and meaninglessness, have the last word" (Griffin, *Evil Revisited*, 35).

21:5). Without hope, we have no reason to believe that good will prevail. Without hope, the doctrine of redemption loses plausibility, and the Christian faith lacks credibility and relevance. So process philosophy's appeal to an open future where good and evil hang in the balance undermines Christian theodicy, and calls into question the entire edifice of PT, which cannot promise any ultimate meaning to suffering, in the final analysis.

Conclusion

PT reframes the contemporary debate about the problem of evil. It frees itself from the intellectual contortions of traditional theodicy by denying a key premise of the logical problem of evil, divine omnipotence: "It was this supernaturalistic doctrine of divine omnipotence that created the insoluble problem of evil."[107] That move opens new possibilities for theodicy, which involves shifting theological metaphors. God becomes the Great Companion, the Fellow-Sufferer whose intimate presence with us in suffering comforts and inspires. God also becomes the Great Persuader who lures us into an indeterminate future that we realize together, hand in hand. Whether or not PT ultimately succeeds at integrating its philosophical and theological commitments, and whether or not it offers a theologically and religiously sustainable vision for the problem of evil, I leave for the reader to decide as we transition to a theodicy that redeploys the concept of divine suffering within an explicitly Christian framework: the cross.

107. Griffin, "Process Theology," 140.

Questions for Discussion:

1. What are PT's objections to the doctrine of divine omnipotence?
2. What are the theological implications for denying divine omnipotence?
3. What does PT mean by divine persuasion? How does it impact the problem of evil?
4. How does the process God help us? Is It worthy of worship? Why or why not?
5. What are the possibilities of process eschatology? How does it impact theodicy?

6

Cruciform Theodicy

Divine Solidarity through the Cross

"Only the suffering God can help."[1]

In the FWD, SMT, and PT we encounter three paradigmatic theodical systems, complete with distinctive cosmologies, theologies, and perspectives on the problem of evil. Over the final three chapters, we will explore three broad themes or trajectories in theodicy that appear in these systems but that also have their own inner intellectual integrity and particular contributions to theodicy. These theodical themes do not address all the questions of theodicy—the origin, nature, problem, reason, and end of evil—but they do inflect the discussion in significant ways, and offer valuable theological resources. To designate it a cruciform theodicy (hereafter CT), then,

1. Dietrich Bonhoeffer, *Letters and Papers from Prison*, Dietrich Bonhoeffer Works, vol. 8, ed. Eberhard Bethge et al. (Minneapolis: Fortress Press, 2010), 479.

does not imply its systematic status. Instead, it frequently informs contemporary theological reflections on the problem of evil, and it has the potential to morph into a theodical system, if it expands beyond its narrow Christological focus to engage the broader questions of theodicy.

CT arises partly out of the ashes of the death and destruction of the two world wars and asks: Where was God amid all the carnage? How do we speak of theodicy in the wake of Auschwitz? To speak of God's impassibility, that is, God's imperviousness to pain and suffering, seems heartless in the face of the horrors of the Holocaust and the other instances of genocide that have occurred since. Is God really unaffected? Does God not feel the wound of humanity's suffering? How do we relate to a God who does not relate to the tears and turmoil of humanity? On July 16, 1944, awaiting execution in a Nazi prison and reflecting on Christ's experience of powerlessness and pain, Dietrich Bonhoeffer penned six words that became the clarion call of the modern theological paradigm shift: "Only the suffering God can help."[2] Jürgen Moltmann famously develops a theology of divine suffering (or passibility) in his landmark *The Crucified God*.[3] In this chapter, we explore New Testament resources for CT, Moltmann's signature contribution, and, finally, Marilyn McCord Adams's conception of redemptive suffering.[4]

2. Bonhoeffer, *Letters and Papers from Prison*, DBWE, vol., 8, 479. On the tension between redemption and "the history of suffering," as well as its implications for theodicy, see also Johann Baptist Metz, *Faith in History and Society: Toward a Practical Fundamental Theology*, trans. and ed. J. Matthew Ashley (New York: Crossroad, 2007), 114–27. "As everyone knows, for as long as God was looked upon as the subject of history the concrete history of suffering was the bane of every theodicy" (119). For a contemporary theological engagement on the question and meaning of human suffering, see Dorothee Söelle, *Suffering* (Philadelphia: Fortress Press, 1975).
3. Jürgen Moltmann, *The Crucified God: The Cross of Christ as the Foundation and Criticism of Christian Theology*, trans. R. A. Wilson and John Bowden (Minneapolis: Fortress Press, 1993).
4. Marilyn McCord Adams, *Horrendous Evils and the Goodness of God* (Ithaca, NY: Cornell University Press, 1999). Adams notes the theological similarities and differences between her and Moltmann on the issue of divine suffering: "So far, Moltmann travels the road of my

The Passion of Christ

The starting point for CT is the passion of Christ. Passion, from the Latin *passio*, means suffering.[5] Christ subjects himself to the entire spectrum of human sorrow, including economic exploitation, political disenfranchisement, social ostracism, rejection and betrayal by friends, and even alienation from his own family. In the Garden of Gethsemane he undergoes intense psychological distress as he faces his impending torture, crucifixion, and death: "Then he said to them, 'I am deeply grieved, even to death; remain here, and stay awake with me.' And going a little farther, he threw himself on the ground and prayed, 'My Father, if it is possible, let this cup pass from me; yet not what I want but what you want'" (Matt. 26:38-39). According to some textual traditions, Christ's acute aguish produced perspiration "like great drops of blood," which signify the depth of his emotional turmoil (Luke 22:44). Moreover, at the pivotal moment, the disciples, his closest friends, abandon him when he needs them most, despite their earnest pledge to stand by his side until the end, made just hours before: "Peter said to him, 'Even though I must die with you, I will not deny you.' And so said all the disciples" (Matt. 26:35). So Christ experiences the breadth and depth of human suffering firsthand in his life and ministry.

At his trial, Christ suffers various forms of injustice and indignity. He faces false accusations and hostile witnesses without any adequate representation. He suffers penalty without a fair conviction, punishment without crime, and stands under the presumption of guilt despite countervailing evidence. In short, his judicial system

Christological approach, in effect, insisting that universal defeat of horrors within the context of the participants' lives requires Divine solidarity with the worst that humans can suffer, be, or do. His distinctive move reaches beyond Christology to claim that only a Trinitarian (at least, multipersonal) God could adequately identify with created misery" (175–76).

5. *Passio, onis*, f. [*patior*]: "I suffer." It also has the related nuance of "enduring." Charlton T. Lewis and Charles Short, eds., *A Latin Dictionary* (New York: Clarendon, 1966 [1879]), 1312.

utterly fails him, and he receives an unfair sentence. He endures abuse and ridicule from the soldiers, crowd, and even one of those executed with him (Luke 23:39). Beyond the excruciating physical pain of the whipping, beating, puncture of the nails in his hands and feet, and asphyxiation, Christ felt the weight of the sins of humanity. On the cross, Christ experiences mutilation, humiliation, and abandonment. His cry of despair on the cross reveals his dejected state of mind: "My God, my God, why have you forsaken me?" (Matt. 27:45).[6] Christ, then, was the victim of injustice, exploitation, abuse, and humiliation. As a victim, he is able to identify with victims, as we will discuss below.

Christ, as the Word made flesh (John 1:14), inhabits the full human condition. Consequently, Christ has firsthand knowledge of human frailty: "For we do not have a high priest who is unable to sympathize with our weaknesses, but we have one who in every respect has been tested as we are, yet without sin" (Heb. 4:15). Despite his consubstantiality (*homoousios*) with God the Father, as the Nicene Creed (325 C.E.) affirms,[7] Christ "empties" and "humbles" himself to assume human form and to suffer for the sins of humanity (Phil. 2:6-7). God does not observe from an impassible perch of divine aloofness; God takes action, gets involved, and subjects himself to the full range of human misery. Since, as the Council of Chalcedon (451 C.E.) spells out in its "Definition of Faith," Christ is "truly God and truly man,"[8] it follows that the incarnation entails God's intimate

6. Echoing Ps. 22:1: "My God, my God, why have you forsaken me? Why are you so far from helping me, from the words of my groaning?"
7. "We believe in one God, Father, all-sovereign, maker of all things seen and unseen; and in one Lord Jesus Christ, the Son of God, begotten from the Father, as only-begotten, that is, from the substance of the Father, God from God, light from light, true God from true God, begotten, not made, *homoousios* with the Father . . ." (The Creed of the Synod of Nicaea [June 19, 325], in *The Trinitarian Controversy*, trans. and ed. William G. Rusch [Philadelphia: Fortress Press, 1980], 49).
8. "Following, therefore, the holy fathers, we confess one and the same Son, who is our Lord Jesus Christ, and we all agree in teaching that this very same Son is complete in his deity and

familiarity with human suffering. God's internalization of human suffering and the corollary concept of divine solidarity with suffering mark a paradigm shift in contemporary theology that has important implications for theodicy.

Divine Suffering and Solidarity with Human Suffering

Classic theism presupposes divine impassibility, that is, the doctrine that God does not suffer. Over the past century, however, divine passibility, or the doctrine of divine suffering, has gained considerable traction.[9] Paul Gavrilyuk aptly notes its pervasiveness in contemporary theology: "With a few significant exceptions, modern theologians advocate the claim that God suffers."[10] Jürgen Moltmann forcefully argues for the doctrine of divine suffering in *The Crucified God*, through which the doctrine has entered into the contemporary

JÜRGEN MOLTMANN: The most influential modern Protestant systematic theologian after Karl Barth (1886–1968), Moltmann (1926–) popularizes the doctrine of divine passibility in *The Crucified God* (1972), where he famously argues that God internalizes human suffering on the cross of Christ.

complete—the very same—in his humanity, truly God and truly a human being, this very same one being composed of a rational soul and a body, coessential with the Father as to his deity and coessential with us—the very same one—as to his humanity, being like us in every respect apart from sin" (The Council of Chalcedon's "Definition of Faith" in *The Christological Controversy*, trans. and ed. Richard A. Norris Jr. [Philadelphia: Fortress Press, 1980], 159).

9. For a concise overview, with helpful footnotes for bibliographic purposes, see Richard Bauckham, "'Only the suffering God can help': Divine passibility in modern theology," *Themelios* 9, no. 3 (April 1984): 6–12.

theological bloodstream: "The God of theism is poor. He cannot love nor can he suffer."[11] Christ's experience of godforsakenness on the cross functions as the theological fulcrum of Moltmann's position.[12] We will briefly discuss the rationale behind these clashing beliefs before we detail Moltmann's "doctrine of *theopathy* [divine suffering]" and examine its significance for theodicy.[13]

In his erudite study, *Does God Suffer?*, Thomas Weinandy clarifies the terms of the debate. Divine impassibility signifies God's ontological independence: "God is impassible in the sense that he cannot experience emotional changes of state due to his relationship to and interaction with human beings and the created order."[14] God, as "Wholly Other," acts within creation without any diminution of divine perfection, and without becoming imprisoned within it. In theological terms, God's immanence does not negate God's transcendence, since God's engagement with creation does not entail God's absorption of its imperfections.[15] Nor, Weinandy argues, does

IMPASSIBILITY: In classical theism, the doctrine of divine impassibility denotes the denial of divine suffering. God does not suffer, nor does God experience emotion. God, as wholly "Other," does not possess human characteristics. The doctrine tries to protect God's perfection and transcendence.

10. Paul L. Gavrilyuk, *The Suffering of the Impassible God: The Dialectics of Patristic Thought* (New York: Oxford University Press, 2004), 1.
11. Moltmann, *The Crucified God*, 253.
12. Moltmann, *The Crucified God*, 200.
13. Moltmann, *The Trinity and the Kingdom*, 25.
14. Thomas G. Weinandy, *Does God Suffer?* (Notre Dame, IN: University of Notre Dame Press, 2000), 38.

divine impassibility imply divine indifference. Quite the contrary, the Trinity, as "pure act" (*actus purus*),[16] exhibits perfect love not through the experience of mercurial emotions anthropomorphically projected onto the divine life, but through God's full immersion into the human condition to transform it. God's passion, then, reflects divine being, not divine emotion: "Being fully in act his love is fully in act and therefore his passion is fully in act. God cannot become more passionate or loving by actualizing, as human beings do, some further potential and so become more passionate or loving."[17] In other words, God expresses love by what he *does*, not how he *feels*. God embodies love to the utmost degree without recourse to feeling.

Theologically, the doctrine of divine impassibility rests on divine otherness and secures divine transcendence: "The ancient and medieval tradition of impassibility is bound up with three principal motives. There is, firstly, the motive which depends upon belief in divine transcendence. . . . Then, secondly, there is the motive which arises out of the conviction that the life of God is a blessed life, and, as such, happy with perfect happiness. . . . And thirdly, there is the motive which springs from the dread of anthropomorphism."[18] Biblically, it draws on passages that underscore God's otherness: "God is not a human being, that he should lie, or a mortal, that he should change his mind" (Num. 23:19).[19] Similarly, the New Testament affirms God's difference from humanity, in whom "there is no variation or shadow due to change" (James 1:17). When passibilists

15. Weinandy, *Does God Suffer?*, 145.
16. Weinandy, *Does God Suffer?*, 123.
17. Weinandy, *Does God Suffer?*, 127.
18. J. K. Mozley, *The Impassibility of God: A Survey of Christian Thought* (Cambridge: Cambridge University Press, 1926), 173.
19. As a caution against anthropomorphism in theology, a driving concern of impassibility, see Isa. 55:8: "For my thoughts are not your thoughts, nor are your ways my ways, says the Lord. For as the heavens are higher than the earth, so are my ways higher than your ways and my thoughts than your thoughts." On divine immutability, which divine impassibility implies, see Mal. 3:6: "For I the Lord do not change."

adduce anthropomorphic passages that indicate the contrary, impassibilists argue that these are metaphorical, not literal, designed to accommodate to human modes of perception.[20] In summary, the doctrine of impassibility protects divine transcendence and felicity. Far from negating divine love, it ensures its effectiveness, and anchors it more securely in the eternal Trinitarian life of God, who displays love through action, not emotion.

PASSIBILITY: In modern theology, the doctrine of divine passibility denotes the affirmation of divine suffering. God suffers with, from, and for humanity on the cross of Christ. The doctrine hinges on divine love and argues that love entails suffering, since the object of love—humanity—suffers.

Divine passibility, on the other hand, denotes God's experience of change and emotion: "For God to be 'passible' then means that he is capable of being acted upon from without and that such actions bring about emotional changes of state within him."[21] God does not stand above creation, observing its anguish from a distance. Instead, God chooses to inhabit human suffering. It appears firstly in English Anglicanism in response to "the demise of nineteenth-century optimism and in the face of the social suffering caused by the Industrial Revolution and the agony of World War I [and later World War II]."[22] It later develops out of the horrendous suffering and moral outrage of the Holocaust, which calls traditional theological paradigms into question. Passibilists point to God's love as

20. Weinandy, *Does God Suffer?*, 59.
21. Weinandy, *Does God Suffer?*, 39.
22. Weinandy, *Does God Suffer?*, 2.

the source of theology, and the cross as the exemplification of divine love, a love that suffers. God suffers because he loves. God's vulnerability arises from God's emotional investment in creation as the creator. True love suffers, it does not stand aloof.

Theologically, the doctrine of divine passibility rests on divine love, demonstrated in the cross, which accents divine pathos: "The thought that if God really loves, if His outgoing love is the expression of His innermost nature, then, confronted as He is with such a world as ours, He must suffer, is to be met with again and again among the opponents of the traditional doctrine."[23] Biblically, the doctrine of divine passibility draws on passages that express God's love and suffering for and from the world. Since "God is love" (1 John 4:8, 16), God's felicity depends on our felicity. Love creates space in the self for the other, and that entails the internalization of the delight and despair of the other. If creation suffers, God suffers. God experiences the full emotional spectrum of a parent who worries and wearies over the waywardness of a child (Hosea 11) and of a lover wounded by infidelity and rejection (Hosea 2–3). Loving humanity subjects God to emotional vulnerability and the real risk of disappointment, distress, and even despair. Scripture is replete with depictions of divine passion, including love and hate, joy and sorrow. Genesis 6:6 typifies the passibilist proof-text, where God clearly shows emotion: "And the Lord was sorry that he had made humankind on the earth, and it grieved him to his heart."[24]

Both sides of the debate justify their position with dueling theological rationalizations (divine transcendence/otherness on the impassibilist side, divine presence/love on the passibilist) and rival scriptural passages. Both sides criticize the other as guilty of grave theological error, hermeneutical blindness, and misrepresentation.

23. Mozley, *The Impassibility of God*, 175–76.
24. Mozley, *The Impassibility of God*, 3–4.

Despite the weight of tradition behind the doctrine of impassibility, it has increasingly fallen out of favor. As theologians grapple with the bloodshed and destruction of the twentieth century, many find the emotionally engaged God of divine passibility more theologically palatable and plausible than the seemingly detached God of divine impassibility. "The problem of theodicy," then, stimulated the shift in modern theology.[25] Moltmann crystallizes the emerging consensus in his concise expression of the theological logic of divine passibility: "A God who cannot suffer cannot love either."[26]

In twentieth-century theology, Moltmann has become the flag-bearer for the doctrine of divine passibility. He develops his position in response to theological, historical, and literary considerations. First, for Moltmann, the cross stands at the center of theology: "The death of Jesus on the cross is the *centre* of all Christian theology. . . . All Christian statements about God, about creation, about sin and death have their focal point in the crucified Christ."[27] As the theological center, the cross serves as the primary criterion for theological questions. Moltmann appeals to Luther's *theologia crucis* to develop his cruciform theology.[28]At the Heidelberg disputation on April 26, 1518, Luther distinguishes between the theologian of glory and the theologian of the cross as a way to discuss the mystery of divine suffering: "One deserves to be called a theologian, however, who comprehends the visible and manifest things of God seen through suffering and the cross (Thesis 20). A theologian of glory calls evil good and good evil. A theologian of the cross calls the thing what it actually is (Thesis 21)."[29] Luther's emphasis on the "God hidden

25. Weinandy, *Does God Suffer?*, 6.
26. Moltmann, *The Trinity and the Kingdom*, 38.
27. Moltmann, *The Crucified God*, 204.
28. Moltmann, *The Crucified God*, 212.
29. Martin Luther, *Heidelberg Disputation*, in *Martin Luther's Basic Theological Writings* [3rd edition], ed. William R. Russell (Minneapolis: Fortress Press, 2012), 15.

in suffering" sounds the theological refrain that Moltmann expands on in *The Crucified God*.[30] Impassibility belongs to the theologian of glory, whereas passibility belongs to the theologian of the cross. The cross reveals God's nature as love, and love suffers.[31]

At issue is whether the suffering of the incarnate Son reverberates into the intra-Trinitarian life of God. Does the Father suffer *in se* through the suffering of the Son, with whom he is consubstantially united? The doctrine of the *communicatio idiomatum*, or communication of attributes between the divine and human natures of Christ, comes into debate.[32] This doctrine posits that the unity of Christ's natures allows the attributes of one to be applied to the other, so that we may say "God suffers," but only in the context of the incarnation, not outside of it. If, however, we posit the identity between the "economic Trinity" and the "immanent Trinity," to borrow from Karl Rahner's formulation, then it becomes difficult to justify the exclusion of God's inner life from the experiences of the incarnation.[33] If God *pro nobis* (for us) is identical to God *in se* (in himself), then does it not follow that God internalizes human suffering in his transcendent being, that is, in the life of God outside of creation and the incarnation?

The church fathers retained the doctrine of divine impassibility through the restriction of the *communicatio idiomatum* to the incarnate life of God. Moltmann decries this as an unjustifiable capitulation to

30. Luther, *Heidelberg Disputation*, Thesis 21: "This is clear: He who does not know Christ does not know God hidden in suffering. . . . God can be found only in the suffering and the cross, as has already been said" (22).
31. Moltmann, *The Crucified God*, 212: "This [distinction between the theology of glory and the theology of the cross] presupposes that while indirect knowledge of God is possible through his works, God's being can be seen and known directly only in the cross of Christ and knowledge of God is therefore real and saving."
32. Moltmann, *The Crucified God*, 232.
33. "The 'economic' Trinity is the 'immanent' Trinity and the 'immanent' Trinity is the 'economic' Trinity." Karl Rahner, *The Trinity*, trans. Joseph Donceel (New York: Crossroad, 1999 [1970]), 22. Moltmann, *The Crucified God*, 240.

impassibility. In the incarnation, God himself, in his eternal being, really suffers. God does not pretend to suffer (contra Gnosticism), nor does he simply suffer as a substitute for sinful humanity, crying out in godforsakenness on our behalf, not his own.[34] God the Father experiences the death of the Son, and the Son experiences death itself. Moltmann attempts to dodge the ancient heresy of patripassianism through his specification of the types of suffering particular to each person: "The suffering and dying of the Son, forsaken by the Father, is a different kind of suffering from the suffering of the Father in the death of the Son. . . . The Son suffers dying, the Father suffers the death of the Son."[35] God, then, experiences both sides of death personally, as both the deceased and the bereaved: "The Son suffers death in this forsakenness. The Father suffers the death of the Son. So the pain of the Father corresponds to the death of the Son."[36] God's experience of death enables his solidarity with us as we face it from both sides.

Moltmann employs the controversial language of the "death of God."[37] On the cross, the Trinity experiences an internal breach between the Father and Son: "[W]hat happened on the cross was an event between God and God."[38] Divine suffering, Moltmann insists, extends beyond the incarnation to the inner life of God: "What happens on Golgotha reaches into the innermost depths of the Godhead, putting its impress on the Trinitarian life in eternity."[39] God endures self-alienation and, paradoxically, divine abandonment. God the Father rejects and abandons God the Son: "In the cross, Father and Son are most deeply separated in forsakenness. . . . It

34. Moltmann, *The Crucified God*, 229.
35. Moltmann, *The Crucified God*, 243.
36. Moltmann, *The Trinity and the Kingdom*, 81.
37. Moltmann, *The Crucified God*, 200.
38. Moltmann, *The Crucified God*, 244.
39. Moltmann, *The Trinity and the Kingdom*, 81.

was a deep division in God himself, in so far as God abandoned God and contradicted himself."[40] The Father, conversely, feels the grief of the loss of the Son. Nevertheless, even in their state of alienation, they remain united in their surrender to his death, which opens space for God's love for forsaken humanity. Moltmann applies the Trinitarian language of *homoousios* to divine love and God's determination to suffer for humanity: "The Son suffers in his love being forsaken by the Father as he dies. The Father suffers in his love the grief of the death of the Son."[41] *Homoousios* signifies for Moltmann their partnership in suffering for humanity, even as death interposes between them until the Spirit transmutes death into life, love, and salvation.[42]

Moltmann's affirmation of divine passibility, then, follows from his Christological reflection on the centrality of the cross, where God embodies and internalizes human suffering. His Christological moves, however, draw from historical as well as theological influences. While Christ is the conceptual center of Christian theology, the Holocaust is the historical center, he argues. As a "young German prisoner" during the Second World War, Moltmann gained intimate familiarity with "how unjust social and political systems impoverish, oppress, and terrorize."[43] Elie Wiesel's recounting in *Night* about the prolonged death of the youth at the gallows galvanizes his position: "'Where is God now?' And I heard a voice in myself answer: 'Where is he? He is here. He is hanging there on the gallows.' . . . Any other answer would be blasphemy. There cannot be any other Christian answer to the question of

40. Moltmann, *The Crucified God*, 244.

41. Moltmann, *The Crucified God*, 245.

42. Moltmann, *The Crucified God*, 244: "What proceeds from this event between Father and Son is the Spirit which justifies the godless, fills the forsaken with love and even brings the dead alive, since even the fact that they are dead cannot exclude them from this event of the cross; the death in God also includes them."

43. Adams, *Horrendous Evils and the Goodness of God*, 175.

this torment. To speak here of a God who could not suffer would make God a demon."[44] As a synecdoche for the Holocaust and for all horrendous evils, Moltmann speaks of the prospects of "theology after Auschwitz."[45] Any theology after Auschwitz must speak from within it, in the face of the hung youth and the countless other victims of unspeakable horror, and must relate its propositions to those experiences. Whatever it says about God, then, must have credibility in the gas chambers, in the mass graves, in the silent sites of slaughter, if it is to have relevance outside of them. Moltmann's Christology, then, internalizes the slaughterhouse of history: "God in Auschwitz and Auschwitz in the crucified God—that is the basis for a real hope which both embraces and overcomes the world, and the ground for a love which is stronger than death and can sustain death."[46] God, as the paradigmatic victim, can speak to it, and redeem it, as we will discuss momentarily.

In conjunction with these theological and historical pressures, a strong literary current underwrites Moltmann's theology of divine suffering. Dostoevsky's indictment against innocent suffering in *The Brothers Karamazov*, Book V, Chapter IV, titled "Rebellion," ignites Moltmann's disdain for divine impassibility.[47] In strongly evocative terms, Ivan Karamazov recounts gruesome stories of disturbing brutality against children and declares his rejection of a world where innocent suffering weaves into eternal harmony: "Listen! If all must suffer to pay for the eternal harmony, what have children to do with it? . . . And if the sufferings of children go to swell the sum of sufferings which was necessary to pay for truth, then I protest that the truth is not worth such a price."[48] Driven by Karamazov's protest

44. Moltmann, *The Crucified God*, 274.
45. Moltmann, *The Crucified God*, 277–78.
46. Moltmann, *The Crucified God*, 278.
47. Moltmann, *The Crucified God*, 220.

against God's instrumentalization of evil for higher theological purposes, Moltmann responds by joining his voice to the protest and placing God on the side of the victim: "The only way past protest atheism is through a theology of the cross which understands God as the suffering God in the suffering of Christ and which cries out with the godforsaken God, 'My God, why have you forsaken me?'"[49] The ghost of Ivan Karamazov haunts Moltmann's theology, especially as it relates to the question of suffering.

To summarize, Moltmann objects to the doctrine of divine impassibility for three reasons. First, divine impassibility negates divine love, the cornerstone of Christian theology: "The theology of the divine passion is founded on the biblical tenet, 'God is love' (1 John 4:16)."[50] Moltmann associates divine impassibility with divine disengagement and distance: "For a God who is incapable of suffering is a being who cannot be involved. Suffering and injustice do not affect him. And because he is so completely insensitive, he cannot be affected or shaken by anything. He cannot weep, for he has no tears. But the one who cannot suffer cannot love either. So he is also a loveless being."[51] Weinandy and other impassibilists would object that Moltmann veers dangerously close to anthropomorphism and that he wrongly equates impassibility with apathy. Whereas Moltmann characterizes the God of impassibility as "a stone,"[52] Weinandy and others would characterize him as fully active to restore

48. Fyodor Dostoevsky, *The Brothers Karamazov*, trans. Constance Garnett, ed. Ralph E. Matlaw (New York: W. W. Norton, 1976), 225–26.

49. Moltmann, *The Crucified God*, 227.

50. Moltmann, *The Trinity and the Kingdom*, 57.

51. Moltmann, *The Crucified God*, 222. "Were God incapable of suffering in any respect, and therefore in any absolute sense, then he would also be incapable of love. . . . The one who is capable of love is also capable of suffering, for he also opens himself to the suffering which is involved in love" (230).

52. Moltmann, *The Crucified God*, 222.

creation.[53] For Moltmann, however, divine love entails divine engagement with human suffering in the inner divine life.

Second, the doctrine of divine impassibility is extrinsic and foreign to Christian theology. It filters into the church fathers through the theological sensibilities of Hellenistic philosophy: "If, in the manner of Greek philosophy, we ask what characteristics are 'appropriate' to the deity, then we have to exclude difference, diversity, movement and suffering from the divine nature."[54] Salvation history, however, relays the story of God's passionate engagement with the world: "But if we turn instead to the theological proclamation of the Christian tradition, we find at its very centre the history of Christ's passion."[55] To affirm the doctrine of divine passibility, for Moltmann, means to reclaim and reaffirm the distinctive Christian story and to wrest theology from the iron grip of Greek philosophy. To answer Tertullian's famous question as it relates to the doctrine of impassibility, the apathetic God of Athens does not have anything to do with the suffering God of Jerusalem. Christian theology must deny the former to stay true to its proclamation. Paradoxical language of impassible suffering is contradictory and unsatisfactory, in his view.[56]

Finally, the doctrine of divine impassibility trivializes the depth of human suffering. Impassibility loses all emotional and moral credibility in the face of the half-glazed eyes of the young man remembered in *Night*: "For more than half an hour he stayed there, struggling between life and death, dying in slow agony under our eyes. And we had to look him full in the face. He was still alive when I passed in front of him. His tongue was still red, his eyes

53. "I believe a passible God is actually less personal, loving, dynamic, and active than an impassible God" (Weinandy, *Does God Suffer?*, 26).
54. Moltmann, *The Trinity and the Kingdom*, 21.
55. Moltmann, *The Trinity and the Kingdom*, 21.
56. Moltmann, *The Trinity and the Kingdom*, 22.

were not yet glazed."[57] What God could witness this nightmare impassively, without any emotion and without any moral outrage? No, Moltmann inveighs, that would not be God. God does not watch from above. God enters the gallows with him, as God enters into all human suffering, through the cross. Hence, God identifies with human suffering, and stands in solidarity with all who suffer: "But anyone who cries out to God in this suffering echoes the death-cry of the dying Christ, the Son of God."[58] God's solidarity with human suffering throughout history enables Christian theology to speak to these situations in constructive and comforting ways.

God suffers because God loves humanity, so when we suffer, God necessarily suffers with us. God's empathy with humanity's sorrow does not diminish divine perfection; it reveals it, since true love always suffers with its beloved. True love internalizes the pain of its beloved, and works toward its alleviation. In the incarnation God participates in human suffering directly, without an impassible firewall. As God works toward our redemption, God subjects himself to rejection and humiliation, resistance and disbelief. In the suffering of Christ, Moltmann concludes, the world witnesses the personification and exemplification of divine love: "The suffering of God with the world, the suffering of God from the world, and the suffering of God for the world are the highest forms of his creative love, which desires free fellowship with the world and free response in the world."[59] The question that will detain us in the dialogue section will be: Does Moltmann's conception of divine suffering undermine God's ability to redeem suffering, and does it inadvertently project an anthropomorphic conception of love unto God?

57. Elie Wiesel, *Night*, trans. Stella Rodway (New York: Bantam, 1982 [1960]), 62.
58. Moltmann, *The Crucified God*, 252.
59. Moltmann, *The Trinity and the Kingdom*, 60.

Redemptive Suffering

As a corollary to divine suffering, the concept of redemptive suffering also informs cruciform perspectives on the problem of evil. God's suffering with, from, and for the world reshapes God's relationship with humanity beyond God's capacity to empathize. God does not simply experience suffering through Christ's passion, God transforms it, which opens new existential possibilities for the nature and meaning of suffering: "First, because God in Christ participated in horrendous evil through His passion and death, human experience of horror can be a means of identifying with Christ, either through sympathetic identification (in which each person suffers his/her own pains, but their similarity enables each to know what it is like for the other) or through mystical identification (in which the created person is supposed literally to experience a share of Christ's pain)."[60] As Christ's suffering redeems humanity and, in the process, redeems suffering, so our suffering can have redemptive value when intentionally aligned with his.[61]

Marilyn McCord Adams sketches her distinctive version of cruciform theodicy in "Redemptive Suffering: A Christian Solution to the Problem of Evil," as well as in her other works on evil.[62] Like Moltmann, she begins with a cruciform starting point: "Christians believe that God is effectively dealing with the problem of evil through the cross—primarily the cross of Christ and secondarily their

60. Marilyn McCord Adams, "Horrendous Evils and the Goodness of God," in *The Problem of Evil*, ed. Marilyn McCord Adams and Robert Merrihew Adams (New York: Oxford University Press, 1990), 218–19.

61. For a discussion on the alignment of human and divine suffering, see Eduardo J. Echeverria, "The Gospel of Redemptive Suffering: Reflections on John Paul II's *Salvifici Doloris*," in *Christian Faith and the Problem of Evil*, ed. Peter van Inwagen (Grand Rapids, MI: Eerdmans, 2004), 111–47.

62. Marilyn McCord Adams, "Redemptive Suffering: A Christian Solution to the Problem of Evil," in *The Problem of Evil: Selected Readings*, ed. Michael L. Peterson (Notre Dame, IN: University of Notre Dame Press, 1992), 169–87.

own."[63] She notes that Jesus instructs his disciples to take up their cross not once but daily in order to follow Christ truly, effectively linking Christ's suffering with ours (Luke 9:23-25). Despite its centrality to Christian spirituality, this identification often eludes philosophy: "Yet these points are rarely mentioned in discussions of the problem of evil by analytic philosophers," she observes as a doyen of that guild, because they involve paradox, and philosophers recoil in the face of paradox.[64] She boldly proposes that innocent suffering witnesses to the transformative power of redemption rather than against the goodness of God, inverting the standard expectations, and offering a distinctly Christian contribution to the problem of evil for analytic philosophers of religion, regardless of their religious beliefs.[65]

Martyrdom, she argues, epitomizes redemptive suffering: "I have proposed martyrdom as a paradigm of redemptive suffering."[66] She begins, as any sound analytic philosopher, by defining her terms: "A martyr is simply a witness, in the sense relevant here, someone who gives testimony about a person, some events, or an ideal and who is made to pay a price for doing it."[67] That price ranges from social and economic marginalization to imprisonment and death, with countless permutations in between and within each. When endured as an expression of love for the truth, rather than chosen as a manipulation tactic, martyrdom assumes redemptive value: "Given this characterization, I want to suggest that martyrdom is an expression of God's righteous love toward the onlooker, the persecutor, and even the martyr himself."[68] Martyrs inspire onlookers

63. Adams, "Redemptive Suffering," 169.
64. Adams, "Redemptive Suffering," 169.
65. Adams, "Redemptive Suffering," 170: "My bold contention will be that the Christian approach to evil through redemptive suffering affords a distinctive solution to the problem of evil, for believers and unbelievers as well."
66. Adams, "Redemptive Suffering," 181.
67. Adams, "Redemptive Suffering," 177.
68. Adams, "Redemptive Suffering," 177.

through their perseverance, convict the persecutors through their dramatic expression of love, and reinforce the bonds of love between themselves and the object of their martyrdom. Christ, the paragon of martyrs, exemplifies these characteristics and serves as a model for his followers and indicates the redemptive power of martyrdom for all involved.

Adams entertains objections to her identification of martyrdom as spiritually redemptive. First, not all instances of suffering allow the martyr to experience the benefits of martyrdom, as in the cases of swift death or atheistic examples, where they have closed themselves to deepening relationships with God. Nevertheless, even in these cases, their martyrdom inadvertently creates redemptive possibilities for onlookers and persecutors. Similarly, even when suffering arises from natural causes, that is, where there is no "personal persecutor," it still enables redemptive outcomes for the martyr and onlooker.[69] Finally, some might question its cost-effectiveness, since "the price for the victim is too high and the success rate is too low, both in relation to God's goals with the persecutor and in relation to his purposes with the martyr."[70] Too often suffering fails to produce any higher order goods, and fails to generate redemptive outcomes.

To combat these and other philosophical and moral objections to redemptive suffering, Adams appeals to the afterlife, specifically to the "incommensurate good" of the beatific vision: "In my opinion, suffering cannot seem a wise, justifiable, or loving redemptive strategy except when embedded in the larger context of a Christian world view."[71] She argues that ultimate human felicity hinges on the "face-to-face" encounter with God in the afterlife, an experience of eternal intimacy that will engulf the horrendous evils of life, as

69. Adams, "Redemptive Suffering," 181.
70. Adams, "Redemptive Suffering," 181–82.
71. Adams, "Redemptive Suffering," 182.

she explains in a profound and provocative passage in *Horrendous Evils*: "Retrospectively, I believe, from the vantage point of heavenly beatitude, human victims of horrors will recognize those experiences as points of identification with the crucified God, and not wish them away from their life histories."[72] God's identification with suffering enables our identification with God through suffering, so the moments we wish away from our lives here will take on new significance in the afterlife, when we will understand them fully (1 Cor. 13:12) and see God face to face (1 John 3:2; Rev. 22:4). Following Rom. 8:18, Adams argues that the beatific vision recasts our perception of temporal suffering, which, negatively, will pale into insignificance by contrast to our future glory and, positively, align our suffering with Christ's, imbuing it with eternal personal significance.[73]

Adams summarizes her views on redemptive suffering well in the "Afterword" in *Encountering Evil*. First, God's identification with horrors on the cross transforms suffering. It makes it spiritually redemptive, not merely physically and emotionally destructive. Moreover, God's incarnate suffering creates an existential and spiritual link between his suffering and ours: a cosmic compatibility that situates individual experiences of horror within the salvific framework of Christ's redemption. When we suffer, we experience God, if we suffer in solidarity with him, and that allows the integration of these experiences into our lives. Second, full integration of these experiences only occurs in the afterlife, with the beatific vision, when all parties involved (victims *and* perpetrators of evil) recognize and appropriate God's presence in suffering and

72. Adams, *Horrendous Evils and the Goodness of God*, 167. Cf. Adams, "Redemptive Suffering," 183: "Nevertheless, retrospectively, from the viewpoint of the beatific vision, no one would be disposed to blame God for not eliminating or preventing various evils or to regard God's love as limited or insufficient." Cf. Adams, "Horrendous Evils and the Goodness of God," 218–20.
73. Adams, "Redemptive Suffering," 183.

its mysterious contribution to God's redemptive plan: "I take it that everlasting beatific intimacy with God is incommensurately good for individual persons."[74] Finally, God would have to eliminate the possibility of suffering, to close the circle of redemption.[75] In short, God, who is "Goodness Itself,"[76] engulfs evil with his goodness, which turns out to be the only power in the universe capable of undoing the damage it causes: "The worst evils demand to be defeated by the best goods. Horrendous evils can be overcome only by the goodness of God."[77]

Adams's reliance on the beatific vision faces the classic objection of Ivan Karamazov about the cost of the eternal harmony, but she insists her position does not deny, trivialize, or instrumentalize the evil she enfolds in a Christian mystical vision of God's presence in suffering: "Christian mysticism invites the believer to hold that a perfectly good God further sanctifies our moments of deepest distress so that retrospectively, from the vantage point of the beatific vision, the one who suffered will not wish them away from his life history—and this, not because he sees them as the source of some other resultant good, but inasmuch as he will recognize them as times of sure identification with and vision into the inner life of his creator."[78] Only the mystery of God answers the mystery of evil, Adams avers: "For Christians as for others in this life, the fact of evil is a mystery. The answer is a more wonderful mystery—God himself."[79] As we will discuss in the final chapter, some cry foul at appeals to mystery. It shifts the ground of the debate from the logical to the mystical, and strikes the skeptic as intellectual evasion in the face of logical defeat or the exhaustion of

74. Adams, "Afterword," in *Encountering Evil*, 199.
75. Adams, "Afterword," in *Encountering Evil*, 200.
76. Adams, "Afterword," in *Encountering Evil*, 199.
77. Adams, "Horrendous Evils and the Goodness of God," 220.
78. Adams, "Redemptive Suffering," 187.
79. Adams, "Redemptive Suffering," 187.

resources. For Christian theology, however, mystery lies at the heart of faith, so when pondering the great mystery of evil, deep must call to deep (Ps. 42:7). For those who find mystical appeals logically hazy, Adams's perspective will seem deficient.

Dialogue

As God's definitive response to evil, the cross takes on central importance in Christian theodicy. On the cross, God suffers with, from, and for humanity. As the Son of God, Christ's suffering and death means, paradoxically, God suffers and dies, although whether or not God suffers impassibly (Cyril of Alexandria) or passibly (Jürgen Moltmann) has been the subject of intense theological dispute in Christian theology. For theodicy, two powerful insights arise from the cross. First, God's internalization of suffering in the incarnation means that God identifies with human suffering, and stands in solidarity with us when we suffer. Divine solidarity with human suffering has powerful implications and applications for theodicy. Second, God's redemption of humanity through the suffering, death, and resurrection of Christ opens new vistas in theodicy, and enables theodicy to look for the redemptive possibilities of human suffering. Divine solidarity with human suffering and human identification with the redemptive significance of Christ's suffering recasts the problem of evil and creates exciting new pathways that Christian theodicy has only begun to explore. What are the strengths and weaknesses of these pathways?

Strengths

Emotionally and spiritually, cruciform theodicy (CT) resonates with a broken world. Rather than explain the brokenness, CT explains how God experiences brokenness, and how a broken God encounters and transforms a broken world. God's internalization of human suffering through Christ entails God's identification with experiences of despair and divine abandonment. God does not sit above human suffering, God stands within in it, and walks beside us in our valleys. To know that God stands in solidarity with us in the darkest of nights and through the fiercest of storms brings tremendous comfort and suggests a spirituality of sacred suffering. Adams points to Julian of Norwich's *Revelations of Divine Love* as a vivid illustration of the mystical possibilities available to Christian theological reflection on suffering. She cites Julian of Norwich's vision of God's expression of gratitude to us in the afterlife, and the unspeakable joy it will elicit, when God says: "Thank you for your suffering, the suffering of your youth!"[80]

But God does not simply experience suffering on the cross, God redeems and transforms it. God's utilization of Gethsemane and Golgotha as the means of attaining salvation for humanity suggests the redemptive power of suffering, historically exemplified in the lives and deaths of the martyrs. As we suffer in solidarity with Christ, we participate in the redemptive power of suffering, which allows us to view it in a new light. We suffer, not in a crypto-Pelagian sense, to save ourselves, but rather, in an *imitatio Christi* sense, to participate in the suffering of Christ. As such, suffering need not signal divine rejection, but, paradoxically, divine presence and, even in the midst of suffering, hope. CT points to the resurrection as the

80. Adams, *Horrendous Evils and the Goodness of God*, 162–63. Cf. Adams, "Horrendous Evils and the Goodness of God," 219.

definitive transmutation of suffering and the promise of its eventual elimination in the eschaton. While it does not depend on a detailed eschatology, it implies, through the resurrection, the eventual end of evil and the dramatic restoration of broken bodies and broken hearts in the afterlife.

Finally, theologically, CT works from within the center of Christian theology: the cross. Its historical relevance and responsiveness to the world wars and the Holocaust is matched by its fidelity to its fundamental proclamation of God's love for a broken world. In fact, divine love drives CT from start to finish, and determines its theological and theoretical orientation. For Moltmann, God's love demands that God suffers because love always suffers with its beloved. An impassible God does not love, he argues. While he hastily equates impassibility with indifference, he nonetheless rightly points to the outward nature of love, which moves beyond itself to promote the good of the beloved. God demonstrates his love for the world through the cross (Rom. 5:8), so Moltmann touches on a core truth when he sees the cross as the superlative manifestation and expression of divine love, and as the locus of divine revelation. CT, then, goes to the heart of the gospel for insight into God's relationship with suffering.

Weaknesses

Problematically, CT does not technically meet the threshold of a theodicy, at least not according to the traditional definition as the vindication of divine justice. It does not address the central questions of theodicy: the origin, nature, problem, reason, and end of evil. It aspires to explain *what God does about evil* rather than explain *why God allows it* in the first place, the classic task of theodicy. So, as it relates to the exculpatory and explanatory function of theodicy, it falls short, and operates more as a crutch than as a critical explanation, according to some detractors. CT operates within theodicy as a theme, trend, or trajectory, not as a system. Nevertheless, in its explication of God's solidarity with suffering and its redemptive prospects, it significantly contributes to and advances the conversation. To transform from a theodical theme, trend, or trajectory to a theodical system it would have to incorporate elements from other theodicies, and engage the standard questions of theodicy within its cruciform matrix.

Philosophically, CT is too narrow to contribute to broader theistic conversations on the problem of evil, especially in philosophical theology. For the typical philosopher of religion, operating within a general theistic context, CT comes across as too exclusive, too particular, and too reliant on distinctively Christian resources to have wider heuristic value. How does the cross contribute to Jewish or Muslim theodicies? How does it translate to analytic philosophy? As we often observe, weaknesses from one perspective double as strengths from another. From a Christian theological perspective, its relevance and resonance stems from its Christological focus and cruciform character. Christian theodicies ought to draw from their distinctive theological resources, irrespective of whether or not these directly transfer to other religious and philosophical contexts. Besides, religious and theological distinctiveness does not preclude mutual intellectual enrichment, as interreligious and interdisciplinary dialogue demonstrates.

Theologically, CT tends to subscribe to the doctrine of divine passibility, although it does not necessarily entail that position. Divine passibility, however, raises several theological issues. Does it chain God to creation, and trap him in the ditch with us, so to speak? Does it negate divine transcendence? Does it compromise God's perfection and felicity? After all, would not God's experience of suffering *outside of* the incarnation permanently imprint it on the divine life, and thus imperil eternal felicity, for God and for us? Moreover, does the doctrine of divine passibility anthropomorphically project the human psychology and experience of love onto God? Might God's love exist completely outside the human emotional-intellectual grid? In short, divine otherness and human epistemological limitations should restrain the hasty ascription of human affectivity to God, since it runs the risk of projection. Theology, particularly the cataphatic tradition, cautions against hasty affirmations that outstrip our intellectual capacities. We really are in no position to know exactly how *God* experiences God's love for humanity, and what the cross means for God's eternal intra-relations between the three Persons. What matters, from a Christian point of view, is that *we* experience God's love for humanity through the cross.

Conclusion

Cruciform theodicy depicts God as both in the ditch with us (divine solidarity with human suffering) and outside of the ditch to help us (redemptive suffering). It draws from the central elements of the gospel: God's indefatigable love for humanity, his suffering in the incarnation, and his victory over sin and death on the cross. These themes, beloved in Christian hymnology, shape Christian perspectives on evil: "The universal significance of the crucified Christ on Golgotha is only really comprehended through the theodicy question."[81] The cross, then, furnishes us with the definitive lens through which to interpret the problem of evil and suffering. God suffers with us, from us, and for us. God's identification with human suffering in the incarnation enables our identification and participation with Christ in our suffering. God stands in solidarity

81. Moltmann, *The Trinity and the Kingdom*, 52.

with us in suffering, sometimes walking alongside us, and sometimes carrying us, as the famous "Footprints in the Sand" poem expresses. God knows about unanswered prayers, divine silence, and divine abandonment: "He suffered from the prayer which went unanswered, from his forsakenness by the Father."[82] And although CT does not explain where evil comes from and why God allows it, it assures us that God knows how to bring beauty from ashes. That transformation culminates in the afterlife, which we will discuss in the final chapter.

Questions for Discussion:

1. Which do you find more persuasive, divine impassibility or divine passibility, and why?
2. Must love always suffer? Give some examples and explore some counterexamples.
3. What are some practical applications of the doctrine of divine solidarity in suffering?
4. What are the implications of Christ's redemption for our experiences of suffering?
5. Are all experiences of suffering redeemable? Why or why not, in your view?

82. Moltmann, *The Trinity and the Kingdom*, 81.

7

Antitheodicy

Intellectual and Moral Critiques

> "I am at a loss. I have read the theodicies produced to justify the ways of God to man. I find them unconvincing. To the most agonized question I have ever asked I do not know the answer. I do not know why God would watch him fall. I do not know why God would watch me wounded. I cannot even guess."[1]

At the end of the day, what does theodicy have to do with "real life"?[2] Does it ameliorate or illuminate the lived experience of suffering? Does it contribute to the betterment of the world at all? If not, does that fact invalidate the task of theodicy, and should we discard it as more useless theory? Must theodicy have practical dimensions?

1. Nicholas Wolterstorff, *Lament for a Son* (Grand Rapid: Eerdmans, 2001 [1987]), 68.
2. Theologians must wrestle with the question of the practical value of theology, that is, its relevance to "real life." See Miroslav Volf, "Theology for a Way of Life," in *Practicing Theology: Beliefs and Practices in Christian Life*, ed. Miroslav Volf and Dorothy C. Bass (Grand Rapids, MI: Eerdmans, 2002), 245.

After all, many theories do not have concrete applications in the "real world." If theodicy does in fact mitigate suffering in some way or mobilize ethical action, does that involve a paradigm shift in the concept of theodicy? These are the kinds of questions that have emerged in recent treatments of theodicy. In this chapter, we will inspect where the rubber of theodicy meets the road of real life, and see if we gain any traction.

We begin with an analysis of the two forms of antitheodicy: atheistic and theistic.[3] Antitheodicy rejects theodicy on multiple intellectual and moral grounds, often with the underlying critique that theodicy trivializes suffering and silences the voice of the victim.[4] Whereas atheistic antitheodicies link the failure of theodicy with the failure of theism, theistic antitheodicies reject theodicy while retaining theism despite the purported failure of theodicy. After detailing these two types of antitheodicy, we will then discuss the practical turns that have arisen in response to these critiques. Practical turns in theodicy do not reject theory. Rather, they reject theory that does not take the experiential reality of suffering into account. We will end the chapter with an assessment of the problems and prospects of these practical turns.[5]

3. For a general introduction, see N. N. Trakakis, "Antitheodicy," in *The Blackwell Companion to the Problem of Evil*, ed. Justin P. McBrayer and Daniel Howard-Snyder (Malden, MA: Wiley Blackwell, 2013), 363–76. "The term 'antitheodicy' is a neologism coined by Braiterman ([*(God) After Auschwitz*] 1998) where he defines antitheodicy as 'any religious response to the problem of evil whose proponents refuse to justify, explain, or accept as somehow meaningful the relationship between God and suffering' (p. 31)" (363).
4. See, for instance, Terrence W. Tilley, *The Evils of Theodicy* (Washington, DC: Georgetown University Press, 1991): "As the predominant modern theological and philosophical discourse practice about God and evil, theodicy misportrays and effaces genuine evils. . . . It silences powerful voices of insight and healing" (1).
5. Philosophically, these practical turns draw upon Immanuel Kant. See Immanuel Kant, "On the miscarriage of all philosophical trials in theodicy," in *Religion within the Boundaries of Mere Reason and Other Writings*, trans. and ed. Allen Wood and George Di Giovanni (Cambridge: Cambridge University Press, 1998 [2003]), 17–30.

Antitheodicy

ANTITHEODICY: The repudiation of theodicy for intellectual and moral reasons. Intellectually, it fails to solve the logical problem of evil. Morally, it justifies evil rather than condemns it. Antitheodicy takes two forms: atheistic (rejects theodicy and theism) or theistic (rejects theodicy, not theism).

First, some reject theodicy on purely intellectual grounds, arguing for the logical incompatibility between God and evil, and thus the nonexistence of God. We call these atheistic antitheodicies. In his influential article "Evil and Omnipotence," J. L. Mackie argues against the rational coherence of theism.[6] According to Mackie, the "traditional problem of evil" *disproves* the existence of God: "Here it can be shown, not that religious beliefs lack rational support, but that they are positively irrational, that the several parts of the essential theological doctrine are inconsistent with one another, so that the theologian can maintain his position as a whole only by a much more extreme rejection of reason than in the former case [of belief in God based on nonrational grounds]."[7] As a logical problem, rather than a scientific or practical problem, the problem of evil remains a fixed intellectual contradiction that discounts theism, despite the maneuverings of

6. Originally published as a journal article in *Mind* 64 (1955): 200–212, it has been reproduced in two influential anthologies on the problem of evil: J. L. Mackie, "Evil and Omnipotence," in *The Problem of Evil*, ed. Marilyn McCord Adams and Robert Merrihew Adams (New York: Oxford University Press, 1990), 25–37, and *The Problem of Evil: Selected Readings*, ed. Michael L. Peterson (Notre Dame, IN: University of Notre Dame Press, 1992), 89–101. I will utilize Peterson's version.
7. Mackie, "Evil and Omnipotence," 89.

theodicy, since no new data or observations will abate its force, he argues.

J. L. MACKIE: John Leslie Mackie (1917–1981) was an Australian philosopher whose influential essay "Evil and Omnipotence" famously argues that the logical problem of evil demonstrates "not that religious beliefs lack rational support, but that they are positively irrational."

For Mackie, theologians find themselves in a bind: on the one hand, they *must* affirm divine goodness, omnipotence, and the reality of evil, but, on the other hand, they *cannot* affirm these without logical contradiction. Theists may affirm any two of these propositions, but the inclusion of the third renders it illogical, as the following set of equations illustrates:

Mackie's Bind

Evil + Goodness–Omnipotence=logical

Evil + Omnipotence–Goodness=logical

Goodness + Omnipotence–Evil=logical

Goodness + Omnipotence + Evil=illogical

To seal the insuperability of the argument, Mackie adds two additional premises: "good is opposed to evil" and "there are no limits to what an omnipotent thing can do."[8] When stated in these

8. Mackie, "Evil and Omnipotence," 90.

stark terms, the logical problem of evil controverts classic theism, in Mackie's view.

According to Mackie, theodicy unsuccessfully attempts to circumvent these premises through logical subterfuge and linguistic equivocation. "Half-hearted solutions" explicitly reject one of the three premises, thereby neutralizing the problem, only to smuggle it in later. "Fallacious solutions" explicitly affirm all three premises, but ultimately implicitly reject or modify one of them later in the argument: "I suggest that in all cases the fallacy has the general form suggested above: in order to solve the problem one (or perhaps more) of its constituent propositions is given up, but in such a way that it appears to have been retained, and can therefore be asserted without qualification in other contexts."[9] The trick, for Mackie, is not to discover whether or not a particular theodicy is fallacious. The trick, rather, is to discover where the fallacy lies, since all theodicies are fallacious.[10] Although he does not examine all the theodicies we have explored, he would argue that all of them, at some point in their argument, commit a fallacy.[11] The FWD, SMT, PT, and CT implicitly deny divine omnipotence, he would argue. Moreover, he might argue that the FWD and SMT deny the reality of genuine evil. Mackie, then, illustrates the atheistic rejection of theodicy on rational grounds.

Some theists, however, also problematize theodicy on rational grounds. Kenneth Surin, in *Theology and the Problem of Evil*, notes three "socio-historical" reasons for theodicy's failure. First, the Enlightenment, while intensifying the problem of evil, undercut

9. Mackie, "Evil and Omnipotence," 91.
10. Mackie, "Evil and Omnipotence," 91, 101.
11. Mackie, "Evil and Omnipotence," 101: "There may be other solutions which require examination, but this study strongly suggests that there is no valid solution of the problem which does not modify at least one of the constituent propositions in a way which would seriously affect the essential core of the theistic position."

the religious worldviews underwriting classic theodicies.[12] Second, theodicy's excessive intellectualization of the logical problem of evil fails to do adequate justice to the social, historical, and existential dimensions of the problem.[13] Third and finally, theodicy fails because the problem of evil defies intellectual resolution.[14] It fundamentally transcends reason and recedes into the realm of mystery. These objections problematize the viability of theodicy without denying theism. Surin, in the face of these objections, recommends a shift from theory to praxis, from the abstract to the concrete, and from the conceptual to the historical, and, lastly, from description to participation. Surin does not reject theodicy *in toto*, but rather rejects overly theorized, historically underdeveloped theodicies. Surin's theistic antitheodicy, or critiques of traditional approaches to theodicy, sets the stage for practical turns in theodicy, which we will explore below.

D. Z. Phillips's essay "Theism without Theodicy," far from simply problematizing and qualifying theodicy, rejects theodicy outright, but, significantly, without rejecting theism.[15] Phillips explicitly differentiates his theistic antitheodicy from Mackie's atheistic antitheodicy: "I am not an antitheist, like J. L. Mackie, whose opposition is expressed within a theodicist framework. I want to probe the character of that framework."[16] He argues that theodicy "fails to do justice to the things of the world," particularly to the

12. Kenneth Surin, *Theology and the Problem of Evil* (Eugene, OR: Wipf & Stock, 2004 [1986]), 39–46.

13. Surin, *Theology and the Problem of Evil*, 46–52. "Theodicy might be first and foremost a form of rational discourse about the phenomenon of evil, but the theodicist cannot afford to overlook the fact that rationality itself has social roots, and that occurrences of evil and suffering, and human responses to these occurrences, are likewise located in quite specific historical and material configurations" (48).

14. Surin, *Theology and the Problem of Evil*, 52–54.

15. D. Z. Phillips, "Theism without Theodicy," in *Encountering Evil: Live Options in Theodicy*, ed. Stephen T. Davis (Louisville: Westminster John Knox, 2001), 145–61.

16. Phillips, "Theism without Theodicy," 146.

empirical reality of evil and suffering.[17] According to Phillips, theodicists are guilty of deception and insensitivity in their attempts to justify evil. They are, however, also the victims of deception.[18] Theodicy, by its very definition, minimizes evil in its effort to demonstrate its compatibility with theism. Phillips argues that theodicy undermines theism, and opts for theism without the dubious assistance of theodicy.

Phillips redeploys Wittgenstein's "allegory of bees," which locates in the comparison between the bee's honey and its sting an analogy for human experiences of good and evil. Phillips identifies ten "bee stings," or defects in theodicy, where he takes aim at John Hick and Richard Swinburne. While it does not serve our purposes to detail every sting, which, at any rate, often overlap, he raises three salient objections. First, theodicy inherently justifies evil by instrumentalizing suffering. Second, theodicy shifts the blame from God to victims of suffering. Third, the appeal to mystery, the afterlife, and other postmortem resolutions tends to minimize earthly suffering and obscure the problem rather than solve it. In light of these fatal flaws, Phillips recommends the total rejection of theodicy, not merely its revision.[19]

Why this torment? Phillips repeats these italicized words five times at the close of his essay as a rhetorical refrain to underscore the incomprehensibility of suffering and the inability of theodicy to explain the profusion of evil in the world.[20] This cry of affliction opens the possibility of solidarity with the divine, he admits, gesturing toward a cruciform theodicy, but it does not explain suffering. He stops short of identifying it as the *reason* for suffering, since that would commit the characteristic error of theodicy: "I

17. Phillips, "Theism without Theodicy," 147.
18. Phillips, "Theism without Theodicy," 147.
19. Phillips, "Theism without Theodicy," 152.
20. Phillips, "Theism without Theodicy," 156–60.

repeat: suffering is not for anything. This assumption seduces theodicy."[21] At the end of his essay, Phillips shifts his analogy for theodicy from bees to spiders. He likens theism's construction of theodicy to the spider's self-entanglement in its own web: "In that tangled web I never cease to marvel at a miracle: that theism survives theodicy."[22] So Phillips, in light of the intellectual and moral defects of theodicy, recommends that theism discard theodicy without discarding its theological principles, while Mackie argues that the defects of theodicy discount theism. Both adopt antitheodical positions based on similar criticisms, but they advocate disparate theological responses.

Sarah Katherine Pinnock sounds many of the same critical notes in *Beyond Theodicy: Jewish and Christian Continental Thinkers Respond to the Holocaust*, which examines contemporary political and existential philosophical critiques of theodicy. The very first sentence sets the tone of the book: "Dissatisfaction with theodicy is the passion driving the production of this book."[23] Her dissatisfaction stems particularly from the failure of theodicy to speak to the horror of the Holocaust: "After Auschwitz, theodicy is exposed as perpetrating amoral justifications of evil and rationalistic caricatures of practical faith struggles."[24] Theoretical theodicy fails, she argues, because it inevitably justifies evil as somehow instrumental for God's providential designs and focuses on the global rather than the personal and particular.[25] For these reasons, many "post-Holocaust thinkers widely reject theodicy as morally scandalous."[26] Pinnock probes continental philosophy, specifically Gabriel Marcel

21. Phillips, "Theism without Theodicy," 158.
22. Phillips, "Theism without Theodicy," 161.
23. Sarah Katherine Pinnock, *Beyond Theodicy: Jewish and Christian Continental Thinkers Respond to the Holocaust* (Albany: State University of New York Press, 2002), xi.
24. Pinnock, *Beyond Theodicy*, xi.
25. Pinnock, *Beyond Theodicy*, 7.
26. Pinnock, *Beyond Theodicy*, 7.

(1889–1973), Martin Buber (1878–1963), Ernst Bloch (1885–1977), and Johann Baptist Metz (b. 1928), for philosophical resources to critique and correct theoretical theodicy by attending to the practical dimensions of the problem of evil and employing practical strategies to combat the concrete realities of evil.[27]

Her recommendations take the form of four guidelines for theodicy that will "disrupt the false totality of the discourse of theodicy" and "counteract its moral evasions."[28] We alluded to these guidelines briefly in chapter 2, but, to rehearse them, they are: "(1) epistemic humility, (2) moral sensitivity, (3) religious practice, and (4) narrative memory."[29] The "epistemic humility" criterion cautions against theoretical overreach in theodicy, which offers categorical explanations for why God permits evil, recommending instead theological and philosophical modesty.[30] The "moral sensitivity" criterion resists excessive abstraction and systematization and attends to concrete experiences of suffering and their social, economic, and political causes.[31] The "religious practice" criterion focuses on the "practices of faith" employed in the face of suffering, and the theories that underwrite those practices, rather than focusing on theory in isolation from practices.[32] The "narrative memory" criterion pivots from global theodicy theories to personal stories of suffering and religious engagement with suffering, illustrated classically by the Book of Job.[33] Collectively, these signal the practical turns in theodicy in continental philosophy, which, as we will see, inform theological discourse on theodicy.

27. Pinnock, *Beyond Theodicy*, 7–12.
28. Pinnock, *Beyond Theodicy*, 138.
29. Pinnock, *Beyond Theodicy*, 139.
30. Pinnock, *Beyond Theodicy*, 139–40.
31. Pinnock, *Beyond Theodicy*, 140–41.
32. Pinnock, *Beyond Theodicy*, 141.
33. Pinnock, *Beyond Theodicy*, 141–44.

These theorists from theology and philosophy, despite their disparate vantage points, exemplify the contemporary dissatisfaction with theodicy and the suspicion of its logical and moral bankruptcy. They all, in different ways, accuse theodicy of intellectual and moral failure, and recommend various correctives. Mackie argues that theodicy inevitably falls prey to fallacious solutions and, based on its logical failure, declares theism "positively irrational."[34] Surin, Phillips, and Pinnock discuss the logical and moral failures of theodicy, but, rather than reject theism, they affirm it and recommend that theism either modify or abandon theodicy. These critiques challenge the theodicist to refine the project of theodicy through more rigorous logical explication and through attentiveness and sensitivity to the lived reality of suffering, prompting theodicy to turn sharply from theory to practice, from the global to the personal and local, and from justifying and condoning evil to condemning and confronting it.

Where does that leave traditional theodicy? If theodicy has been typically at home in philosophy departments or as a bridge between philosophy and theology, where does it seem to be moving? The practical turns in theodicy branch in several directions, so before we enter the dialogue section let us examine three directions that have emerged in part from these objections to classic theoretical theodicy and from the imperative to enrich theory with practice and with narratives of suffering. They are, broadly: ethical theodicies, contextual theodicies, and pastoral theodicies. Finally, I will discuss how theodicy might naturally interface with spirituality.

You would not normally associate ethics with theodicy, but the recent practical turns in the field invite the expansion of theodicy in that direction. Ethical theodicies avoid justifying evil and instead theorize ways to identify and overcome the social, economic, and political structures that engender suffering.[35] They may vary from

34. Mackie, "Evil and Omnipotence," 89.

ethical studies on income inequality and its adverse social consequences to studies on the power structures that subjugate groups of people and perpetuate cycles of violence, poverty, and marginalization. Ethical theodicies would vary in scope and substance depending on their scholarly context (e.g., philosophy, theology, sociology, economics, etc.), but they would share the objective to analyze the diverse social and intellectual mechanisms that give rise to evil and suffering and to recommend ways to alleviate suffering.

Contextual theodicies examine the problem of evil from the standpoint of the marginalized or disenfranchised. So, for instance, contextual theodicies might examine specific experiences of suffering for women, African Americans, or the socially disadvantaged, which would naturally intersect with feminist/womanist theology, black theology, and liberation theology.[36] We might designate these allied approaches to the problem of evil *theodicy at the margins*, a new trajectory in theodicy that I have sketched in an article of that title, but that deserves more sustained theological treatment.[37] Beyond the descriptive task of chronicling and confronting systems of oppression, contextual theodicies offer constructive solutions to the plight of the oppressed, drawing on their respective theological resources. Studies have begun to appear that situate theodicy within particular experiences of suffering, and I suspect these will become more frequent.[38] They represent an important shift in theodicy away

35. Tilley, *The Evils of Theodicy*, 246: "Theodicy literally blinds us to the social evils of our day." Hence the need to counteract theodicy's traditional focus on the conceptual over the phenomenological or practical experience of evil.

36. See, as representative examples of feminist, black, and liberation theology's engagement with the lived experience of suffering, Serene Jones, *Feminist Theory and Christian Theology: Cartographies of Grace* (Minneapolis: Fortress Press, 2000), 70–93; James H. Cone, *God of the Oppressed* (Maryknoll, NY: Orbis, 1997, rev. ed.), 150–78; Gustavo Gutiérrez, *A Theology of Liberation: History, Politics, and Salvation* (Maryknoll, NY: Orbis, 1988, rev. ed.), 162–73; *On Job: God-Talk and the Suffering of the Innocent*, trans. Matthew J. O'Connell (Maryknoll, NY: Orbis, 1987), 39–49.

37. Mark S. M. Scott, "Theodicy at the Margins: New Trajectories for the Problem of Evil," *Theology Today* 68, no. 2 (2011): 149–52.

from the global and toward the particular with a view to engaging the lived experiences of suffering more directly.

Pastoral theodicies problematize the facile and insidious theodicies sometimes employed in the church, often by clergy, and offer more theologically, morally, and emotionally sound responses that draw from the lived experiences of suffering, rather than from disembodied theories.[39] John Swinton, in *Raging with Compassion*, argues that traditional theodicies are meaningless in the face of "radical suffering" and that they potentially compound evil.[40] Swinton details the three problematic aspects of traditional theodicy in pastoral contexts: "They can: 1. justify and rationalize evil; 2. silence the voice of the sufferer; 3. become evil themselves."[41] To illustrate these potential problems, Swinton relays the story of a pastor who explained the sudden death of a seven-year-old girl in the congregation as a prod for spiritual growth, a type of SMT:

> During the service, in an attempt to bring some meaning and comfort to the parents, he suggested that God wanted to bring spiritual renewal to the members of the church and had selected one of their most prominent families and had taken their daughter home to be with the Lord, where she was much better off than to live in this world. God's purpose in doing this, the pastor went on to say, was to cause the members of the church to reflect upon the brevity of life and to call them to repentance and renewed commitment to the Lord.[42]

38. Rafael Luévano, *Woman-Killing in Juárez: Theodicy at the Border* (Maryknoll, NY: Orbis, 2012); Emilie Townes, ed., *A Troubling in My Soul: Womanist Perspective on Evil and Suffering* (Maryknoll, NY: Orbis, 1993); Anthony Pinn, *Why, Lord?: Suffering and Evil in Black Theology* (New York: Bloomsbury Academic, 1999) and *Moral Evil and Redemptive Suffering: A History of Theodicy in African-American Religious Thought* (Gainesville, FL: University Press of Florida, 2002).
39. Tilley, *The Evils of Theodicy*, 3: "Denunciations of academic theodicy from pulpits or platforms outside academia are not effective because academics find them easy—often justifiably easy—to ignore."
40. John Swinton, *Raging with Compassion: Pastoral Responses to the Problem of Evil* (Grand Rapids, MI: Eerdmans, 2007), 13.
41. Swinton, *Raging with Compassion*, 17.
42. Swinton, *Raging with Compassion*, 19. The story comes from Ray Anderson.

Most pastors, to be fair, would react to that pastor's insensitive and inane remarks with horror. For him to suggest that the little girl died for their spiritual benefit obviously obfuscates and obviates the problem and, inadvertently, harms the family. It justifies evil, silences the sufferer, and compounds evil in the misguided attempt to explain it. Swinton proposes an alternative: to replace explanation with resistance and transformation in the Christian community, shifting from the *why* of traditional theodicy to the *what* of pastoral theodicies that focus on the "life and practices of the Christian community," not "disembodied arguments."[43]

Finally, how might Christian theodicy naturally interface with Christian spirituality?[44] If theodicy attempts to explain evil, to enfold it within a larger theological narrative, might it intersect with spirituality, that is, the care of the soul? So, for instance, if you interpret evil as a sickness of the soul that arises, at least partially, from the misuse of freedom, your theodicy might include a spiritual programmatic of renunciation. Or, if you interpret evil as part of a spiritual battle, you might employ a spirituality of cosmic battle (Ephesians 6). Lastly, if you interpret evil as suffering that defies explanation and must be suffered in solidarity with Christ, you might appeal to the venerable tradition of *imitatio Christi* in Christian spirituality. Origen's cosmic theodicy, to illustrate, includes a spirituality of restoration, or theology of ascent, whereby the fallen soul returns to God after it undergoes the necessary purification.[45] In

43. Swinton, *Raging with Compassion*, 4, 244–47. For another example of pastoral theodicy, particularly as it relates to preaching theodicy, see Thomas G. Long, *What Shall We Say? Evil, Suffering, and the Crisis of Faith* (Grand Rapids, MI: Eerdmans, 2011).

44. The term "spirituality" is notoriously difficult to define, and, consequently, has been employed in a variety of ways in different contexts. I would refer the reader to standard texts on Christian spirituality for an introduction into these important terminological debates. For our purposes, we define spirituality simply as the care of the soul.

45. For an extended discussion of the intersection between theodicy and spirituality in Origen, see Mark S. M. Scott, *Journey Back to God: Origen on the Problem of Evil* (New York: Oxford University Press, 2012), 101–28.

other words, his logical treatment of the problem of evil includes his spiritual treatment of fallen souls: he unites the explanatory task of theodicy with the soteriological task of spirituality.[46]

Dialogue

Antitheodicies problematize traditional theodicies on several intellectual and moral fronts. Fundamentally, they argue: (1) theodicy fails to solve the problem of evil and salvage theism; (2) theodicy fails to explain radical, horrendous, or dysteleological evil; (3) theodicy contributes to evil by justifying it and by shifting blame from God to humans, which (4) condones evil rather than condemns it. These are some of the failures and deficiencies of theodicy, and they serve as an impetus for either the wholesale rejection of theodicy or its radical reformation along practical lines. They call for the integration of theory and practice, greater attentiveness to the lived experience of suffering, and the reframing of theodicy in practical directions, if retained at all. What are the merits and demerits of these new trajectories? What are their strengths and weaknesses?

Strengths

In the first place, critiques against theodicy rightly repudiate tendencies in theoretical theodicy to overlook or elide real-life experiences of suffering. Even when they illustrate the problem of evil, they tend to draw from literature or the distant past, rather than contemporary situations of oppression, marginalization, and victimization. These examples often sanitize the problem and transfer it from the existential to the historical, pushing it away from the

46. Scott, *Journey Back to God*, 164–65.

consciousness of the writer and the reader. Moreover, the high level of abstraction in especially philosophical theodicies removes it from the raw affective experience of the sufferer, thus calling into question its relevance, cogency, and even morality. When theodicy speaks too coolly about evil and suffering, it loses all moral and intellectual credibly. It must always keep the disturbing, disruptive horror of evil in view as it constructs its theories. To put it starkly, "No statement, theological or otherwise, should be made that would not be credible in the presence of burning children."[47] In other words, if theodicy fails in the crucible of the Holocaust and other examples of horrendous evils, it fails everywhere, which calls for a rethinking of the task of theodicy.

Moreover, moral critiques in particular have encouraged theodicy to move from the theoretical to the practical, including the ethical, contextual, pastoral, and spiritual. These have opened new vistas for theodicy, and have reinvigorated the task of theodicy. Practical turns in theodicy allow for more interdisciplinary work, more innovation, and more social action, developments that will transform the nature of theodicy and the way we think about the problem of evil. Theodicy will increasingly integrate theory and practice, rather than keeping them in hermetically sealed compartments, which will make it more robust and relevant. The more theoretical theodicies draw from and respond to the lived experience of suffering, the more engaged they will become with questions of social, economic, and political inequality, and the more they will deploy the resources of theology to speak to these issues within the context of theodicy.

Furthermore, these new practical trajectories in theodicy encourage a renewed focus on "narratives of suffering," not simply

47. J. Greenberg, "Cloud of Smoke, Pillar of Fire," in *Auschwitz: Beginning of a New Era?*, 23, cited in Phillips, "Theism without Theodicy," 158. See also Elisabeth Schüssler Fiorenza and David Tracy, eds., *The Holocaust as Interruption* (Edinburgh: T. & T. Clark, 1984).

detached "theories of suffering," specifically the stories of suffering that sometimes fail to make the pages of academic or theoretical theodicies.[48] Narratives of suffering surface the voice of the marginalized and oppressed and examine the problem of evil through their perspective.[49] As we see in the Book of Job and the story of the man born blind in John 9, stories are valuable entry points into theodicy. They give the problem of evil a face and a name, which helps to obviate the depersonalization and desensitization often associated (sometimes unfairly) with traditional academic or theoretical theodicy.

Practical turns in theodicy signal the moral imperative of theodicy to avoid insensitivity through the uninvited and inartful employment of specious theodicies at inopportune times. It reminds theodicists to understand the proper context of theodicy and to measure their words when responding to tragedies, if they are asked to respond in the media or in academia or even in their private lives. That does not mean that theodicy must keep silent, for people ask for explanations and the theologian and pastor have the duty to speak when asked. Instead, theodicy must find new registers to speak in and new resources to mine. Theodicy cannot prevent evil, but it can at least not compound it, and it can offer resources for the sufferer to interpret their own experience, rather than unhelpfully foisting the theodicist's own perspective onto the victim.

48. Pinnock, *Beyond Theodicy*, 138. See also Swinton, *Raging with Compassion*, 245, and the magisterial treatment of the problem of evil by Eleonore Stump, *Wandering in Darkness: Narrative and the Problem of Suffering* (Oxford: Oxford University Press, 2010), especially 23–81.

49. See, for example, Carol Winkelmann, "'In the Bible, It Can Be So Harsh!' Battered Women, Suffering, and the Problem of Evil," in *Christian Faith and the Problem of Evil*, ed. Peter van Inwagen (Grand Rapids, MI: Eerdmans, 2004), 148–84.

Weaknesses

Some of the critiques of theodicy, however, are guilty of oversimplification and overstatement. Not all theoretical theodicies downplay or ignore the experiential dimension of suffering. In fact, I have found most treatments of the problem of evil in theology and philosophy to be sensitive to real-life experiences of suffering, so the charge of theodicy's oversight of real-life suffering does not, in my view, withstand careful scrutiny. That does not mean, of course, that theodicy should not take even greater care to keep the practical dimension of the problem in view, but it does mean that we should avoid sweeping indictments that do not fairly characterize the subfield of theodicy and the scholars who devote their time and attention to exploring the problem of evil.[50]

We should also, moreover, not conflate the theoretical task of theodicy with the ethical task of overcoming evil in practical ways. They may, at times, be related enterprises, but they are not, strictly speaking, identical: they belong on a spectrum where they may mutually reinforce each other, but where they also inhabit different spheres at the outer poles of the continuum. So to indict theodicy for failing to eliminate social, economic, and political evils makes a category mistake, similar to berating an environmental scientist for not picking up trash, and for condoning litter through their study of its effects and implications. They certainly should pick up trash,

50. I disagree, naturally, with Tilley's unnuanced assertion: "It is not possible to write an 'untainted' theodicy" (Tilley, *The Evils of Theodicy*, 249). His view of theodicy has itself been tainted by his exclusive focus on its deficiencies, a myopia that prevents him from perceiving the productive analysis and employment of theodicy inside and outside of the academy and its inherent value as an intellectual strand in the history of western thought. In my disagreement with Tilley, I enjoy good company. See Marilyn McCord Adams, *Horrendous Evils and the Goodness of God* (Ithaca, NY: Cornell University Press, 1999), 185–86. "My point is that many (though, to be sure not all) participants in horrors, sooner or later, not at every stage but eventually, over and over, raise questions of meaning: of why God allowed it, of whether and how God could redeem it, of whether or how their lives could now be worth living, of what reason there is to go on?" (187–88).

but that does not invalidate their scholarly studies on environmental degradation.

Furthermore, antitheodicy declares victory prematurely. Does Mackie really think he has definitively refuted theodicy and, in the process, theism, in thirteen pages?[51] It is a little hasty. Moreover, do Tilley, Surin, Phillips, and Pinnock really think that their critiques have decisively refuted theodicy, in all its manifestations and permutations? That would be a precipitous assumption. Certainly they have rightly and helpfully drawn attention to the defects and dangers of theodicy, but that does not discount the task of theodicy. As just mentioned, theoretical theodicy should not be abandoned simply because it does not always have practical outcomes, any more than quantum physics should be abandoned because it does not always have concrete applications. Practice cannot bypass theory any more than theory can bypass practice without injury. Grafting practical considerations into theodicy does not negate the need for complex theory, and complex theory sometimes makes for dry reading, and often feels disconnected from real life, despite its necessary function. So while we ought to subject theoretical theodicy to rigorous logical and moral interrogation, these should be done to refine, modify, strengthen, and contextualize theodicy, not to discard it prematurely.

Many readers will have asked themselves at some point in their reading of the chapter: "Are we even talking about theodicy anymore?"[52] What counts as theodicy once we have moved drastically in practical directions? It is a valid, crucial question. When

51. Alvin Plantinga, for instance, mounts a spirited defense of theism in his book *God, Freedom, and Evil*, even while accepting the force of Mackie's argument against theodicy proper. See Alvin C. Plantinga, *God, Freedom, and Evil* (Grand Rapids, MI: Eerdmans, 1977 [1974]), 12ff.

52. Tilley, I suspect, would ask this question: "For theodicy as it is now practiced is an academic discourse, created in the context of Enlightenment theism and developed throughout the modern era" (Tilley, *The Evils of Theodicy*, 3).

do practical turns in theodicy veer so far away from its explanatory center that it ceases to be theodicy? When does theodicy morph into ethics, advocacy, ministry, or spirituality rather than the intellectual enterprise of making sense of suffering, of addressing its central theological question: "Why does God permit evil?" If we are to expand the boundaries of theodicy, we must ensure that it stays moored to its primary explanatory function, and that necessitates theory. That does not preclude the experiential and practical, since they enrich and extend theory, but they must remain organically connected to the explanatory task of theodicy to stay in its orbit, however wide we might expand that orbit to make room for new lights. Those who maintain a strict definition of theodicy as *simply* the rational justification of God in light of the logical problem of evil will reject these new trajectories as transgressing the bounds of theodicy.

Conclusion

What does theodicy have to do with real life? If you have read books about theodicy or taught or taken courses on the problem of evil, you have probably asked yourself this question more than once. It is an important question to answer for ourselves or for others struggling to understand the relevance of theodicy. When theodicy turns its back on the experiential dimension of suffering, it blinds itself to the stakes of the problem of evil and the multifaceted ways suffering intrudes into real life. When it incorporates the lived experiences of suffering into its theory, it enhances its ability to speak to the problem of evil. Global theories often overreach and fail to do justice to the gritty reality of suffering. The critiques of theodicy and the practical movements it impels remind us that when theories have outstripped experience we must return to the basics. As Voltaire perceptively conveys in *Candide*, his "satirical novel of misfortune," optimistic theories distort and downplay the reality of suffering.[53] In the face of inexplicable, excessive suffering, optimistic theories fall flat. In this valley of tears, sometimes the best we can do is to "cultivate our garden."[54] What Voltaire, in all his dark comedic brilliance, failed to realize was that the determination to embrace life simply without casuistry comes at the end of extensive (albeit futile) theorization of the problem of evil, and is itself theoretically grounded.

53. Pinnock, *Beyond Theodicy*, 3: "Leibniz is notorious for making the claim that the universe we live in is the 'best possible world' that God could have actualized. He neutralizes the badness of evil by claiming that evil is a necessary component in the overall aesthetic goodness, harmony, and plenitude of the universe as a whole. Already during his lifetime, the optimism of Leibniz's best possible world argument was ridiculed. Notable among his critics is the French writer Voltaire who expressed scathing objections to Leibniz's view in his satirical novel of misfortune *Candide* through the character of the priest Pangloss, and also in response to the cataclysmic Lisbon earthquake of 1755."
54. Voltaire, *Candide*, chapter 30, in Voltaire, *Candide or Optimism*, trans. Robert M. Adams (New York: W. W. Norton, 1991 [1966]), 75. "That is very well put, said Candide, but we must cultivate our garden."

Questions for Discussion:

1. What logical and moral arguments against theodicy do you find most persuasive?
2. Do the deficiencies of theodicy entail the defeat of Christian theology? Why or why not?
3. How should theodicists incorporate real-life experiences of suffering into theodicy?
4. What are the strengths and weaknesses of pastoral approaches to theodicy?
5. What are some ethical applications of the practical turns in theodicy?

8

Beyond Theodicy

The Afterlife and Mystery

"Augustine says the Lord loves each of us as an only child [*Confessions* III.11.19], and that has to be true. 'He will wipe the tears from all faces' [Rev. 21:4]. It takes nothing from the loveliness of the verse to say that is exactly what will be required."[1]

Christian theology posits the continuation of human life beyond death, and that core belief impacts theodicy. All Christian theodicy, if it stays true to its biblical and theological heritage, will appeal to the afterlife in some way. The nature of that appeal and the vision of the afterlife it hinges on will vary widely, but the expansion of the time frame of human existence beyond the terrestrial life is a basic instinct of Christian theodicy, grounded on eschatology, that is, theological reflection on the last or final things, including heaven and hell. Jürgen Moltmann defines eschatology as the "theology of

1. Marilynne Robinson, *Gilead* (New York: Picador, 2004), 245–46.

hope,"[2] so the question of the chapter is: How does hope of heaven and/or hell shape theodicy, and does it contribute to the task of explaining evil?[3]

ESCHATOLOGY: A technical term in Christian systematic theology, eschatology refers to the last, final, or end things, especially heaven and hell. Jürgen Moltmann defines eschatology as "the theology of hope," which, in theodicy, involves the ultimate resolution of the problem of evil in the afterlife.

Appeals to eschatology, however, face an immediate objection: that it transgresses the rational principles and parameters of theodicy and resorts to baseless speculation. Why, once we have exhausted reason, do we abandon it in favor promises of "pie in the sky in the sweet by and by"?[4] It strikes opponents as intellectual evasion. When reason fails to untie or cut the knot of theodicy, we change the rules and say that reason only takes us so far. That might be cheating, or it might be the only way to access the depths of the mystery of suffering. Either way, appeals to the afterlife and mystery are central trajectories in theodicy, which

2. Jürgen Moltmann, *Theology of Hope: On the Ground and the Implications of a Christian Eschatology*, trans. James W. Leitch (Minneapolis: Fortress Press, 1993). "Eschatology was long called the 'doctrine of the last things' or the doctrine of the end. . . . In actual fact, however, eschatology means the doctrine of the Christian hope" (15–16).
3. For a recent papal encyclical on Christian hope, see Benedict XVI, *Spe salvi*, November 30, 2007.
4. C. S. Lewis, *The Problem of Pain* (New York: HarperOne, 2001 [1940]), 148–49: "We are afraid of the jeer about 'pie in the sky.'. . . But either there is 'pie in the sky' or there is not. If there is not, then Christianity is false, for this doctrine is woven into its whole fabric. If there is, then this truth, like any other, must be faced, whether it is useful at political meetings [or departmental meetings or academic conferences, we might add] or not."

we must, in deference to mystery, briefly explore, admitting at the outset the speculative nature of the enterprise.

Heaven

In the theodical equation we outlined at the outset of the book, the problem of evil was confined to the mundane or terrestrial experience of evil. It does not take into consideration the afterlife because that reality lies beyond human experience and reason. Nevertheless, every theodicy we have explored invokes the afterlife, with the possible exception of process theodicy. Eschatology is necessary in theodicy because, in *this* life and in *this* world, evil too often destroys and disfigures. In the cosmic scales of justice, evil too often outweighs the good, and that puts pressure on theodicy to appeal to the afterlife to balance the cosmic ledger, to set things to rights.

Marilyn McCord Adams maintains that the great good of the beatific vision, the face-to-face encounter with God (1 Cor. 13:12; 1 John 3:2), does not simply *outweigh* evil, it *defeats* it.[5] The beauty of the divine gaze in the afterlife transforms us and radically alters our perspective on our personal experience of suffering, making it all worthwhile: "Retrospectively, I believe, from the vantage point of heavenly beatitude, human victims of horrors will recognize those

BEATIFIC VISION: The soul's "face-to-face" or direct encounter with God in heaven (1 Cor. 13:12; 1 John 3:2). The beatific vision signifies the eternal intimacy and felicity between the soul and God, which transforms the soul's perspective of its terrestrial experiences, particularly its experience of evil.

experiences as points of identification with the crucified God, and not wish them away from their life histories."[6] Paul makes a similar point when he says the suffering of the world is not worthy to be compared with the glory that will be revealed to us (Rom. 8:18). In the afterlife, God will make "all things new" (Rev. 21:5) and in the new world no evil or suffering exists.

Life in this world has often been described as a vale of tears. Heaven, by contrast, will be a place or state of laughter and endless celebration. In heaven, according to the Book of Revelation, God wipes away all tears (Rev. 21:4). It is an intimate, personal image: God will dry our tear-stained faces and enfold us in the divine embrace that engulfs all traces of evil and suffering. God takes it upon himself to end the sorrow of creation, and to initiate the new age of joy. Biblical symbolism of heaven accents the cessation of suffering and the commencement of celebration. There will be no more crying, no more heartache, no more pain, and no more loss.

Heaven does not simply balance the cosmic ledger, it engulfs the suffering of the world, and thus reframes the problem of evil entirely. The problem with the problem of evil, from the perspective of eschatology, is that it works with incomplete information. An incomplete equation will always remain unsolved until the missing variables are inserted. Heaven, as the ultimate missing variable, casts the equation of evil into new light. It not only solves the problem of evil: it renders it obsolete. From the perspective of the vale of tears, of course, this seems outrageous and offensive, exactly the type of resolution Ivan Karamazov categorically rejects because it seems to minimize human suffering. From the perspective of the beatific

5. Marilyn McCord Adams, *Horrendous Evils and the Goodness of God* (Ithaca, NY: Cornell University Press, 1999), 155.
6. Adams, *Horrendous Evils and the Goodness of God*, 167.

vision, however, the problem of evil will recede as the outgoing tide in the infinite ocean of divine goodness.

Hell

Hell functions in theodicy as the obverse of heaven.[7] While heaven rewards those who suffer unjustly or disproportionately in this life, hell punishes those who sin with impunity and inflict suffering on others. It is, without a doubt, the most emotionally unpalatable doctrine in Christian theology, perhaps tied with the related doctrine of double-predestination. Nevertheless, as C. S. Lewis points out, while the doctrine is "intolerable" to our emotional sensibilities, it is not immoral.[8] In relation to theodicy, hell safeguards divine justice by punishing the wicked. Those who reject the doctrine must ask themselves: Would it be just, or even desirable, to share heaven with unrepentant sinners, serial killers, child molesters, and perpetrators of genocide?

The concept of hell, therefore, contributes to the restoration of cosmic justice. It is the final destiny of those who refuse divine grace. It exacts punishment on those who misused their freedom for evil rather than for good. God's gift of freedom means the possibility of rejecting divine grace. Hell, in this sense, represents the choice of self-centeredness over God-and-other-centeredness. In a memorable line, Lewis says that the gates of hell are locked from the inside: "I willingly believe that the damned are, in one sense, successful, rebels

7. For an introduction to the issues, see Marilyn McCord Adams, "The Problem of Hell: A Problem of Evil for Christians," in *Reasoned Faith*, ed. Eleonore Stump (Ithaca, NY: Cornell University Press, 1993), 301–27 and Andrei A. Buckareff and Allen Plug, "Hell and the problem of evil," in *The Blackwell Companion to the Problem of Evil*, ed. Justin P. McBrayer and Daniel Howard-Snyder (Malden, MA: Wiley Blackwell, 2013), 128–43.

8. Lewis, *The Problem of Pain*, 121. "There is no doctrine which I would more willing remove from Christianity than this, if it lay in my power. . . . I too detest it [the doctrine of hell] from the bottom of my heart" (119–20).

to the end; that the doors of hell are locked on the inside."[9] So the doctrine of hell preserves divine justice and protects the integrity of human freedom, but, as we will ask in the dialogue section, at what cost?[10]

It would be as futile to attempt to depict hell as it would be to depict heaven (1 Cor. 2:9). The visualization of hell, however, has been heavily influenced by art, which has been fixated on images of fire and physical torture. Scripture certainly alludes to the fire and torment of hell (Matt. 13:42; 25:46; Rev. 20:14), but those physical images might have psychological and emotional correspondences: the fire of regret and the torment of guilt, for instance. According to tradition, God does not create hell for humans, but for fallen angels. Those who align themselves with them will share their destiny. Hell might not refer to a place as much as it refers to the state of being outside of God's realm, outside of God's grace, through sinful intransigence.

Not all, however, accept the doctrine of hell. Some find it pernicious, outmoded, and immoral. Universalism, in all its permutations, suggests that there might be a reality beyond hell. Once sinners have undergone the necessary purgation and punishment they are able to enter heaven with pristine souls, cleansed of their sinful grime, as prisoners reenter society after they have served their sentence. God, as the source of love, as Love Itself, never gives up on sinners, never tires of pursuing their perfection. Eventually, as Julian of Norwich hears in a vision of Jesus, "all shall be well."[11] God's omnipotent love, Hick argues, eventually finds a way

9. Lewis, *The Problem of Pain*, 130.

10. For an extended analysis of the doctrine of hell and its impact on theodicy, see Charles Seymour, *A Theodicy of Hell*, Studies in Philosophy and Religion, vol. 20 (Boston: Kluwer, 2000).

11. Julian of Norwich, *Revelations of Divine Love*, trans. Elizabeth Spearing (New York: Penguin, 1998), The Long Text 27: "But Jesus, who in this vision informed me of all that I needed to know, answered with this assurance: 'Sin is befitting, but all shall be well, and all shall be well,

to draw all fallen souls unto himself: "And it seems to me a reasonable expectation that in the infinite resourcefulness of infinite love working in unlimited time, God will eventually succeed in drawing us all into the divine Kingdom."[12] Universalism argues that divine love ultimately saves all humanity, but, as we have noted, it also involves conceptual and theological difficulties.

UNIVERSALISM: The controversial affirmation of the universal restoration of humanity whereby all people are ultimately saved, perhaps after an extensive period of purgation. Universalism argues that divine love precludes eternal torment, which would undermine divine benevolence and justice.

Mystery

In the same eschatological vein, some appeal to the mystery of divine providence when confronted by the problem of evil.[13] God orchestrates the music of the universe with sheets we have not yet read and with notes we have not yet heard. In the afterlife, the discordant notes of this life will be harmonized into the divine symphony of the universe.[14] Since God's arrangement of the universe exceeds our noetic grasp and has not yet been fully

and all manner of things shall be well'" (79). Cf. The Short Text 13: "He supports us willingly and sweetly, by his words, and says, 'But all shall be well, and all manner of things shall be well'" (21–22).

12. John Hick, "An Irenaean Theodicy," in *Encountering Evil: Live Options in Theodicy*, ed. Stephen T. Davis (Louisville: Westminster John Knox, 2001), 69.

13. See, for instance, John Hick, *Evil and the God of Love* (New York: Palgrave Macmillan, 2007 [1966]), 333–36. "Our 'solution,' then, to this baffling problem of excessive and undeserved suffering is a frank appeal to the positive value of mystery. Such suffering remains unjust and inexplicable, haphazard and cruelly excessive. The mystery of dysteleological suffering is a real

revealed to us, we can only submit to God's better judgment and trust in God's goodness and love. When people say that an event was "part of God's plan," they appeal to the mystery of divine providence. It is an admission of the limits of reason and the broader narrative framework of our lives. Since we know only in part, we are in no position to indict God's providential designs for the universe. John Calvin's theodicy, for instance, turns entirely on the concept of divine hiddenness.[15]

The Book of Job illustrates the appeal to mystery.[16] Job suffers unjustly. God himself declares him a "righteous man" who God blesses with family and fortune (Job 1–2). Without his knowledge, God puts Job to the test to vindicate Job's righteousness to "the Accuser," who questions his motivations. Job's obedience, he argues, depends on divine reward. It is merely a transactional form of righteousness that would end the moment God withholds his blessings. Once Job loses everything, he stays faithful to God, refuses to "curse God and die," and instead praises him: "The Lord gave, and the Lord has taken away; blessed be the name of the Lord" (Job 1:21). When his friends accuse him of sin, that is, when they employ a punishment theodicy to interpret his suffering, he denies any wrongdoing, and demands an audience with God.

mystery, impenetrable to the rationalizing human mind. It challenges Christian faith with its utterly baffling, alien, destructive meaninglessness" (335).

14. Providential theodicies often correlate with aesthetic theodicies, which are woven into many theodicies, and are typically illustrated with the analogy of a painting where individual blots contribute to the beauty of the whole. For an extended treatment, see Philip Tallon, *The Poetics of Evil: Toward an Aesthetic Theodicy* (New York: Oxford University Press, 2012). "Aesthetic theodicy, then, seeks to relate the task of theodicy to aesthetic works, criteria, or values" (xviii).
15. Paolo de Petris, *Calvin's Theodicy and the Hiddenness of God: Calvin's* Sermons on the Book of Job (New York: Peter Lang, 2012).
16. See Immanuel Kant's philosophical exegesis of Job and the mystery of evil in, "On the miscarriage of all philosophical trials in theodicy," in *Religion within the Boundaries of Mere Reason and Other Writings*, trans. and ed. Allen Wood and George Di Giovanni (Cambridge: Cambridge University Press, 1998 [2003]), 25–26. For other examples of the appeal to mystery in the Bible, see James L. Crenshaw, *Defending God: Biblical Responses to the Problem of Evil* (New York: Oxford University Press, 2005), 165–75.

When God finally appears, after protracted wrangling about Job's innocence and God's justice (Job 3–37), he does not answer the question at the heart of the story. God does not say: "It was all a test, and you came through with flying colors!" Instead, he expands Job's perspective, pointing out the vastness of the universe, with its many mysteries, and God's power to subdue chaos. God repudiates the theodicy of the friends (Job 42:7), but he also reprimands Job for overreaching: Who is he to question God's plan (Job 40:2)? Job retracts his accusation of injustice: "See, I am of small account; what shall I answer you? I lay my hand on my mouth" (Job 40: 4). . . . Therefore I have uttered what I did not understand, things too wonderful for me, which I did not know" (Job 42:3). Job's silence in the aftermath of the divine epiphany teaches the wisdom of silence, a silence that laments without indictment against God, but that trusts in God's mysterious designs for the universe and in God's ability to overcome evil in the end.[17]

The appeal to mystery, then, introduces another x-factor or variable into the theodical equation. If God were good and all-powerful he would be willing and able to prevent evil, but, since we do not know the mind of God, and since we cannot know the reasons why God might allow evil for a season, we are in no position to make any final determinations. Theodicy searches for the morally sufficient reasons why God might permit evil, and the appeal to mystery says all such searching is at best provisional and tentative, and at worst totally futile. It highlights the unknown variable that makes solving the theodical equation impossible: the mind of God. So theodicy fails to vindicate God even as the problem of evil fails to disprove God's existence.

17. For an autobiographical reflection on the mystery of divine providence in the face of incurable illness and the role of lament, see J. Todd Billings, *Rejoicing in Lament: Wrestling with Incurable Cancer and Life in Christ* (Grand Rapids, MI: Brazos Press, 2015).

Dialogue

Appeals to the afterlife and to the mystery of divine providence alter the conditions of the logical problem of evil, calling into question the insuperability of the trilemma by expanding the equation into unknown territory. Until we know the ultimate destiny of evil and how providence brings the universe to a close, we must reserve judgment. These appeals limit the range of reason to life on this side of eternity and entertain possibilities of cosmic restoration and retribution on the other side of eternity. Christian eschatology, much beloved in hymnology and utilized in liturgy, is the reflective response of Christian theodicy in the face of dysteleological, inexplicable, and unspeakable evil. What are the benefits and limitations of these appeals?

Strengths

The hope of heaven has two salutary functions in Christian theodicy. First, it rights the wrongs endured in life. Those who suffer unjustly experience the infinite good of the beatific vision. The joy of heaven, beyond description and imagination, does not simply outweigh, it engulfs the miseries of life. Joyful reunions, resurrected bodies, eternal celebrations, these are some of the images the mind conjures, but they are dim shadows of the healing, wholeness, and beauty that await us. Second, it brings comfort to many in times of distress as the default response of Christians in the face of evil, which builds a bridge between the theoretical and practical. So heaven sets to rights the injustices of life and holds out hope to those who suffer loss.

Second, the concept of hell serves a necessary, albeit painful, function in Christian theodicy: it protects divine justice through the righteous judgment of the wicked after death. It rectifies the injustices of the world through the punishment of those who inflicted harm without retribution. Would we want the murderer, the rapist, the SS officer to escape judgment? That kind of mercy would undermine divine credibility. God's justice and holiness demand the satisfaction for guilt from unrepentant sinners and the eradication of evil from the cosmos. While the doctrine of hell has fallen into disfavor for many theodicists, they often make the mistake of preserving divine love at the expense of divine justice, not realizing the theological maxim that divine simplicity means that all of the divine attributes blend into each other seamlessly.

Third, the appeal to the mystery of divine hiddenness, so prominent in the theology of John Calvin, for instance, prevents theoretical overreach in theodicy. It reins in theodicy, reminding it of its limitations and context. We cannot access the mind of God, and we cannot know how God might untie or break the knot of the problem of evil in the afterlife. Theodicists formulate the problem based on reason and experience, and they develop theodicies based on these as well, but they sometimes forget that they are working with partial information, and the missing details will change the equation entirely. In the words of Hamlet: "There are more things in heaven and earth, Horatio, than are dreamt of in our philosophy."[18] Mystery respects God's hiddenness, human limitations, and the possibilities that lie beyond the grave.

Weaknesses

If theodicy operates rationally, as the *logical* vindication of divine justice in the light of evil, then appeals to postmortem equalization ring hallow. We cannot prove the existence of heaven, despite

18. William Shakespeare, *Hamlet* 1.5.174–75, ed. G. R. Hibbard (Oxford: Oxford University Press, 2008 [1987]), 195.

popular stories about out-of-body experiences, which might have scientific explanations, so how can we factor it into our discussions? It would be intellectually dishonest. A skeptic might grant that heaven possibly exists, but that possibility does not rise to the level of fact that we can then apply to the problem of evil. Moreover, Ivan Karamazov would argue that the tears of innocent children are "too high a price" for heaven.[19] And, finally, even though the hope of heaven brings comfort to those who have lost loved ones or who face death themselves, that has no bearing on the *intellectual* task of theodicy. We are doing *theodicy*, not *therapy*.

Moreover, the doctrine of hell raises many problems, both emotional and theoretical.[20] Does not the loss of a single soul defeat divine omnipotence and/or call divine love into question? Does not their loss preclude eternal felicity, permanently marring the bliss of heaven? How could *we* be happy knowing that our loved ones are in torment or have undergone the second death (Rev. 20:14)? How could *God* be happy, granting his moral superiority? And does it not seem excessive that the choices we make in the finite realm, more often than not under adverse conditions, should result in eternal damnation? Hell seems drastically disproportional punishment for finite sins, for which there are many mitigating factors, including the external forces that condition human freedom. Why not give the lost another chance?[21]

19. Fyodor Dostoevsky, *The Brothers Karamazov*, trans. Constance Garnett, ed. Ralph E. Matlaw (New York: W. W. Norton, 1976), 226. "It's not worth it, because those tears are unatoned for. They must be atoned for, or there can be no harmony. But how? How are you going to atone for them? Is it possible?" (225–26).

20. Lewis addresses many of these in *The Problem of Pain*, 119–31.

21. Lewis has an interesting response to the question of second chances in the afterlife: "I believe that if a million chances were likely to do good, they would be given. But a master often knows, when boys and parents do not, that it is really useless to send a boy in for a certain examination again. Finality must come some time, and it does not require a very robust faith to believe that omniscience knows when" (Lewis, *The Problem of Pain*, 126).

Finally, the appeal to mystery, while intriguing, strikes the skeptic as little more than intellectual evasion. Theodicy is a rational, not speculative, enterprise, so all appeals to the mysteries of the afterlife and the unveiling of divine providence are invalid from the outset. Theodicy cheats if it begins by playing by the rules of reason only to discard them once the going gets tough intellectually, once it comes up against evils that do not fit neatly into its theoretical system. The appeal to mystery, then, obfuscates the problem rather than illuminates it. It defers the problem of evil rather than solves it with the intellectual tools at its disposal. It belongs, therefore, more to the realm of mysticism than theology or philosophy, and merely cloaks the failures of theodicy in the mists of mystery to avoid facing the cold, harsh reality of defeat.

Conclusion

Marilyn McCord Adams describes theodicy as a "puzzle."[22] The difficulty, however, is that the pieces of the puzzle, divine goodness, omnipotence, and evil, do not easily fit together, and thus do not give us a clear picture of divine justice, the very reality theodicy seeks to vindicate. Nicholas Wolterstorff poignantly expresses the perplexing tension between his beliefs and the tragic loss of his son, whose life was "cut off in its prime": "I cannot fit these pieces together. I am at a loss."[23] The turn to eschatology and mystery in Christian theodicy acknowledges this disconnect, and recognizes the absence of justice in the cosmos at the present time. The appeal to heaven and hell expands the theodical equation to new data from new horizons of existence. So the theodical equation remains unsolved because it includes significant unknown variables, and the puzzle of theodicy

22. Adams, *Horrendous Evils and the Goodness of God*, 7.
23. Nicholas Wolterstorff, *Lament for a Son* (Grand Rapids, MI: Eerdmans, 2001 [1987]), 68.

remains unfinished because we do not have all the pieces yet. In the beatific vision, the picture of the universe will come into clear focus, and the theodical equation will be solved. At that point, however, perhaps the question will not matter anymore. So Christian theodicy cautions that it would be premature for the logical problem of evil to declare victory over God. It is too soon to call the game. There is more to the story. Theodicy appeals to the afterlife for future resolution of the problem of evil. The rewards of heaven and the punishments of hell balance the cosmic ledger, and the beatific vision engulfs human suffering. That move always risks the twin charges of moral insensitivity and intellectual evasion, but Christian theodicy does not answer only to "the tribunal of reason,"[24] it answers also to the tribunal of faith, and faith operates in the realm of mystery, the mystery of God and the mystery of suffering. Christian theodicy lives in hope that God will right all wrongs and make beauty out of ashes, as the teacher says, "he has made everything beautiful in its time" (Eccles. 3:11). Scripture declares that in heaven there will be no more tears, no more pain, no more heartache, and no more death. God wipes away our terrestrial tears as we fall into the divine embrace, wherein we shed tears of joy, the only tears possible. And then the music begins . . .

24. Kant, "On the miscarriage of all philosophical trials in theodicy," 17.

Questions for Discussion:

1. Do the rewards and punishments in the next life atone for the injustices in this life?
2. How does the concept of heaven contribute to theodicy? How does it defeat evil?
3. How does the concept of hell contribute to or detract from theodicy, in your view?
4. Does the appeal to mystery strike you as intellectually evasive or theologically necessary?
5. Does theodicy belong to the realm of reason or faith or both? Share your reasons.

Conclusion

The title of our study, *Pathways in Theodicy*, expresses the multiplicity of options available in the critical theological analysis of the problem of evil. It signifies the varied paths that have been traversed and hints at others that await exploration. As a rule, I have not promoted a particular theodicy, nor have I adopted a particular theological perspective, at least not intentionally. Instead, I have tried to shed light on the entire landscape of the problem of evil in Christian theology, and to highlight the resources available to those who seek to embark on the journey in theodicy. I have also tried to clarify the concept of evil, the problem of evil, and the task of theodicy for Christian theology, and to apply clear, coherent criteria to our analysis of theodicy, always trying to present all positions as fairly and sympathetically as possible.

Any path we take in theodicy, as we have discovered, has its unique challenges and obstacles. All have strategic advantages and disadvantages, conceptual assets and liabilities, and theological prospects and problems. Deciding on which path to take involves careful theological orienteering through unfamiliar and dense territory that often impedes our progression. As we learn to negotiate the twists and turns, peaks and valleys, and rough and smooth terrain, we discover points of intersection with other paths. Despite their distinctive shapes and slopes, all of these pathways converge on the same theological destination: to explain why God might permit evil. Although they have disparate starting points and often take radically divergent directions, they all arrive at the same place: the rational explication of the problem of evil.

Given the insufficiency of any theodicy to bear the burden of the problem alone, it would be justified to ask theodicies to share the intellectual burden, to distribute the weight between them, rather than ask for total allegiance. We might be able to creatively combine helpful components of several theodicies to address discrete aspects of the problem. Theodicy, then, would not be the choice between parallel paths but the utilization of different paths on different legs of the journey. I do not recommend the harmonization of theodicies, since they often work at cross-purposes and have mutually exclusive theological commitments. Instead of harmonization, I recommend coordination and cooperation where possible. Plurality need not entail hostility.

In other words, we might think of theodicy as a theological GPS that helps us to navigate different stages of the problem, drawing from various theodicies along the way. The FWD, for example, accents human responsibility. SMT posits the constructive potential of suffering to facilitate our moral, intellectual, and spiritual development. PT illustrates the possibility of integrating theology and science, and underscores God's persuasive—not coercive—love, a powerful model for contemporary theodicy. CT reflects on the redemptive possibility of suffering, and God's solidarity with us in suffering. Recent practical turns register the salient objections to theodicy, closing the gap between the theoretical and the experiential, which enriches the discussion. Concepts of the afterlife expand the scope of the problem, and point to the future resolution of cosmic injustice and suffering. Finally, the appeal to mystery recognizes the limitations of theodicy, and admits that all explanations ultimately fall short. They all have something to contribute to the conversation, even if we do not adopt them *in toto*.[1]

I have designed the book as an introduction to the problem of evil, not as a forum for me to develop my own constructive perspective. That must wait for a future project. Arguing for my own theological position here would foreclose conversation rather than stimulate it, which has been my express desire. Nevertheless, I am willing to identify five touchstones in theodicy, that is, five elements that are, in my view, essential for a compelling, coherent, and viable Christian theodicy: free will, experience, Christology, eschatology, and mystery. What might it look like? First, it would explicate the relationship between free will and evil. Second, it would take stock of real-life experiences of suffering: it would not be purely theoretical. Third, it would revolve around the salvific significance of Christ in overcoming evil. Fourth, it would utilize concepts of the afterlife to offset the injustices of terrestrial life. Finally, it would appeal to the mystery of divine providence, especially God's final resolution of evil, which would underscore the unfinished nature of theodicy and circumvent premature declarations of victory or defeat.

Christian theodicy has an obligation to participate in both ecumenical and interfaith dialogue. The three major branches of Christianity, with their distinctive theological traditions, parse the problem of evil and respond to it with sometimes subtle and sometimes pronounced accents. The point of Christian theodicy is not to arrive at a unified theodicy—one theodicy to rule them all, as it were—but to speak to the problem from within these theological traditions. Moreover, Christian theodicy should invite dialogue with

1. What a patchwork or fragmentary theodicy would lose in systematic coherence it would gain in adaptability, and the fragmentary nature of human reason and experience invites a "quilt-making" approach to the problem of evil.

other religious traditions, for their mutual enrichment. For these dialogues to be productive, they must not elide dissimilarities in an effort to find common ground, nor try to interpret the theodicy of the other through their own theological prism. Rather, they should locate the areas of similarities and differences that might serve as instructive entry points for discussions of a problem that impacts all religion.

As promised, we did not, in the end, uncover the elusive solution to the problem of evil, and I do not have any surprise revelations hidden on the final page. I did not promise definitive answers to life's most perplexing theological question. Theodicy, as we have seen, has less to do with conclusive solutions and more to do with rigorous, creative, ethical, and dynamic theological exploration of a mystery that defies easy answers. My study was always intended as the beginning of a conversation that would continue after you had turned over the final page of this book. Good conversations need focus, parameters, conceptual resources, and, most crucially, enthusiastic and open dialogue partners who enter into the discussion in good faith, not simply to advance their own theological agenda. If you have encountered helpful ideas, discovered new interlocutors, and acquired constructive theological resources to critically engage the problem of evil, then I will have accomplished my goals. Where the conversation turns next depends on you.

Questions for Discussion:

1. Which theodicy do you find most and least persuasive, and why?
2. Which theologian did you find most helpful to the problem of evil, and why?
3. What questions were not addressed in the study that you would like to explore?
4. How might we compare Christian theodicy with theodicies in other religions?
5. How would you construct a theodicy? How would you address the questions of theodicy?

Bibliography

Adams, Marilyn McCord, and Robert Merrihew Adams, eds. *The Problem of Evil*. New York: Oxford University Press, 1990.

———. *Horrendous Evils and the Goodness of God*. Ithaca, NY: Cornell University Press, 1999.

Aquinas, Thomas. *On Evil*. Translated by John A. Oesterle and Jean T. Oesterle. Notre Dame, IN: University of Notre Dame Press, 1995.

Augustine. *Confessions*. Translated by Maria Boulding. New York: New City Press, 2001.

———. *The City of God against the Pagans*. Translated and edited by R. W. Dyson. Cambridge: Cambridge University Press, 1998.

———. *The Problem of Free Choice*. Translated by Dom Mark Pontifex. Ancient Christian Writers 22. New York: Newman Press, 1955.

Barth, Karl. *Church Dogmatics* III/3. Translated by G. W. Bromiley and R. J. Ehrlich. Edited by G. W. Bromiley and T. F. Torrance. Edinburgh: T. & T. Clark, 1960.

Batto, Bernard F. *Slaying the Dragon: Mythmaking in the Biblical Tradition*. Louisville: Westminster John Knox, 1992.

Bauckham, Richard. "'Only the suffering God can help': Divine Passibility in Modern Theology," *Themelios* 9, no. 3 (April 1984): 6–12.

Berger, Peter. *The Sacred Canopy: Elements of a Sociological Theory of Religion*. New York: Anchor, 1990.

Billings, Todd J, *Rejoicing in Lament: Wrestling with Incurable Cancer and Life in Christ*. Grand Rapids, MI: Brazos Press, 2015.

Bonhoeffer, Dietrich. *Letters and Papers from Prison*. DBWE, vol. 8. Edited by Eberhard Bethge et al. Minneapolis: Fortress Press, 2010.

Boyd, Gregory A. *Satan and the Problem of Evil: Constructing a Trinitarian Warfare Theodicy*. Downers Grove, IL: IVP Academic, 2001.

Cobb Jr., John B., and David Ray Griffin. *Process Theology: An Introductory Exposition*. Philadelphia: Westminster, 1976.

Cohen, S. Marc, Patricia Curd, and C.D.C. Reeve, eds. *Readings in Ancient Greek Philosophy: From Thales to Aristotle*. Indianapolis: Hackett, 1995.

Cone, James H. *God of the Oppressed*. Maryknoll, NY: Orbis, 1997.

Couenhoven, Jesse. "Augustine's Rejection of the Free-Will Defence: An Overview of the Late Augustine's Theodicy," *Religious Studies* 43 (2007): 279–98.

Crenshaw, James L. *Defending God: Biblical Responses to the Problem of Evil*. New York: Oxford University Press, 2005.

Davies, Brian, and Brian Leftow, eds. *Thomas Aquinas: Summa Theologiae* Questions on God. Cambridge: Cambridge University Press, 2006.

Davis, Stephen T., ed. *Encountering Evil: Live Options in Theodicy*. Louisville: Westminster John Knox, 2001.

Dostoevsky, Fyodor. *The Brothers Karamazov*. Translated by Constance Garnett. Edited by Ralph E. Matlaw. New York: W. W. Norton, 1976.

Ehrman, Bart D. *God's Problem: How the Bible Fails to Answer Our Most Important Question—Why We Suffer*. New York: HarperOne, 2008.

———. *The New Testament: A Historical Introduction to the Early Christian Writings*. New York: Oxford University Press, 2008.

Evans, G. R. *Augustine on Evil*. Cambridge: Cambridge University Press, 1982.

Flesher, Andrew Michael. *Moral Evil*. Washington, DC: Georgetown University Press, 2013.

Flint, Thomas P., and Michael C. Rea, eds. *The Oxford Handbook of Philosophical Theology*. New York: Oxford University Press, 2009.

Fuller, B. A. G. *Plotinus and the Problem of Evil*. Cambridge: Cambridge University Press, 1912.

Gavrilyuk, Paul L. *The Suffering of the Impassible God: The Dialectics of Patristic Thought*. New York: Oxford University Press, 2004.

Griffin, David Ray. *God, Power, and Evil: A Process Theodicy*. Philadelphia: Westminster, 2004 [1976].

———. *Evil Revisited: Responses and Reconsiderations*. Albany: State University of New York Press, 1991.

———. "Process Theology," *A Companion to Philosophy of Religion (Blackwell Companions to Philosophy)*. Edited by Philip L. Quinn and Charles Taliaferro. Malden, MA: Blackwell, 1999, 136–42.

Guinness, Os. *Unspeakable: Facing up to the Challenge of Evil*. New York: HarperOne, 2006.

Gutiérrez, Gustavo. *A Theology of Liberation: History, Politics, and Salvation*. Maryknoll, NY: Orbis, 1988.

———. *On Job: God-Talk and the Suffering of the Innocent*. Translated by Matthew J. O'Connell. Maryknoll, NY: Orbis, 1987.

Hengel, Martin. *Judaism and Hellenism: Studies in Their Encounter in Palestine during the Early Hellenistic Period*, vol. 1. Philadelphia: Fortress Press, 1974.

Hick, John. *Evil and the God of Love*. New York: Palgrave Macmillan, 2007 [1966].

———. *Death and the Afterlife*. Louisville: Westminster John Knox, 1994.

Hobbes, Thomas. *Leviathan*. Edited by Edwin Curley. Indianapolis: Hackett, 1994.

Howard-Snyder, Daniel, ed. *The Evidential Argument from Evil*. Bloomington: Indiana University Press, 1996.

Hume, David. *Dialogues Concerning Natural Religion*. Edited by Martin Bell. New York: Penguin, 1990.

Hunter. Cornelius G. *Darwin's God: Evolution and the Problem of Evil.* Grand Rapids, MI: Brazos Press, 2001.

Johnson, Luke Timothy. *The Writings of the New Testament: An Interpretation.* Minneapolis: Fortress Press, 2010.

Jones, Lindsay, ed. *The Encyclopedia of Religion*, 2nd edition, vol. 13. Detroit: Macmillan Reference USA, 2005.

Jones, Serene. *Feminist Theory and Christian Theology: Cartographies of Grace.* Minneapolis: Fortress Press, 2000.

Kant, Immanuel. "On the miscarriage of all philosophical trials in theodicy," in *Religion within the Boundaries of Mere Reason and Other Writings*, Trans. and ed. Allen Wood and George Di Giovanni. Cambridge: Cambridge University Press, 1998 [2003].

Kropf, Richard W. *Evil and Evolution: A Theodicy.* Eugene, OR: Wipf & Stock, 2004.

Küng, Hans. *On Being a Christian.* Translated by Edward Quinn. Garden City, NY: Doubleday, 1976.

Leibniz, Gottfried Wilhelm. *Theodicy: Essays on the Goodness of God, the Freedom of Man, and the Origin of Evil.* Chicago: Open Court Classics, 1998.

Lewis, C. S. *The Problem of Pain.* New York: HarperOne 2001 [1940].

Long, Thomas G. *What Shall We Say? Evil, Suffering, and the Crisis of Faith.* Grand Rapids, MI: Eerdmans, 2011.

Luévano, Rafael. *Woman-Killing in Juárez: Theodicy at the Border.* Maryknoll, NY: Orbis, 2012.

Matthewes, Charles. *Evil and the Augustinian Tradition.* Cambridge: Cambridge University Press, 2007.

McBrayer, Justin P., and Daniel Howard-Snyder, eds. *The Blackwell Companion to the Problem of Evil.* Malden, MA: Wiley Blackwell, 2013.

McCabe, Herbert. *God and Evil in the Theology of St Thomas Aquinas.* Edited by Brian Davies. New York: Continuum, 2010.

Meister, Chad. *Evil: A Guide for the Perplexed*. New York: Continuum, 2012.

———, and James K. Dew Jr., eds. *God and Evil: The Case for God in a World Filled with Pain*. Downers Grove, IL: InterVarsity, 2013.

Metz, Johann Baptist. *Faith in History and Society: Toward a Practical Fundamental Theology*. Translated and edited by J. Matthew Ashley. New York: Crossroad, 2007.

Milton, John. *Paradise Lost*. Edited by Stephen Orgel and Jonathan Goldberg. Oxford World's Classics. New York: Oxford University Press, 2008.

Moltmann, Jürgen. *The Trinity and the Kingdom: The Doctrine of God*. Translated by Margaret Kohl. Minneapolis: Fortress Press, 1993.

———. *The Crucified God: The Cross of Christ as the Foundation and Criticism of Christian Theology*. Translated by R. A. Wilson and John Bowden. Minneapolis: Fortress Press, 1993.

———. *Theology of Hope: On the Ground and the Implications of a Christian Eschatology*. Translated by James W. Leitch. Minneapolis: Fortress Press, 1993.

Mozley, J. K. *The Impassibility of God: A Survey of Christian Thought*. Cambridge: Cambridge University Press, 1926.

Norris Jr., Richard A., trans. and ed. *The Christological Controversy*. Philadelphia: Fortress Press, 1980.

Norwich, Julian. *Revelations of Divine Love*. Translated by Elizabeth Spearing. New York: Penguin, 1998.

de Petris, Paolo. *Calvin's* Theodicy *and the Hiddenness of God: Calvin's* Sermons on the Book of Job. New York: Peter Lang, 2012.

Peterson, Michael L., ed. *The Problem of Evil: Selected Readings*. Notre Dame, IN: University of Notre Dame Press, 1992.

Pinn, Anthony. *Why, Lord?: Suffering and Evil in Black Theology*. New York: Bloomsbury Academic, 1999.

———. *Moral Evil and Redemptive Suffering: A History of Theodicy in African-American Religious Thought.* Gainesville, FL: University Press of Florida, 2002.

Pinnock, Sarah K. *Beyond Theodicy: Jewish and Christian Continental Thinkers Respond to the Holocaust.* Albany: State University of New York Press, 2002.

Plantinga, Alvin C. *God, Freedom, and Evil.* Grand Rapids, MI: Eerdmans, 1974.

Rahner, Karl, "Why Does God Allow Us to Suffer?" in *Theological Investigations* XIX, *Faith and Ministry*. Translated by Edward Quinn. New York: Crossway, 1983 [1961].

———. *The Trinity*. Translated by Joseph Donceel. New York: Crossroad, 1999 [1970].

Robinson, Marilynne. *Gilead.* New York: Picador, 2004.

Rodin, Scott R. *Evil and Theodicy in the Theology of Karl Barth.* New York: Peter Lang, 1997.

Rusch, William G., trans. and ed. *The Trinitarian Controversy*. Philadelphia: Fortress Press, 1980.

Russell, William R., ed. *Martin Luther's Basic Theological Writings* [3rd edition]. Minneapolis: Fortress Press, 2012.

Scott, Mark S. M. *Journey Back to God: Origen on the Problem of Evil.* New York: Oxford University Press, 2012.

———. "C. S. Lewis and John Hick: An Interface on Theodicy," *Journal of Inklings Studies* 4, no. 1 (2014): 19–31.

———. "Theodicy at the Margins: New Trajectories for the Problem of Evil," *Theology Today* 68, no. 2 (2011): 149–52.

———. "Suffering and Soul-Making: Rethinking John Hick's Theodicy," *Journal of Religion* 90, no. 3 (2010): 313–34.

———. "Guarding the Mysteries of Salvation: The Pastoral Pedagogy of Origen's Universalism," *Journal of Early Christian Studies* 18, no. 3 (2010): 347–68.

———. "God as Person: Karl Barth and Karl Rahner on Divine and Human Personhood," *Religious Studies and Theology* 25, no. 2 (2006): 161–90.

Seymour, Charles. *A Theodicy of Hell* (Studies in Philosophy and Religion, vol. 20). Boston: Kluwer, 2000.

Söelle, Dorothee. *Suffering*. Philadelphia: Fortress Press, 1975.

Solzhenitsyn, Aleksandr Isayevich. *The Gulag Archipelago 1918-1956 Abridged: An Experiment in Literary Investigation (P.S.)*. New York: Harper Perennial, 2007.

Schüssler Fiorenza, Elisabeth, and David Tracy, eds. *The Holocaust as Interruption*. Edinburgh: T. & T. Clark, 1984.

Southgate, Christopher. *The Groaning of Creation: God, Evolution, and the Problem of Evil*. Louisville: Westminster John Knox Press, 2008.

Stackhouse, John G. Jr. *Can God Be Trusted? Faith and the Challenge of Evil*. New York: Oxford University Press, 1998.

Stump, Eleonore. *Wandering in Darkness: Narrative and the Problem of Suffering*. Oxford: Oxford University Press, 2010.

———, ed. *Reasoned Faith*. Ithaca, NY: Cornell University Press, 1993.

Surin, Kenneth. *Theology and the Problem of Evil*. Eugene, OR: Wipf & Stock, 2004 [1986].

Suchocki, Marjorie Hewitt. *The End of Evil: Process Eschatology in Historical Context*. Albany: State University of New York Press, 1988.

Swinton, John. *Raging with Compassion: Pastoral Responses to the Problem of Evil*. Grand Rapids, MI: Eerdmans, 2007.

Tallon, Philip. *The Poetics of Evil: Toward an Aesthetic Theodicy*. New York: Oxford University Press, 2012.

Teilhard de Chardin, Pierre. *The Future of Man*. Translated by Norman Denny. New York: Harper & Row, 1969.

Tilley, Terrence W. *The Evils of Theodicy*. Washington, DC: Georgetown University Press, 1991.

Townes, Emilie, ed. *A Troubling in My Soul: Womanist Perspective on Evil and Suffering*. Maryknoll, NY: Orbis, 1993.

Van Inwagen, Peter. *The Problem of Evil*. New York: Oxford University Press, 2006.

———, ed. *Christian Faith and the Problem of Evil*. Grand Rapids, MI: Eerdmans, 2004.

Vermes, Geza, trans. and ed. *The Complete Dead Sea Scrolls in English*. New York: Allen Lane/Penguin, 1997.

Volf, Miroslav. "Theology for a Way of Life," in *Practicing Theology: Beliefs and Practices in Christian Life*, ed. Miroslav Volf and Dorothy C. Bass. Grand Rapids, MI: Eerdmans, 2002.

Voltaire, *Candide or Optimism*. Translated by Robert M. Adams. New York: W. W. Norton, 1991 [1966].

Weinandy, Thomas G. *Does God Suffer?* Notre Dame, IN: University of Notre Dame Press, 2000.

Whitehead, Alfred North. *Process and Reality: An Essay in Cosmology*. Edited by David Ray Griffin and Donald W. Sherburne. New York: Free Press, 1978 [1929].

———. *Adventures of Ideas*. New York: Macmillan, 1956 [1933].

Whitney, Barry L., ed. *Theodicy: An Annotated Bibliography on the Problem of Evil: 1960-1991*. Charlottesville, VA: Bowling Green State University Press, 1998 [1993].

Wiesel, Elie. *Night*. Translated by Stella Rodway. New York: Bantam, 1982 [1960].

Wolterstorff, Nicholas. *Lament for a Son*. Grand Rapids, MI: Eerdmans, 2001 [1987].

Wright, N. T. *Evil and the Justice of God*. Downers Grove, IL: IVP, 2006.

Index

CPSIA information can be obtained
at www.ICGtesting.com
Printed in the USA
JSHW020413291222
35475JS00006B/66

9 781451 464702